PENG

HOME REMED

T.V. Sairam, a senior mem master's degree in botany and a doctorate in alternative medicine. For the past three decades he has been gathering and documenting data relating to the household use of medicinal plants.

Home Remedies

Volume Three

T.V. Sairam

Illustrations by Amitabh

PENGUIN BOOKS

PENGUIN BOOKS
Published by the Penguin Group
Penguin Books India Pvt. Ltd, 11 Community Centre, Panchsheel Park, New Delhi 110 017, India
Penguin Group (USA) Inc., 375 Hudson Street, New York, New York 10014, USA
Penguin Group (Canada), 90 Eglinton Avenue East, Suite 700, Toronto, Ontario, M4P 2Y3, Canada (a division of Pearson Penguin Canada Inc.)
Penguin Books Ltd, 80 Strand, London WC2R 0RL, England
Penguin Ireland, 25 St Stephen's Green, Dublin 2, Ireland (a division of Penguin Books Ltd)
Penguin Group (Australia), 250 Camberwell Road, Camberwell, Victoria 3124, Australia (a division of Pearson Australia Group Pty Ltd)
Penguin Group (NZ), 67 Apollo Drive, Rosedale, North Shore 0632, New Zealand (a division of Pearson New Zealand Ltd)
Penguin Group (South Africa) (Pty) Ltd, 24 Sturdee Avenue, Rosebank, Johannesburg 2196, South Africa

Penguin Books Ltd, Registered Offices: 80 Strand, London WC2R 0RL, England

First published by Penguin Books India 2000

10 9 8 7 6 5 4 3

While every effort has been made to verify the authenticity of the information contained in this book, it is not intended as a substitute for medical consultation with a physician. The publisher and the author are in no way liable for the use of the information contained in the book.

Typeset in Garamond by Digital Technologies and Printing Solutions, New Delhi
Printed at Chaman Offset Printers, New Delhi

Contents

Introduction to Volume One

For cutting off the tender sprouts, a fine of six panas will be imposed; for cutting off the minor branches, twelve panas and for cutting off the big branches, twenty-four panas. Cutting off the trunk will be punished with the first amercement; and felling will be punished with the middlemost amercement.

—Arthashastra, III 19: 197

The writing of this book was undertaken of fill what I perceive to be a serious void between the ethnic discovery of herbs and their scientific rediscovery.

It was felt that collecting and categorizing available data from folklore as well as the Western scientific literature on medicinal herbs would facilitate an informed understanding that could better evaluate the premises and methodology of the complicated and often misunderstood role of herbalism and alternative medicine. Herbs are often seen as the last resort once all other avenues of treatment have been exhausted. Being approached as last-minute miracle workers serves to reinforce the mystic aura associated with such systems of medicine, thus discounting the sophisticated and ancient herb lore that its practitioners draw on. The hereditary household remedial system handed down by often unlettered women, the village vaids, hakims and ojhas and their travelling counterparts represent the fragmentary remnants of systems evolved to perfection to meet the needs of localized communities, drawing on familiar plants and locally available materials to treat ailments. Such practices are however fast becoming extinct, and I have often noted on my travels that even in a far-flung village, it has become the fashion to go for a tablet of aspirin rather than a piece of ginger, unmindful of the feeble voice of a family elder or the village physician.

Systematic documentation of this knowledge becomes an urgent necessity in the face of such onslaughts, as has been made clear to me time and again on my frequent trips to remote areas. The Kotas, among one of the ancient inhabitants of the Nilgiris, have all but lost their familiarity with their native medicines. Their villages which till recently boasted a village physician, now totally depend on the nearby hospitals for treating even the simplest of ailments.

An identical situation prevails in a village near Hyderabad. Almost the entire village was suffering from malnutrition due to vitamin deficiency. The villagers squarely blamed the government for their plight and pointed out that the local dispensaries never maintained adequate stocks of vitamins. All this was in spite of the surprisingly large number of drumstick trees which were growing almost everywhere in the village! The vitamin-loaded leaves of the trees were ironically ending up as manure or cattle feed.

The ancient methods designed for optimum beneficial use of local resources are in danger in ways that classical systems such as Ayurveda, Unani and Siddha have overcome. These classical systems have been elaborately documented in the form of verses, which survive as manuscripts in the written form, or are passed on from generation to generation orally. Herbal folklore however continues to be unrecorded and as a consequence, endangered.

India has always been a treasure trove of herbs. Historically, in traditional Indian cuisine, there was hardly any distinction between food and medicine. Herbs were seen as agents of satisfaction and well being. Centuries before the birth of the Greek and Roman empires, Indian ships carried herbs and their derivatives like perfumes and textiles to far-off destinations like Arabia, Mesopotamia and Egypt. The subcontinent's wealth of flora derives from the wide variations in geo-climactic and ecological endowments—tropical, temperate, alpine and arid zones, fluctuating factors such as relative humidity, temperature, monsoon, etc. The sheer variety of herbs and spices available to early shamans and physicians and their rich herb mythology and herb lore lured human migration not only from the neighbourhood but also from distant lands.

Later, it was Indian spices that wrote a fascinating history of adventure, exploration, conquest and colonialism. Bitter sea battles were fought over the spice growing colonies. The treasures of herbs and spices have always been indicators of wealth and status and have dictated the policies of nations. Indian herbalism was developed by the ancient seers, sages, wanderers and tribals who through intuition and observation discovered the many properties of plants and their products. The wisdom and experience of generations was consolidated in its growth. Over the millenia, other herbal systems and herbs brought into the subcontinent grew and added to indigenous lore.

Today it is easy to forget that the original sources of modern medicine were unsung folk prescriptions: morphine from poppy, quinine from cinchona, ephedrine from ma-hung, digitalin from foxglove. Today too, there are people who still treat minor ailments inexpensively with remedies taught to them by their forebears. This is especially true of folk medicine and simple home remedies and beauty aids taught to young girls by their grandmothers in many parts of the country. The body of information accumulated in these and other systems of medicine, dealing with the specific medicinal applications of herbs for specific complaints, has been tested innumerable times over the millenia in actual practice.

Scientific Interest in Herbs

The term 'herb' technically refers to a non-woody plant that dies down to the ground after flowering. In general use, it refers to any plant species, including trees. Plants are the chemical factories of nature. The spectacular progress in organic chemistry has rendered most of the natural products amenable to synthesis. In the late eighteenth century and the nineteenth century, organic chemists occupied centre-stage. Recognizing the importance of plant materials, they isolated the active ingredients of many plants and plant products—nimbidin from *Azadirachta indica* (Neem), hyosine from *Datura metel* (Green Thorn Apple), and reserpine from *Rauwolfia serpentina* (Sarpagandha). In the twentieth century, the sixties saw the phytochemists working with randomly chosen plants. In the seventies growing interest in folkloric drugs urged these qualified researchers to select and work on plants used in traditional medicine. In the eighties and nineties these studies, aimed at the isolation and structure elucidation of the chemical constituents of the chosen plants, were pursued further. Despite such investigation, it is estimated that ninety per cent of recorded flora remains unstudied. However, the ultimate aim of scientific interest in traditional drugs is neither to ascribe them formal recognition nor to explore their use as just alternatives or supplements to modern medicine.

The medical recipes and therapies gathered by me from diverse sources deserve very serious and urgent consideration by scientific and medical researchers. I think the time has come for the scientific community not to rest content with the isolation of 'active principles' alone from these plants. This 'classical' approach by scientists seeking to pinpoint single active substances and either extract them as they are or synthesize them in the laboratories serves only a limited purpose, since we are already aware that plants also contain secondary enhancing and/or side-effect-eliminating substances, which are lost for good in the process of isolation of active principles. Besides, there is greater scope for researchers to discover which chemical appears in which part of the plant and when. Apart from verifying existing scientific findings and explaining the role of plants in modern biochemical terms, which I understand that the Herb Society in London has recently undertaken, there is a need for a scientific understanding of systems of alternative medicine that have proved useful for suffering humanity, and for which no scientific explanation has yet emerged. The scientific community by transcending its mindset would perhaps be able to find a satisfactory answer to this in the coming years.

Herbalism in India is today beset by myriad problems. The value of the medicinal plant depends on its active principle content and not on its abundant growth or harvest. This aspect distinguishes the herbal industry from the others as the norms of production of agricultural crops differ.

Moreover, it is often found that the same plant grown in different localities differs widely in its medicinal value. Several factors such as soil, rainfall, latitude, altitude, method of cultivation, time of collection, storage, transport, etc. play an important role in the medicinal value of drugs.

A wholesome and uniform *Materia Medica* appears a distant dream even today.

What is worse, there is no attempt to identify correct plant species mentioned in various vernacular literatures. There is also no serious attempt to document even today all available information on herbs mentioned in the vernacular treatises lying scattered over the length and breadth of the country, or to confirm and consolidate information relating to the affective part of the plant or its dosage and the application-methodology, particularly the details relating to combining the herbs.

Although most of the vernacular treatises make an attempt to broadly communicate the uses of plants, there is little other detail in them, meant as they are for the expert practising physician. Particulars such as exact dosage, duration of treatment, etc. are often left to the imagination of the lay and often unlettered present-day practitioners. There is thus a need for formulating the effective dosage and treatment-duration in respect of each herb/herbal product.

There is also widespread practice of substitution of herbs and ingredients. This is a very serious offence which unfortunately goes unnoticed or un-reported. It is necessary that some institutional checks are initiated with a view to ensure purity and quality of herbal products.

I can find no better way to end than with this beautiful story that emphasizes the need to preserve our ancient skills. The story tells of the legendary Jivaka, who was the royal physician during Buddha's time.

On completion of his seven-year medical course at Taxila, Jivaka was given the following problem by the examiner: 'Take this spade and seek around Taxila, a yojana on every side, and whatever plant you see which is not medicinal, bring it to me.'

Jivaka, so the legend goes, examined all the plants in the specified area and was forced to return to the examiner empty-handed!

How to Use the Book

The book deals with forty commonly found herbs in the subcontinent, most of them familiar kitchen and spice box staples that are invariably accompanied by some minimal knowledge of their therapeutic properties, even in urban homes. The majority of these herbs are indigenous, though some like fenugreek and chillies were brought into the country by incoming invaders, colonizers and migrants. Over a period of time, they have merged so much with Indian gastronomy and medicine that their place of origin appears to be irrelevant. While dealing with each herb, I have recorded its traditional use along with recent scientific information, particularly its efficacy as a drug. A list of references from scientific research work indicating the composition and efficacy of herbs and their constituents will enable each reader to arrive at his or her own evaluation of the relevance of both the traditional practices and the scientific literature. The *In Tradition* pages record the accepted remedies for specific ailments that draw upon each herb's unique therapeutic properties. The ailments are arranged not in alphabetical order, but in groups under the system of related organs to which they belong, as usually classified in medical terminology. They are in their order of presentation in the book, the skeletal and muscular systems (bones, joints, sprains, muscle pulls), the circulatory system (heart, blood, blood vessels, glands, lymph, etc.), the digestive system, the excretory system, all fevers and ailments relating to the head, neck and throat, the nervous system, the reproductive system, the respiratory system, the integumentary system (skin, pigmentation, etc.) and miscellaneous ailments that do not fall under just one of these heads.

While each entry has been alphabetized, certain groups of

related symptoms that cover more than one system have not been separated, since all or a few of them may occur simultaneously. The extensive index at the back of the book allows quick location of multiple remedies for the same ailment, and a choice of herbs. The intuitive preference of certain herbs over others is the best pointer in choosing the appropriate remedy. As many Indian language names as possible have been recorded, thus enabling easy identification of the herbs. The multi language index facilitates the location of herbs by their familiar names, rather than the botanical or English ones. The detailed line drawings that accompany each herb further underline their familiarity while linking us to forgotten healing traditions.

The book records traditional medicinal remedies that are in danger of falling into disuse in forms in which they have been handed down across generations of practitioners. Traditional household practices regarding dosage, application and combination of herbs for alleviating symptoms and curing ailments were all gathered by me mostly through word of mouth from hundreds of housewives, illiterate grandmothers, vaids and ojhas, who voluntarily came forward to reveal them, including specialized tips derived from a lifetime of experience. These living herbals of folk usage will hopefully be the starting points for a comprehensive *Herbal Materia Medica.* Tips on certain herbal preparations that serve as inexpensive substitutes for their chemical-based brethren in the markets are included wherever possible. A comprehensive medical and herbal glossary and one of Non-English terms explains technical concepts from various systems of medicine.

Herbal Preparations: Some Guidelines

There could be some confusion regarding the preparation of home remedies for lay readers. An attempt is made here to explain the various procedures, processes and preparations dealt with in this book.

Notes on Preparation

In traditional systems of medicine, particularly the ones prevalent in South India, one often comes across the practice of mixing honey with almost every herbal powder or *bhasma,* etc. Honey is regarded as an essential vehicle that aids easy digestion and assimilation of the drug. Whenever honey is not available, other sweet substances such as jaggery, sugar candy, etc. are powdered and mixed with the drug. As in Ayurveda, balancing of tastes is an important phenomenon and drugs which are bitter, sour or astringent are often mixed with sweet substances and administered.

Resins and Gums. Resins and gums exude from the branches of several trees, especially *Acacia.* They are generally harvested in the dry seasons, by making cuts on their branches and trunks. The liquid exudate which solidifies quickly is then scraped off the tree with the help of a knife. In the case of myrrh (*Commiphora myrrha*), the exudate is initially pale yellow in colour but as it solidifies, it becomes brown-black.

Jams. Herbal jams are solid or semi-solid preparations. The herbal paste or powder is cooked in liquid (water or milk), and ghee, sugar syrup, etc. are added while cooking. A jam is ready when it achieves single or double thread consistency and when a dollop skins into water *en masse* without spreading. A jam made of fresh ginger is a common household remedy used to strengthen the digestive fire, while another made of dry ginger powder is used as a winter tonic. There is a wide variety of jams used therapeutically for indigestion, diarrhoea, piles, bleeding disorders, respiratory problems, reproductive disorders, etc. *Chyavanaprasa,* the most well-known among jams, consists mainly of amla in addition to as many as forty herbs and at times, is fortified with even minerals. It is a rejuvenator and also a remedy for debility and old age.

Medicated Oils and Fats. Sneha are prepared by boiling a drug-fat-water mixture until the water evaporates and the remnants are strained. There are four textures distinguishable in Kerala preparations: flowing, soft, waxy and hard. While hair oils (often medicated with amla, Chinese rose, etc.) are flowing, certain preparations like medicated ghee are in various semi-solid states (soft, waxy or hard). Soft fats are used for nasal medication. Waxy fats are used for internal consumption and the hard greasy ones are applied to the body. The hard fat often contains charred herbs.

Nasal and Eye Drops. Nasal and eye medication is preferred for purification in all diseases of the head, lungs, throat and eyes. A good daily routine includes introduction of a couple of drops of medicated oil or ghee into the nose or eyes as the case may be. Whenever any fresh juice is required to be introduced, sufficient caution is to be exercised to avoid any contamination. Sterilized cotton and clean hands are necessary. Never use more than 2-3 drops at a time.

Application of Warmed Leaves. Some leaves are applied on boils, etc. after warming over a flame. The leaves which are otherwise hard or leathery get softened and pliable by such treatment and are rendered handy for bandaging the affected area. Sometimes a coating of oil (such as sesame oil) is applied on the surface of the leaves before warming them.

Burning the Plant Materials. This process is quite common and releases the aroma (e.g., resins, incense, etc.) of the plant parts which helps in relieving nasal congestion, etc. In certain cases, plant parts are burnt over hot coals and the ash obtained is used as medicine.

Roasting the Plant Materials. Roasting plant parts such as seeds is a common method before they are used as medicine. By roasting in the skillet, the volatile oil content in seeds is gradually released and the efficacy of the plant parts, when used as medicine, increases. In Siddha medicine, roasting of leaves, etc. is also done in mud pots. Such a roasting process removes traces of moisture, besides wilting the leaves.

Notes on Dosage

> *A doctor should treat taking account of the patient,*
> *the illness and the time.*
>
> —Tirukkural 949

Prescribing the optimal dosage of the plant material for a particular ailment and for the particular constitution of the patient has always been a challenging task for any herbalist. The main reason for this is the fact that the content of the so-called 'active principle' of a plant part varies widely due to factors such as climate, altitude, latitude, soil type, nutrition, temperature, relative humidity, season, time of plucking, packing, storage, etc. Determining the nature of the constitution of the patient has also been a crucial factor for determining the dosage of the drug.

As such, the dosage should vary from person to person and from drug to drug, the judgement being based on the close observation by the physician of the individual constitution and reaction of the patient, with a view to enhancing or decreasing the dose already prescribed by him. In other words, a close rapport between the physician and the patient is a *sine qua non* before making any such attempt. The practitioner should be fully aware of the inherent weakness in prescribing the dosage, or a particular dose of a drug, in a general or casual way, overlooking the importance of both the dynamism that a drug exhibits and the individuality of a patient's constitution. The crude manner in which dosage has been prescribed in this book is merely to broadly document roughly how much of the drug could be required. It has been assumed that the patient is fully grown and mature. The dosage indicated is therefore subject to modification by the prudent user.

Finally, I make no apologies for the fact that I approach patients like a 'primitive' shaman. For me, they represent highly complex psycho-physico-spiritual creatures rather than mechanical devices taken up for servicing or repair. I am fully convinced that when a man suffers from an ailment, all he needs is relief best suited to his bodily constitution and in the least harmful way. It is in such a spirit that I hope readers too will approach the book.

Notes on Preparing Plant Parts

Collection. Although there are no hard and fast rules, the following principles are generally adhered to:

Roots, Rhizomes and Bark: They are collected in late autumn or early spring when vegetative growth has ceased.

Leaves and Flowering Tops: They are collected at the time of development of flowers and before maturing of fruit and seeds as the photosynthetic activities are maximum at this time. The active principle content is also high.

Fruits: They are collected when fully grown, but unripe.

Seeds: They are collected when fully matured and if possible, before the fruits open for dispersal. Seed-like fruits such as coriander, saunf, ajwain, etc. are harvested a little before they are fully ripe, to retain their fresh and bright appearance.

Drying: The object of drying is to remove moisture and to preserve the plant and its parts. Under natural conditions, the drug could be dried under the sun or in shade, according to the nature of its content or the active principle. Greater success is encountered in commercial drying, where the temperature and flow of air are controlled. Certain delicate drugs such as digitalis need a specific temperature for drying.

Garbling: The final stage in the processing of a drug is garbling. In the process, extraneous matter such as dirt, unwanted plant parts, adulterants, etc. are removed.

Packing: Different drugs need different types of packing. Basically, packing should ensure protection against moisture, fungus, insects, etc.

Storage and Preservation: Conditions for storage and preservation vary from plant to plant. In case of drugs such as digitalis, which deteriorate in the presence of moisture, the insertion of a suitable dehydrating substance in the container itself is a prerequisite. In general, the ideal conditions for preservation of all drugs are refrigeration or low temperatures.

Infusion: An infusion, like tea, is made by combining boiling water with herbs (usually the green parts of flowers) and steeping for 5 to 10 minutes to extract their active ingredients. Due to exposure to heat only for a short duration, this method ensures that the volatile elements and vitamins are not totally lost. It is recommended that a porcelain, enamel or glass pot be used while steeping the herbs. The pot should be covered with a tight-fitting lid to minimize evaporation. Sometimes sugar or honey can be added to the infusion to improve its taste. Most herb-teas (also called tisanes) are taken in small regular doses ranging from a teaspoon to a mouthful over a period of time. They are taken hot, if the intention is to break up a cold or cough. Otherwise they can be taken either lukewarm or cold.

Decoction: Hard materials such as wood-pieces, bark, roots, seeds, etc. require prolonged boiling to extract their active ingredients. About ½ cup of plant parts can be boiled in 1 cup water. It is better to use a non-metallic or enamelled pot. Green plant parts and flowers can be added to cold water, brought to a boil and allowed to remain so for 3-4 minutes. Or they can be added straight to boiling water and allowed to be immersed at a galloping boil for a few minutes. In either case the pot should be covered with a lid. Harder materials need to be boiled longer. Plant parts need to be strained out from the decoction. The Kerala physicians often strain the decoction and boil it again until it is reduced to one-and-a-half times the original weight of the herbs. For cooking decoctions clay pots are considered the best. However, copper pots for *kapha* problems, silver or bronze for *pitta* problems and gold or iron pot for *vata* problems are also considered acceptable and good.

Cold Extract: To ensure effective extraction of delicate or volatile compounds the herbs are steeped in a non-metallic or enamelled pot containing cold water (1:6 ratio of herb and water) for 8 to 12 hours. Strain and the drink is ready. Through this method, only minor amounts of mineral salts and bitter principles can be extracted. Compared to hot infusions, cold extracts would need double the quantity of plant material. This method is recommended for very delicate herbs such as hibiscus, sandalwood, jasmine, marigold, rose, coriander, vetiver, etc. and for the treatment of *pitta* conditions.

Juice: While extracting juice from the plant material, a little cold water could be added. This is a good method for extracting water-soluble constituents, vitamins and minerals from the plant.

The juice should be consumed immediately after pressing, as otherwise the vitamin content is denatured and the fermentation process starts. This method is used in the case of all juicy plants particularly aloe, amlaki, brahmi, coriander, garlic, ginger, tulsi, lime, neem, onion, etc.

Syrup: The plant materials can be boiled in honey and strained through cheesecloth. This is an easier way of administering medicines to children.

Powder: Dried plant parts can be ground with the help of a traditional mortal and pestle or with a grinder or blender. Powders made from a combination of a number of drugs are popular in Ayurveda. The versatile *Triphala* is a shining example. The powder can be taken with water, milk or soup. It can be just swallowed with water or sprinkled on food. The common dosage is stated as the quantity that you can lift on the tip of a knife! These days, gelatine capsules can be used to facilitate swallowing. Sometimes powders are used externally as in the case of *Dashanga Lepa,* which contains liquorice, valerian, red sandalwood, cardamom, turmeric, etc. It is dusted on boils, mumps, abscesses, erysipelas and neuralgia.

Poultice: Also called cataplasms, the poultice is used to apply a herbal product to a skin area with moist heat. Often, the herb is made into a pulpy mass and warmed up. The warmed pulp is spread on a wet, hot cloth and wrapped around the affected area. In the case of mustard pulp or similar herbs, which are quite irritable to the skin, two layers of cloth could be used. After removing the poultice, the area could be washed with water or herbal tea to wipe out any left-over residue on the skin. Poultices are used to soothe, to irritate, or to draw out impurities from the body. Such an action depends on the type of herbs selected for the purpose.

Fomentation: A Turkish towel can be soaked in a hot infusion or decoction and after wringing out the excess liquid, applied as hot as possible on the affected area.

Cold Compress: It is like fomentation, but the infusion or decoction used is cold. The cloth is left on the body until it is warmed by body heat. Usually it is left on for 10 to 15 minutes. This is repeated with another fresh cold compress.

Soap Substitutes: Certain plants contain a compound called saponin, which produces lather when the plant tissues are rubbed in water. They can also be used to make shampoos. The plants which contain saponin in sufficient quantity to produce lather are:

Papaya leaves

Soap-nut powder (reetha) and shikakai

Powder made of dried orange rind, lemon rind, rose petals, etc.

All these can play an effective role as a substitute for soap.

Turmeric powder, which is a germicide, is also used along with besan, *kasturi manjal,* etc. Powdered leaves of neem, curry leaf, etc. also find their use as substitutes for soap.

In combination with milk, these herbs make an ideal wash for the upkeep of skin and in preventing its damage due to weather, old age, bacteria, etc.

Volatile Oils: Volatile oils extracted from various plants have been in use from time immemorial. They are extracted by distilling grass (*Cymbopogon,* etc.), leaves (basil, cinnamon, *Citrus,* etc.), flowers (*Citrus,* jasmine, rose, saffron, etc.), flower buds (lawsonia, mango, etc.) fruits (black pepper, bel, cardamom, nutmeg, etc.), seeds (anise, ajwain, coriander, cumin, saunf, etc.), roots or rhizomes (galangal, ginger, sweet flag, turmeric, vetiver, etc.), wood (aga, camphor, deodar, sandal, etc.), bark (asafoetida, *boswellia,* camphor, commiphora, etc.).

The volatile oils are responsible for the characteristic odour of the plant. Some act on the central nervous system, increase appetite, aid digestion and regularize intestinal action. When placed on intact skin, they can increase the flow of blood, especially of leucocytes. This property associated with the bactericidal properties of certain oils is the basis of their antiseptic use.

Preface to Volume Two

Systematic research in various systems of Indian medicine under the patronage of the Government of India commenced in the year 1969 with the establishment of the Central Council for Research in Indian Medicine and Homoeopathy (CCRIMH). In 1978, this body was split into four separate research councils: one each for Ayurveda and Siddha, Unani medicine, Homoeopathy, and Yoga and Naturopathy.

A recent WHO estimate reveals that around 80 per cent of the global population consumes phyto-medicines, and documents a shift in emphasis from the underdeveloped to the developed countries of the world. This trend has both positive and negative fallouts in society. While the prices of useful herbs skyrocket in the developing world as their main sources are depleted, the rural poor who have long been dependent on them find them unaffordable when compared to synthetic drugs and medicines. Even in the remote corners of rural and tribal India, we notice that branded synthetic medicines manufactured by multinational concerns have begun to percolate.

A survey conducted by researchers at the Beth Israel Deaconess Medical Centre and the Harvard Medical School in Boston reveals that the use of herbal medicines and other alternative therapies has shown a steep rise in the United States, with sales of herbal remedies increasing by 380 per cent during the nineties. The number of visits made by American patients to herbalists, chiropractors and other purveyors of alternative medicine is reported to exceed the total visits to all primary-care physicians.

The trend indicates the changing attitudes in modern society in general with regard to complementary and alternative systems of medicine.

A comparative study of ethno-botanical information contained in ancient Indian literature with folk medical lore, research amongst tribal communities and current scientific findings can go a long way in establishing the direction of future medical exploration.

The recent publication of the *Indian Herbal Pharmacopoeia* is a giant leap in this direction; some herbs have been standardized and twenty herbs have had monographs devoted to them. No doubt much work remains to be done. In order to obtain consistent results, the standardization of the product has to be monitored right from the raw-material stage. The habitat of the plant and the time of collection play a vital role in achieving consistency.

Although there have been attempts at a broader understanding of drugs based on their chemistry and pharmacology, India can perhaps follow China, where experimental results are immediately passed on to clinical investigators, who provide the necessary support in the clinical evaluation of particular drugs.

The Indian subcontinent contains about 25,000 species of vascular plants, of which 7500 are used by folk and other traditional systems. Several are used either alone or in combination with other plants. The current regulations state that if these drugs are prepared in exactly the same way as laid down in ancient literature and if they are preserved as detailed by the tests, such drugs do not require either approval of registration. The drug will however be treated as 'new' whenever a different method of preparation is used.

The subcontinent occupies a unique position in the world, capable of cultivating most of the medicinal plants used both in modern as well as traditional systems of medicine.

While India has to travel a long way to become self-sufficient in pharmaceutical production, the largest chunk of medicines—almost 70 per cent—draws on the indigenous systems of medicine catering to the needs of most of our rural people.

The export value of crude drugs from India in the international market has increased 2.76 times between 1985-86 and 1994-95, and now stands at 53.2 million.

Although India is one of the major suppliers of medicinal plants to the world, the export of value-added materials such as plant derivatives, chemicals, etc. is insignificant compared to the developed countries.

According to an UNIDO study, although there were 3349 units licensed to manufacture plant-based pharmaceuticals in 1987, their contribution to the total production was considered marginal.

A systematic survey of all medicinal flora is the need of the hour. While that may safely be left to dedicated researchers, this book is my attempt to contribute by documenting and making available to a larger public what I have seen practised in the course of my research.

This second volume of *Home Remedies* follows on from where the first had left off, hoping to reclaim a place on our kitchen shelves and in our lives for plants we have come to dismiss lightly.

1

Crab's Eye

Abrus precatorius

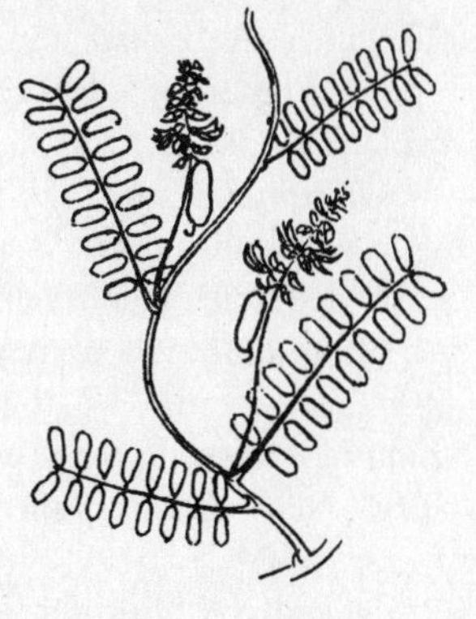

Ganja in eye diseases . . .
— Bhaavaprakasam

Worth Its Weight

Long before the invention of electronic weighing machines, which can accurately determine the weight of precious stones and metals, gold merchants had relied upon the seeds of crab's eye as the standard weight for transactions.

The seeds of this plant are quite shiny and attractive, exhibiting mostly a black-red colour combination. White seeds are also not unknown. It is not surprising that these shiny seeds have captured the hearts of our tribal women, who wear them as necklaces or bangles. At the same time, the tribals are aware of the toxic protein contained in the seeds, which is known to researchers as abrin.

The various plant parts, that is the leaves, roots and seeds, are well known in India for their medicinal use. Several classical writers like Sushruta have referred to the ayurvedic drug 'gunja' which owes its origin to this plant.

Both the leaves and roots of this plant are sweetish, resembling liquorice. They are used in folk medicine as a remedy for colds and coughs. As they are often used as a substitute for liquorice the plant has come to be known as 'Indian liquorice'.

The leaves, which possess laxative properties, are helpful in fighting the accumulation of phlegm in the body. They are also found useful in diminishing excessive thirst.

The roots which are emetic are, like the leaves, also found useful in eliminating phlegm. The root paste is reported to be used as a tribal remedy in the treatment of night blindness. (Bodding, 1986.)

The seeds which contain highly toxic proteins are said to possess various properties: antihistaminic, antiseptic, aphrodisiac, emetic, tonic and vermifuge. Various folk remedies recommend the seeds for the treatment of alopecia. Other common ailments for which the seeds are used are bronchial asthma, breathing problems, diarrhoea, dryness of the mouth, excessive thirst, eye diseases, feverishness, jaundice, pruritus, skin diseases, ulcer, vertigo, vitiation of *vata* and *pitta* etc.

The Unani system has long acknowledged the abortifacient properties of the seeds. Modern science has endorsed this use. A concoction of this indigenous drug was observed to prevent the implantation of the fertilized ovum. (Das, 1977.)

The Profile

Botanical Name	:	*Abrus precatorius* (Linn.)		
English Names	:	Indian liquorice, Crab's eye		
Indian Names	:	Bengali	:	*Kunch*
		Hindi	:	*Chirmiti, Ghumchi, Guncha, Ratti*
		Sanskrit	:	*Gunja*

	Tamil :	*Gundumani, Kunrimani, Kunritittu*
	Telugu :	*Ghurie-ginja*
Ayurvedic Name	:	*Gunja*
Unani Name	:	*Ghonghi*
Family	:	Fabaceae
Appearance	:	A wiry, climbing, twining shrub. Leaves compound with leaflets in 10-20 pairs. Flowers with pink stalks, in bunches (racemes). Pods pubescent. The seeds may be shiny black, white, half black and half scarlet in colour.
Distribution	:	Common upto 1000 m in the semi-arid tropical dry deciduous areas of the country.
Medicinal Parts	:	Leaves, seeds, root.
Ayurvedic Preparations	:	*Gorochandadi gulika*, *Gunjabhadra ras*, *Gunjadi taila*, *Gunjadi lepa*, *Neelibhringadi tailam*, *Svetagunjadi gulika*.

In Tradition

Arthritis, hip pain	:	Warm some sesame oil with finely powdered seeds (3:1) and apply on the affected areas.
Chest pain	:	Apply castor oil and stick some leaves over it.
Convulsions	:	Grind the roots of tree cotton with the leaves of crab's eye into a fine paste. Plaster over the whole body.
Swelling	:	Powder the seeds and mix with coconut oil (1:3) and apply. Grind and apply the seed paste. Mix equal quantities of leaf juice and warm gingelly oil and apply.
Leucoderma, leprosy	:	Grind equal quantities of the seeds of *Abrus precatorius* and the roots of chitraka into a fine paste. Apply and bandage.

HOME REMEDIES

- Muscular pain from over-exertion : Grind the leaves of henna, crab's eye and tamarind. Add a little salt and warm the paste slightly. Plaster the affected part of the body.
- Painful swelling : Mix 1 tbsp leaf juice in ¼ cup coconut oil and apply on the affected areas.
- Chest pain, hip pain : Apply some castor oil on the affected areas. Spread some fresh leaves over them and if necessary bandage so as to hold the leaves for 15-20 minutes.

  Boil the leaf juice with the leaf juice of trailing eclipta and sesame oil (1:2:3) thoroughly till all traces of moisture are gone. Cool and bottle. Apply 1 tbsp of this oil, massage for 10 minutes and take a shower. Repeat 2 to 3 times a week.
- Stiffness of shoulder joints, sciatica, paralysis : Apply the seed paste locally.
- Hair loss : Grind the seeds and mix with gingelly oil. Apply on the hair before a shower.

A Word of Caution

The seeds are POISONOUS as they contain a highly toxic protein.

In Science

Agarwal, S. S. et al. 1970. Anti-fertility activity of roots of *Abrus precatorius* Linn. *Pharmacol. Res. Commun.* 2. 159.

Agarwal, S. S. et al. 1969. Anti-estrogenic activity of alcoholic extract of the roots of *Abrus precatiorius* Linn. *Indian. J. Pharm.* 31: 175.

Agarwal, V. K. et al. 1971. Preliminary pharmacological investigations of the water-soluble portion of the alcoholic extract of the seed kernels of *Abrus precatorius* Linn. *J. Res. Indian Med.* 6: 139.

Agarwal, V. K. 1975. Anthelmintic activity of the seeds of *Abrus precatorius. J. Res. Indian Med.* 10 (3): 138. (Could kill all the earthworms.)

Akhtar, N. et al. 1972. Polysaccharide components of *Abrus precatorius. Sci. Ind (Karachi)* 9: 304; *Chem. Abstr.* 1874. 81: 101858p. (Sugar units identified.)

Basu, A. P. 1973. Studies on the antibacterial activity of *Abrus precatorus. Indian J. Pharm.* 35 (6): 203. (Water extracts could inhibit the growth of several Gram-positive and Gram-negative bacteria.)

Bharadwaj, D. K. et al. 1980. Flavanoids from *Abrus precatorius. Phytochemistry.* 19: 2040. (Chemical identification of the red-colouring matter of the seeds.)

Bodding, P. O. 1986. Studies in Santal Medicine and Connected Folklore. Calcutta: The Asiatic Society. (Reprint). (In *Santal Medicine.*)

Central Council, R. S. 1969. *Science*, 166: 44. (Glycyrrhizin, the active ingredient found in liquorice is also found in the leaves of this plant.)

Chakravarthy, R. S. 1969. *Science*, 166:44. (Glycyrrhizin, the active ingredient found in liquorice is also found in the leaves of this plant.)

Chowdhury, R. R. and M. Haq. 1980. Review of plants screened for anti-fertility activity. Part IV. *Bull. Medico-Ethno-Not Res.* 1 (4): 546. (A glycoside, abrin, and an alkaloid, abraline, responsible for anti-fertility activity.)

CSIR, 1948. *The Wealth of India*, Raw Materials, New Delhi, I, 3 and 1985, I. 18 (On amino acid content of the seeds.)

Das, P. C. 1977. Oral contraceptive. *Chem. Abstr.* 86: 21786b. (Role of crab's eye in controlling human population.)

Desai, R.V. and E. N. Rupawala. 1967. Anti-fertility activity of the steroidal oil of the seeds of *Abrus precatorius* Linn. *Indian J. Pharma* 29: 235. (An experiment on rats with seed oil.)

Desai, V. B. and M. Sirsi. 1966. Anti-microbial activity of *Abrus precatorius* Linn. *Indian J. Pharm.* 28: 164. (Alcoholic extracts of the seeds could inhibit the growth of micro-organisms such as *S. Aureus,* enteric micro-organisms, pathogenic fungi etc. in vitro.)

Desai, V. B. et al. 1970. Anti-tumour activity and some pharmacological properties of *Abrus precatorius* Linn. Part II. *Indo-Soviet Symposium on the Chemistry of Natural Products including Pharmacology.* 148.

Ghosal, S. and S. K. Dutta. 1971. Alkaloids of *Abrus precatorius. Phytochemistry.* 10: 195. (Pictorine and trigonelline identified.)

Gupta, N. C. et al. 1969. Steroids and triterpenes from *Alangium lamarckii, Allamanda cathartica, Abrus precatorius* and *Hoioptelea integrifolia. Phytochemistry.* 8: 791-7922.

Gupta S.C. et al. 1976. Preliminary pharmacological studies on *Abrus precatorius* seed-kernel (Gunja). *J. Res. Indian Med.* 11 (3): 94-97.

Lalitha Kumari, H. et al. 1971. Purification of proteins from *Abrus precatorius* Linn. and their biological properties *Indian J. Biochem. Biophys.* 8: 321. (A protein extract isolated from the seeds exhibited anti-cancer properties.)

Li Jung Yin et al. 1970. Purification of abrin from *Abrus precatorius. Chem. Abstr.* 1970. 72: 98695b. (Abrin, the highly toxic protein.)

Maiti, P. C. et al. 1970. Chemical examination of seeds of *Abrus precatorius. J. Indian Acad. Forensic Sci.* 9:64.

Prakash, A. O. et al. 1980. Effect of oral doses of *Abrus precatorius* (seeds) on oestrus cycles, body weight, uterine weight and cellular structure of uterus in albino rats. *Probe* 19(4): 286-292. (Seed powder administered to rats for 21 consecutive days exhibited anti-fertility effect.)

Saxena, U. K. 1973. Anti-fertility agents of plant origin. *J. Res. Indian Med.* 8(3): 79-86. (The plant exhibited oxytoxic activity in guinea pigs.)

Sivarajan. V. V. and I. Balachandran. 1994. *Ayurvedic Drugs and their Plant Sources.* New Delhi: Oxford & IBH. 158-159.

Subba Reddy, V. V. and M. Sirsi. 1968. Effect of *Abrus precatorius* L. on experimental tumours. *Indian J. Pharm.* 30: 288. (A protein extract isolated from seeds exhibited anti-tumour activity against Yoshida sarcoma in rats and fibro-sarcoma in mice.)

Thakur, R. S. et al. 1989. *Major Medicinal Plants of India.* Lucknow: CIMAP. 7-10

Zia-ul-Haque, A. et al. 1983. Studies on the anti-fertility properties of active component isolated from the seeds of *Abrus precatorius* L. *Pak. J. Zool.* 15(2): 129-139.

2

Dill

Anethum graveolens

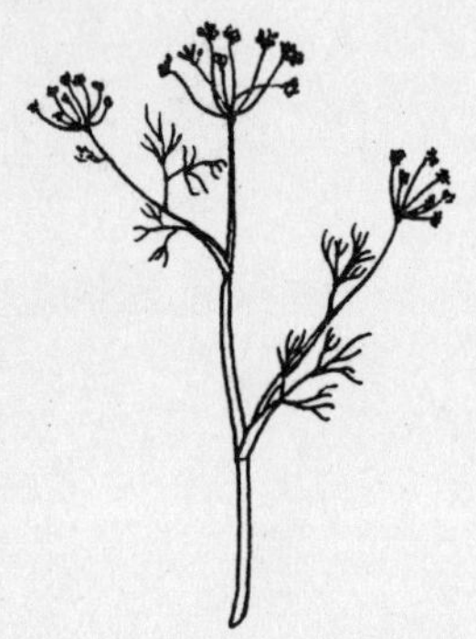

Satapushpa—destroyer of kapha and pitta . . .
—Nighantu Ratnakara

Dill to Dull and Lull

The common English name 'dill' probably originated from the Saxon word 'dillon', meaning to dull or lull. Historically, dill was given to restless babies to calm them and hence this name.

Both the seeds (botanically speaking, they are the fruits!) and leaves of this plant find their use in home remedies, across the continents. Dill's pungent and characteristic flavour is however, less pronounced and more delicate in the leaves than in the seeds.

The leaves are popularly called 'dill weed' by Continental cooks. Though both the seeds and the leaves are quite pungent, as the flavour is much less pronounced and more delicate in the leaves, they are ideal for those preparations which need subtle flavours such as cheese, pickles, salads, soups, sauces, poultry, fish etc. The leaves also impart an appetizing 'green' accent to otherwise colourless food.

Dill tea made with water or white wine is a popular remedy in the West for an upset stomach. A decoction of dill is also taken to cure insomnia and stomach aches due to flatulence. For hundreds of years, the nursing mothers in Europe have been using dill to promote milk secretion. For this purpose, the dill seeds are often used in combination with aniseed, caraway, coriander and saunf.

Properties: Anti-inflammatory, antispasmodic, calmative, carminative, diuretic, galactagogue, stomachic.

Leaves: cure haemorrhage, headache, ear ache, induce appetite.

The essential oil from the seed, known as Indian dill oil forms a main ingredient of 'gripe water' for infants.

In the Middle Ages, it was believed that dill would safeguard one against witch-craft.

The Profile

Botanical Names	:	*Anethum graveolens* L.		
		Peucedanum graveolens Benth. & Hook.		
English Names	:	Dill, Dilly, Garden dill		
Indian Names	:	Bengali	:	*Sowa, Soya*
		Punjabi and Urdu		
		Gujarati	:	*Surwa*
		Hindi	:	*Soya, Sowa, Soi*
		Kannada	:	*Sabasige*
		Kashmiri	:	*Soi*
		Marathi	:	*Shepu, Surva*
		Sanskrit	:	*Satapushpi*
		Tamil	:	*Sadakuppai, Satakuppi, Soyikkeerai, Madhurikai*
		Telugu	:	*Sabasige, Satakuprivuttulu*

Ayurvedic Name	:	*Satapushpi*
Unani Name	:	*Soya*
Other species	:	*Anethum sowa* (Indian Dill)
Family	:	Umbelliferae (Apiaceae)
Appearance	:	An annual erect, shiny, aromatic plant upto 1 m. tall with a hollow, finely grooved stem with 5 longitudinal, parallel lines. Leaves bipinnate, bluish green with thread-like leaflets; the base dilates into a sheath surrounding the stem. Flowers, yellow, in clusters (umbels). Seeds, convex, flat, variable in size and form.
Distribution	:	Native of Eurasia, cultivated in Jammu and Kashmir, Madhya Pradesh (around Neemuch) and in some parts of Gujarat.
Medicinal Parts	:	Leaves, flowers, seeds.
Ayurvedic Preparations	:	*Satapushpadi churan, Satapushpa arka.*
Unani Preparations	:	*Lubab-al-asrar, Ma'jun muurawahul-Arwah, Ma'jun nanakwah mushaki, Ma'jun sohag sonathi.*

In Tradition

- Swelling : Smear some castor oil on the leaves. Slightly heat and apply.
- Flatulence, insomnia, stomach ache, noise in stomach : Grind the seeds into a fine powder and bottle. Dose: Soak 1 tsp in 1 glass hot water for 5 minutes and take the decoction with 1 tsp honey.
  Soak 1 tbsp dill flowers (after thoroughly cleaning them) in a jug of drinking water. Drink it frequently.
- Insomnia (due to nervous problems) : Mix equal quantities of the following: aniseed, camomile, dill and hops. Dose: 1 tsp of the mixture steeped in ½ cup boiling water for 3 to 5 minutes. Add some honey and take at bed time.
- Insomnia due to exhaustion : Mix equal quantities of dill, pudina and saunf. Dose: 1 tsp steeped in ½ cup boiling

		water with some honey just before retiring.
❧ Phlegm, headache, earache, loss of appetite	:	Dry the leaves, powder. Add equal quantities of sugar and bottle. Dose: 1 to 2 tsp taken with 1 glass hot water.
❧ To disinfect a patient's room	:	Burn the dried leaves with dhoop.
❧ To promote delayed menstruation	:	Bruise ½ tsp dill seeds and steep them in 1 glass boiling water. Strain out seeds and drink.
❧ To promote lactation in nursing mothers	:	Mix equal quantities of dill, aniseed and sweet marjoram. Steep 1 tsp in ½ cup boiling water. Add honey to taste. Take 2 to 3 times daily.
❧ To strengthen the stomach and to achieve peak digestion	:	Mix equal quantities of the following: aniseed, caraway, dill and saunf. Add dried pudina leaves to this mixture (1:1). Dose: steep 1 tsp in ½ cup boiling water. Take 30 minutes before a meal.
❧ Intestinal worms	:	Crush the fresh leaves and take 20 drops of juice along with 1 tsp honey.
❧ Arthritic swelling	:	Grind dill seeds and roots (equal quantities) into a smooth paste and steam in a pressure cooker. Use the resultant paste to cover the affected parts. Allow to remain for 30 to 45 minutes, before wiping away with a cotton rag.

A Word of Caution

In Ayurveda fennel is sometimes identified as *satapushpi.*

No clinical data on the pharmacological efficacy of the drug is forthcoming at present.

Intake can cause hiccups, nausea, vomiting, giddiness. It is often advised to take the drug with lime juice to avoid such side effects.

In Science

Bandopadhyay, M. P. and T. R. Seshadri. 1972. Comparative study of *Anethum graveolens* and *Anethum sowa*. *Curr. Sci.* 41: 50. (The two showed certain differences in their chemical constituents.)

Buchman, D. D. 1996. *Herbal Medicine.* New York: Wings Books. 89.

Chakravarty, K. K. and S. C. Bhattacharya. 1954. Examination of Indian dill oil—Isolation of dihydrocarvone. *Indian Pharmacist.* 9: 218. (The chemistry of oil obtained from the seeds.)

Chou, J. S. T. and J. I. Iwanura. 1978. Studies on an unknown terpenoid obtained in dill oil-extract of *Anethum graveolens* L. from USA and on the analysis of some other dill oils. *Taiwan Ke Hsueh.* 32:131; *Chem. Abstr.* 1979. 91:52719. (Gas chromatographic analysis of the oil-extract).

Lust, J. B. 1974. *The Herb Book.* New York: Bantam Books. 173.

Pruthi, J. S. 1976. *Spices and Condiments.* New Delhi: National Book Trust. 110-113.

Shah, C. S. et al. 1972. Indian dill as a substituent for the European dill. *Indian J. Pharm.* 34:60. (Similarity between the two.)

Thakur, R. S. et al. 1989. *Major Medicinal Plants of India.* Lucknow: Central Institute of Medicinal and Aromatic Plants. 65-67.

Tomar, S. S. and S. K. Mukherji. 1981. Dillapional, a new constituent of *Anethum sowa*. *Indian. I. Chem.* 20B: 723.

3

Soap Pod

Acacia concinna

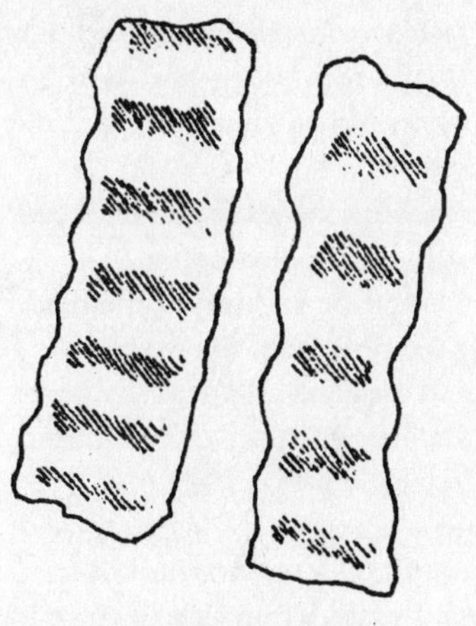

Sigaikai induces vomiting . . .
—From a Tamil verse by Agathiar

A Fruit for the Hair

Known in India as shikakai, the 'fruit for the hair', the soap pod has been in use as a common hair cleanser from time immemorial. As the pods are loaded with saponin (upto about 5% of its content), it qualifies as an ideal shampoo offered by Mother Nature. In addition, the soap pod seldom interferes with the natural oils of the skin, while flushing out dirt. In that way, it is the 'first' shampoo-cum-conditioner ever used by human beings! Folk wisdom has acknowledged its contribution fighting those lice or pathogens that are harboured in the hair roots or the skin surface, as the case may be.

The traditional textile processors of India have also employed the soap pod as an an effective detergent in the manufacture of both silk and woollen fabrics.

As a folk remedy the pod is used in various ways.

An infusion could be a substitute for modern day chemical antiseptics and can be used for cleaning and washing wounds and bruises; as a first aid, this can prevent pus formation and the resulting complications.

Soap pod can be called a poor man's analgesic particularly in the treatment of pain in legs, hips and joints. First you apply some castor oil on the limbs that ache and foment the area with a hot water bag. Then sprinkle the area with a fine soap pod powder, massage and later wash it with hot water. When you wipe it dry, the pain should have also been wiped away!

An infusion of the pod, after removing the seeds, when drunk with 1 tsp honey is a simple way of fighting constipation.

A dilute decoction of soap pod could be an ideal home-made gargle to drive away odour-causing bacteria from the mouth. As a consequence, several mouth-related diseases such as halitosis, gum bleeding, mouth ulcers and the like, that may over a period, tend to uproot the teeth can be effectively prevented.

Several folk remedies prescribe soap pod for fighting skin infections. A simple method is just to boil a teaspoonful of soap pod powder in 1 cup water and use the decoction as a tincture to wash frequently the affected areas of the skin. This could be the most affordable and economical way to locally treat itch, pimples, psoriasis, skin rashes etc.

The Profile

Botanical Name	:	*Acacia concinna* DC
English Name	:	Soap pod

Indian Names	:	Bengali	:	*Banritha*
		Gujarati	:	*Chikakai*
		Hindi	:	*Banritha, Kochi, Shikakai*
		Kannada	:	*Sige*
		Malayalam	:	*Chikaka*
		Marathi	:	*Shikakai*
		Tamil	:	*Sigaikai, Seekai*
		Sanskrit	:	*Saptala*
		Telugu	:	*Seekai, Shikaya*
Family	:	Mimosaceae		
Appearance	:	A prickly bush occurring in the tropical jungles in India, especially in Deccan. The pods appear wrinkled and brown when dry. Each pod contains 6 to 10 seeds.		
Distribution	:	Found all over the tropical parts of India, particularly in Andhra Pradesh, Assam, Bihar and along the West Coast.		
Medicinal Parts	:	Leaves, fruits (pods).		
Medicinal Preparations	:	Powder of dried pods.		

In Tradition

- **Pain in chest, hip, limbs etc.** : Apply a little castor oil on the affected area. Foment the area with a hot water bag (it should be bearably hot) and gently massage with powdered soap pod for 15 minutes. Wash the area with hot water and wipe it with a dry towel.
- **Constipation** : Take 3 leaf buds and grind them along with ¼ tsp tamarind paste, 2 tbsp each pudina leaves and coriander leaves, a pinch each of asafoetida and black pepper and salt to taste . Mix this powder in cooked rice or rice porridge and eat.
- **Constipation, fever** : Grind 3 leaf buds along with 3 peppers, 2 cloves of garlic and salt to taste. Take this paste mixed with cooked rice or rice porridge.

Constipation, jaundice	Crush a fruit, discard seeds and soak the rest in 1 glass of water for 1 hour. Take the infusion.
Dandruff :	Boil powdered soap pod in water (1:50 ratio) for 10 minutes. Cool and filter. Use this decoction to rinse hair.
Dandruff, lice :	Grind the following into a fine powder: dried fruits (after discarding the seeds) 10, ½ cup each of fenugreek seeds, zedoary roots, roots of Indian sarsaparilla and sandalwood chips. Bottle. Massage the head thoroughly with coconut oil and apply this powder. Rinse the head with water after half an hour.
Freckles :	Apply a finely ground paste of the fruit rind every day. Wash off after 15 minutes.
Gum infection, mouth odour	Boil ½ tsp powdered soap pod in 2 cups water. When lukewarm, gargle 3 to 4 times a day.
Mouth odour :	Apply a few drops of gingelly oil on the tongue and the interior of the mouth. Allow it to remain for 5 minutes. Mix a few drops of water into ¼ tsp powdered soap pod and make the whole thing a paste and apply carefully on the tongue and rub gently with the index finger. Wash the mouth with lukewarm water. (*Note*: Avoid swallowing.). Repeat 3 to 4 times a day and particularly after each meal.
Itch, psoriasis, wounds	Boil 1 tsp powdered soap pod in 1 cup water. Cool and apply on the affected parts.
Jaundice :	Grind 1 tbsp tender leaves with 3 peppercorns, tsp tamarind pulp, ½ red chilli and a little salt into a fine paste. Eat it with cooked rice or chapati. Soak a crushed fruit (after removing the seeds) in 1 glass drinking water stored in a mud pot for at least half an hour and drink this infusion. (*Caution*: This treatment may stimulate bowel movements and cause

frequent loose motions.) *Note*: In addition to the fruit, the following can also be added to the drinking water: coriander seeds (½ tsp) and galangal root powder (1 pinch).

A Word of Caution

Soap pod is clearly distinguishable from soap nut which grows in the northern parts of India.

While using soap pod, care is to be exercised to remove the seeds.

Soap Pod Body Wash

Powder equal quantities of the following, mix together and bottle. Use it with milk (1:10) for your ayurvedic luxury bath that is also an antiseptic guard against infection:

1. Soap pod
2. Green gram
3. Dried lime peel
4. Indian sarsaparilla roots
5. Zedoary roots

Soap Pod Hair Wash

Powder equal quantities of the following, mix together and bottle. Use it with the requisite amount of water for cleaning and washing the hair.

1. Soap pod
2. Green gram
3. Dried amla
4. Dried curry leaves
5. Dried lime peel
6. Fenugreek seeds

In Science

Arcilla, L. et al. 1986. In-vitro sensitivity testing of Mycobacterium tuberculosis using bawang, duhat, granada, latundan, acacia and betel. Bull. S. P. H. Public Health Thesis, Univ. of the Philippines, Manila. 49.

Chopra, R. N. et al. 1994. Chopra's Indigenous Drugs of India. Second Edn. Calcutta: Academic Publishers. 492.

CSIR, *The Wealth of India*, Vol. I. Raw Materials. Delhi. 13.

Mital, S. P. and B. Singh 1986. Introduction of genetic resources of some important medicinal and aromatic plants in India. *Indian J. Genet.* 46(1): 209216.

Sairam, T.V. 1999. Fruit for the Hair. *Holistic Healing*, September issue.

4

Babul

Acacia nilotica

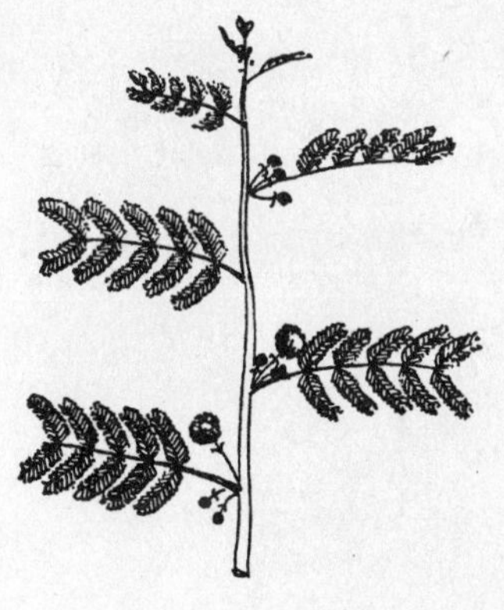

Babbula removes kapha and pitta . . .
—Nighantu Ratnakara

A Tree or a Drugstore?

The babul is a large tree indigenous to Sind. It also grows wild in India and Africa. It is often cultivated for its bark and gum which have a commercial use.

In native medicine, the bark is used in the treatment of gum diseases, fevers, mouth ulcer, etc. The gum is also medicinal. It vitalises the body and cures a number of common ailments: cough, dysentery, fevers, respiratory diseases, stomach ulcer, throat infections, leucorrhoea and spermatorrhoea. It is supposed to form a soothing, protective layer over the wounds and swellings that may occur on the inner surface of the throat, alimentary canal, urinary passage, respiratory tract etc.

The tender leaves of the babul are used in folk remedies for stopping diarrhoea and premature ejaculation.

The roots of the babul do not lag behind when it comes to healing. They are found useful in curing blood-dysentery.

The Profile

Botanical Names	:	*Acacia nilotica* (L.) Willd. Ex Del. *Acacia arabica auct.* Non (Lam.) Wild.
English Names	:	Acacia, Babul, Indian gum arabic tree
Indian Names	:	Bengali : *Babul* Hindi : *Babul* Marathi : *Babul* Gujarati : *Baval* Kannada : *Gobli, Jali* Malayalam : *Karuvelam* Punjabi : *Kikar* Tamil : *Karuvelam, Arimedham* Telugu : *Nallatumma*
Arabic name	:	*Ummughilan*
Persian name	:	*Khare Mughilan*
Ayurvedic name	:	*Babbula*
Family	:	Mimosaceae (Fabaceae)
Appearance	:	A large tree, distinguishable by the dark brown or black, longitudinally fissured bark. Leaves, bipinnate. Spines, white, sharp and straight. Flowers, yellow in colour crowded in globose heads. Pods, white, compressed, constricted at sutures, containing 8-12 seeds. Flowers during summer and fruits during winter.
Distribution	:	In dry areas of the country.
Medicinal Parts	:	Bark and gums; also tender leaves, seeds and root.

Ayurvedic Preparations	:	*Babbula churna, Babbularishta, Iremadadi taila, Lawang-adi-vati.*
Unani Preparations	:	*Bah Ral, Hub Awazkusha, Qurs Didan, Sunam Poast Mughlian.*

In Tradition

Anaemia	:	Fry 1 tsp each of the gum, sweet basil and purslane in an adequate quantity of olive oil for 10 minutes. Remove and soak in 1 cup rose-water for 1 hour. (Dosage: 1 tsp three times a day.)
Bed-wetting	:	Fry 1 tsp coriander seeds in a skillet till brown. Mix in 1 tsp each of pomegranate flowers, sesame seeds and babul gum and grind the mixture into a very fine powder. Add brown sugar equal to the powder. Dose: 1 tsp at bedtime.
Blood-dysentery	:	Soak 1 tsp crushed roots in a jar containing water for a few hours. Drink this water frequently.
Burns	:	Mix the gum in equal quantities of powdered turmeric and coconut oil and apply.
Cough	:	Take ¼ tsp tender-leaf paste with 1 tsp honey and a little warm water.
Cough, diabetes, excessive urination, dryness, impotency, throat infection	:	Chew a small portion of the gum.
Diarrhoea accompanied by stomach ache	:	Take the Karuvelam Bark Syrup (SEE below) in doses of 1 to 2 tsp twice a day.
Eczema	:	Boil 3 tbsp each of powdered bark of babul and mango in 4 cups water. Allow the

		vapour to foment the affected parts. After fomentation with vapours, anoint the area with ghee.
Conjunctivitis, sore eyes	:	Grind some tender leaves of babul in water into a fine paste. Fold the paste in a clean handkerchief and bandage it over the closed eyes at bedtime.
Gum problems, loose teeth	:	Grind 1 cup each of the bark of neem and babul into a fine powder. Add 1 tsp each of powdered cubebs, long pepper and rock salt. Mix thoroughly and use it as a tooth powder after every meal. Chew a small piece of the bark daily.
Poisoning	:	Take ¼ tsp tender leaf paste with 1 cup yoghurt.
Diarrhoea, dysentery	:	Take ¼ tsp powdered gum in water. Soak some leaves in water for 1 hour and take the infusion with 2-3 pinches of black cumin.
Eczema	:	Boil 3 tbsp each of bark of babul with bark of mango in a kettleful of water. Allow the steam vapours to foment the affected area. Finally, apply some ghee.
Leucorrhoea	:	A decoction of the bark is used as a vaginal douche.
Redness of the eyes	:	Grind 1 tsp tender leaves into a fine paste with a little breast milk. Form it like a coin and heat it on a skillet or a pan. When bearably hot, foment the eyes.
Gum diseases, loose teeth, mouth ulcers	:	Boil 1 tbsp tender leaves in 2 cups water. Gargle the decoction. Soak some crushed bark in water kept in an earthernware container for a few hours. Use this water to gargle. Use the finely-powdered bark as tooth-powder.
Sexual debility	:	Fry ¼ tsp powdered gum in 1 tsp ghee and take everyday with 1 glass milk.
Spermatorrhoea	:	Grind equal quantities of gum and the rind of haritaki into a very fine powder. Dosage:

		½ tsp taken with 1 tsp honey for 10 days. Dry the tender (seedless) pod in the shade. Powder. Mix equal quantities of palm sugar and bottle. Dosage: ½ tsp with 1 glass milk at bed time.
Sty	:	Grind a little piece of bark in breast milk into a very fine paste. Apply on the eye lid.
Spermatorrhoea	:	Dry the tender seedless pods in the shade. Powder, mix with equal quantities of raw sugar and bottle. Dosage: ½ tsp taken with 1 glass milk in the morning.
Sore throat, spongy gums, tonsilitis	:	Boil 1 tsp crushed bark in 1 glass water. Mix in a pinch of rocksalt and gargle.
Wounds	:	Grind the tender leaves into a very fine paste. Apply on the wounds. Boil some crushed bark in water and use the decoction for washing the wounds. Dust finely-powdered bark.
Yellow stained teeth due to digestive disorders	:	Grind the following into a fine powder and brush the teeth frequently with it: 5 tbsp of charred bark of babul, 2 tbsp roasted alum and 1 tbsp rock salt.

Karuvelam Gargle: A Home Remedy for Laryngitis and Sore Throat

Mix the following: 5 tbsp bark with ¼ tsp each powdered alum, betel nut, black catechu, and oak galls (masikkai). Boil in 1 litre water till the volume is reduced to half. Use it for frequent gargling.

Karuvelam Bark Syrup: A Home Remedy for Stomach Ache and Diarrhoea

Boil 1 cup bark in 1 litre water thoroughly and filter. Dissolve powdered jaggery (1 cup) into it. In addition, add the following ingredients in powder form: black peppercorns (4), cardamom (2), cinnamon (½ inch piece), cloves (2), nutmeg (¼) and pippali (½ tsp).

Mix all the ingredients thoroughly and allow to remain for a month before it is taken for medicinal use. Dosage: 1 to 2 tsp twice a day.

In Science

Arcilla, L. et al. 1986. In-vitro sensitivity testing of mycobacterium tuberculosis using bawang, duhat, granada, latundan, acacia and betel. *B.S.P.H. Public Health Thesis Document*: Univ. of the Philippines, Manila. 49. (Garlic, leaves of Java plum, seeds of pomegranate, red banana peeling, acacia (*shikakai*) and betel showed different sensitivity: pomegranate seeds produced the most significant inhibitory effects on different mycobacterium.)

Atique, A. and M. G. Siddique. 1989. Ethnopharmacological evaluation of the bark drug of *Acacia leucophloea. Willd. J. Natl. Integr. Med. Assocn.* 31(7): 15-16. (A mixture of the plant gum (Hindi: *safed babul*), turmeric and coconut oil or burnt gum and borax found to successfully cure burns in about 40% of the patients.)

Bakhru, H. K. 1995. *Herbs that Heal—Natural Remedies for Good Health*, Delhi: Orient Paperbacks. 5th Printing. 30-32. (Babul: a brief.)

Baruah, J. N. et al. 1963. Fungitoxicity of different polyphenolic fractions of *Acacia arabica* bark. *J. Inst. Chem. India.* 35(6): 306-308.

Chatterjee, A. and S. C. Pakrashi, (eds.) 1992. *The Treatise on Indian Medicinal Plants.* New Delhi: CSIR. 51-52. (Babul: a profile.)

Hussein-Ayoub, S. M. 1982. Molluscicidal properties of *Acacia nilotica. Planta Med.* 46:181.

Hussein-Ayoub, S. M. 1984. Polyphenolic molluscicides from *Acacia nilotica. Planta Med.* 50:532.

Khan, M. S. Y. et al. 1990. Chemical investigation of the pods of *Acacia leucophloea.* Roxb. *Indian Drugs,* 28(2): 97-98. (Steroids etc.)

Shaykh Hakim Moinuddin Chishti, 1991. *The Book of Sufi Healing.* Vermont: Inner Traditions International, 68 (On gum arabica.)

Thakur, R. S. et al. 1989. *Major Medicinal Plants of India.* Lucknow: CIMAP. 14-16.

Zaka, S. et al. 1986. Composition of the total lipids from *Acacia arabica* and *Acacia farnesiana* seed oils. *Pakistan J. Sci. Industr. Res.* 29(6): 27-29. (Chemistry of fats.)

5

Agar Wood

Aquilaria agallocha

Agil rejuvenates the body shattered by ageing . . .
— From a Tamil Siddha song

The Exotic Aroma

Agar wood when burnt emits a soothing aroma, which calms the nerves. Many people, Arabs and Parsis particularly, seem to be highly fascinated with this fragrance.

The fragrant agar wood is not obtained from all the trees of this species. It occurs rarely in some branches that fork out from the stem of only certain trees. It is interesting to note that it is only the trained eyes of certain tribals like the Garos, that easily spot the right trees among hundreds of others. The rest of the 'non-professional' agar hunters who have not cultivated this tribal sense, may end up felling many trees unnecessarily, thus jeopardizing forests and the eco-system.

Agar wood is sold in the form of blocks, chips or splinters. True agar is hard, brown and loaded with aromatic oleo-resins, whose odour is comparable to that of ambergris or sandal wood. Sylhet agar, a variety of agar, possesses almost all these characteristics and hence fetches a higher premium. Another variety, Dhum, much softer and yellowish white in colour is cheaper and commercially of not much use.

Agar attar, an aromatic oil obtained from agar wood, is as expensive as the otto of roses. It is a valuable perfume sought all over the world. The famous perfumers of Europe and America use it for enhancing the effect of their best grade scents and perfumes.

In Folk Medicine

Agar is a stimulant, carminative and a cardiac tonic. It imparts heat to the body, increases bile secretion, cures fatigue, fevers, headache, itching, migraine, nausea, lack of taste, *vata*-aggravation etc. Powdered agar wood is used in many concoctions such as medicated jams, used by native doctors in treating their clientele. In Malaysia, it is used as a liniment for various skin diseases, besides being used as a cosmetic preparation.

During epidemics such as those of small pox or malaria, there is a practice in many villages of Tamil Nadu to burn agar wood and raise a thick smoke. The patients suffering from cold, cough and toxic fevers who inhale the smoke are believed to overcome all such problems, caused by the wrath of goddesses.

Indian agar also finds its way into China, where it is largely used as incense and in the manufacture of joss-sticks.

The Profile

Botanical Names	:	*Aquilaria agallocha* Roxb. *Aquilaria malaccensis* Lamk.
English Names	:	Agar wood, Aloe wood, Calambac, Eagle-wood
Indian Names	:	Assamese : *Sasi* Bengali : *Agaru* Hindi : *Agar* Kannada : *Krishnagaru* Malayalam : *Akil, Karakil* Sanskrit : *Aguru, Krishnaguru* Tamil : *Agalsandanum, Agil, Agaru, Poozhil, Kagathundam* Telugu : *Agru*
Burmese Name	:	*Akyaw*
Family	:	Thymelaeaceae
Appearance	:	A large evergreen tree with a somewhat straight and fluted stem. Leaves silky and glossy, resembling mango leaves. Flowers, small, green. Fruits, yellow-coloured capsules, somewhat compressed, tomentose.
Distribution	:	Foothills of the Eastern Himalayas, forests of Assam, Bhutan, Bihar, Garo and Naga hills, West Bengal and South India.
Medicinal Parts	:	Resin, wood.
Ayurvedic preparations	:	*Chyavanaprasam, Lavangadi churnam, Mahanarayana tailam, Sankhapushpi tailam, Irimedadi tailam.*

In Tradition

Body odour	:	Rub the agar stick on a smooth stone with a little milk or rosewater and apply the paste so obtained all over the body before bathing.

Flabbiness in the body:		Make a fine paste of agar and apply all over the body.
Fever due to *pitta*-aggravation or heat	:	Boil 1 inch agar wood in 3 cups water in an earthern pot, till the volume is reduced to half. Allow it to cool. Take 1 to 2 tsp.
Fleas and lice	:	Dust all over the affected parts of the skin with fine agar powder frequently.
Burning sensation in the body, liver problems, loss of appetite, vomiting, nausea	:	Burn some agar pieces and inhale the smoke.
Wrinkles and flabbiness of the skin due to ageing	:	Make a paste of agar by grinding it with milk and apply all over the face and body. Repeat every day.
Asthma, breathless-ness, migraine, ailments of ear, nose and throat	:	Boil 5 cups of agar pieces in 2 litres of water till the volume is reduced to 1 litre. To this, add 1 litre each of cow's milk and gingelly oil and boil till the moisture is removed from the mixture. Now add ½ cup each of finely powdered vibhitaki rinds and liquorice root. Cool, filter and bottle the oil. Use this oil once or twice a week as a massage oil for the scalp and after massaging the head thoroughly allow it to remain for 20-25 minutes before washing.

Note: Individual results may vary.

A Word of Caution

Ayurvedic materia medicas mention two varieties of agar wood: black and white. In the southern parts of the country, the white agar (*Dysoxylum malabaricum*) is in use. Many physicians, however, consider the black variety as the possessor of all the medicinal properties of agar.

Agar Hair Oil

Soak 4 cups of broken chips of agar in 2 litres of water over night. Next day boil the water along with the chips till the volume of water is reduced to ½ litre. Now separate the chips and grind them into a fine paste. Remix this paste with the decoction of wood. Boil for 10 minutes and filter. To the filtrate so obtained, add ½ litre each of coconut oil, cow's milk and heat the mixture. Add 1 cup each of zedoary and the rinds of vibhitaki and 2 cups each of flowers of aavaram and Southernwood and ¼ tsp saffron. Boil all the ingredients for 10 minutes and cool. Take out the clear oil and bottle.

This hair oil is reported to be quite useful for avoiding premature greying of hair. It is also believed to be useful for those suffering from any blockage of the nose, dropsy and venereal diseases.

In Science

Chopra R. N. et al. 1994. *Chopra's Indigenous Drugs of India.* Second edn. Calcutta: Academic Publishers. 495

Council of Scientific and Industrial Research. *The Wealth of India—Raw Materials*, New Delhi I: 328. (The main constituent of agar oil is agarol.)

Bhandari, P. et al. 1982. Aquillochin, a coumarinolignan from *Aquilaria agallocha. Phytochem.* 21: 2147-2149

Central Council for Research in Ayurveda and Siddha. 1990. *Phytochemical Investigations of Certain Medicinal Plants Used in Ayurveda.* New Delhi, 34. (Identification of the alkaloids found in the roots.)

Pant, P. and R. P. Rastogi. 1980. Agarol, a new sesquiterpene from *Aquilaria agallocha. Phytochem.* 19: 1869-1870.

6

Areca Nut

Areca catechu

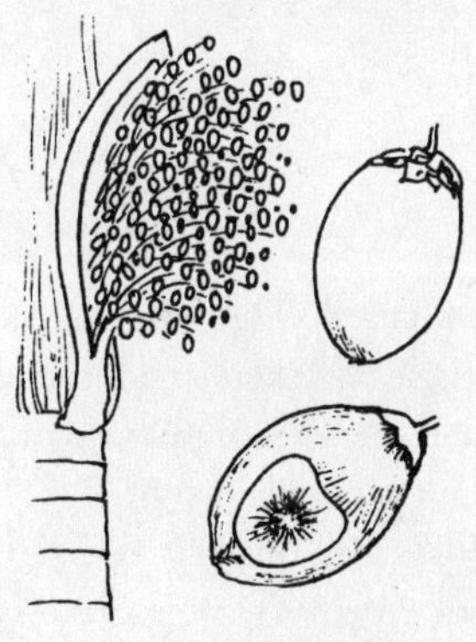

The person who is in the habit of masticating poogiphalam alone, and never in accompaniment with betel leaves and slaked lime, will be in perpetual debt for ten births . . .
— Charaka Samhita

The Areca Spread

Native of the Malay peninsula, the areca palm is widely cultivated in India, particularly in Assam, West Bengal and the West Coast. Even though known as a maritime tree in India, the palms can be found growing even at a distance of 300 kms from the seacoast. They also reach higher elevations, up to 3000 feet above sea level.

The Masticator's Delight

Areca nuts are the masticator's delight throughout the subcontinent. It is traditionally chewed in combination with betel leaves, chuna (slaked lime) and spices like cardamoms, coconut, cloves, fennel, nutmeg, rose-petals or gulkand.

Mastication of nuts, in combination with a variety of spices, can be a useful exercise for teeth. In moderation, it also aids in deodorizing the mouth, improving digestion and cooling the heat in the human body. There is widespread belief in the subcontinent that paan chewing has an aphrodisiac effect and hence it is customarily banned for children, widows and ascetics.

Curing the Nuts

The nuts are used as such (raw) or cured. The latter is more popular in southern India. The expert pickers exercise a lot of care in picking the right quality of nuts as it is the level of ripeness of the nut that determines its quality and eventually its price. They normally gather the nuts which are just three-quarters ripe.

Curing the raw nuts is an elaborate process. It is done in a variety of ways. Broadly, the process of curing involves the following steps: shelling the fruits; slicing the kernels into finer fragments; boiling the pieces of the kernels in a mixture of water and the previous year's nut extract called chogaru in earthen or copper pots; and finally sun-drying the resultants.

To satisfy the taste buds of connoisseurs, the kernels are at times boiled in coconut water or milk. When fully boiled, the embryos drop out as the cut surfaces assume a slightly concave appearance. They are then removed from the fire and sun-dried. The remnant decoction, which is called chogaru, is preserved for the following year's requirement, after desiccating it in the sun.

Another method of curing involves boiling the fruits as such, i.e. without husking. They are, however, peeled and sliced later.

Cracking the Nut

Areca nuts contain as an active principle, tannoids (15 to 20%) and a host of alkaloids (30 to 50%) which impart a mild astringency. Folk medicine makes full use of this potential, particularly in the treatment of diarrhoea and urinary infections. Village veterinarians use the nuts for their livestock as a vermifuge for eradicating tapeworms and various other parasites.

Of the several alkaloids present in the nuts, the four major ones are arecoline, arecaidine, guracine and guvacoline. Arecoline is used in combination with other drugs as a desiccating agent of blood and lymph. Arecoline hydrobromide, recognized in a number of pharmacopoeias, is the secret behind the success of the village veterinarians: it not only drives away worms and parasites, but it also stimulates the bowels.

The Profile

Botanical Name	:	*Areca catechu* Linn.		
English Names	:	Areca nut, Betel nut		
Indian Names	:	Hindi	:	*Supari*
		Kannada	:	*Adike*
		Malayalam	:	*Adakke*
		Sanskrit	:	*Poogiphalam*
		Tamil	:	*Paakku*
		Telugu	:	*Vaaka*
Arabic Name	:	*Fofal*		
Persian Name	:	*Popal*		
Family	:	Palmaceae		

Appearance	:	A very tall (60 feet) slender palm with a smooth, whitish stem, surmounted by a crown of pinnate leaves. Fruit: brightly orange when ripe, egg-shaped containing a greyish brown seed, couched in a hard fibrous pericarp. Seed, a hard nut to crack, has reddish brown lines.
Distribution	:	Cultivated in Assam, Karnataka, Maharashtra, Tamil Nadu and West Bengal.
Medicinal Parts	:	Root, seeds (nuts).

In Tradition

Constipation, intestinal worms	:	Boil ¼ tsp tender nut in 1 cup water. Cool and drink.
Fracture and injuries	:	Dust the injured areas with powdered katha. Place the bark of the areca palm over it and tie a bandage.
Gum infection	:	Burn one nut till its ash is obtained. Mix in 2 tbsp finely-powdered cloves and ¼ cup katha. Use it for washing the mouth thrice daily.
Gum infection, ulceration in lips	:	Boil 2 tsp root powder in 2 glasses of water till the volume of water is reduced to half. Wash the mouth/lips with this solution thrice daily.
Yellowing of teeth	:	Burn some nuts till charred. Powder and bottle. Rub the affected teeth frequently with this powder every day.
Diarrhoea, urinary diseases	:	Finely-powdered nut. Dosage: ¼ tsp powder along with 1 tsp jaggery in 1 cup warm water.
Intestinal worms	:	Mix well ¼ tsp finely powdered nut in the juice of one lime. Add 1 glass warm water and drink. Mix ¼ tsp finely powdered nut in ½ cup milk and drink.

- Gum infection : Frequently gargle with 1 cup warm water in which 1 tsp finely-powdered nut has been boiled.
- Gum inflammation, halitosis : Fry 2 tsp finely-powdered nut in 2 tbsp ghee and powder. Add equal quantities of ajwain, katha and rock salt. Grind them together into a very fine powder and apply all over the mouth thrice daily.
- Leucorrhoea : Mix 1 tsp betel nut powder in a mug of water and use it as a vaginal douche.

Note: Individual results may vary.

A Word of Caution

The chewing of raw (uncured) nut is not recommended, as there are possibilities of getting severe giddiness, tightness in the throat or profound secretion of mucus due to its intoxicating properties.

While areca nut no doubt in moderation prevents halitosis, it can be harmful in excess: it blackens the teeth, to begin with, which eventually results in their loosening and loss. It is also reported to cause leucophlegmatia, incipient jaundice, with paleness and bloating of the face.

Arecoline, the alkaloidal constituent in the nut, acts on central and peripheral nervous systems. It is suspected to cause paralysis, which may be preceded by convulsions. The habit of chewing nuts may, therefore, prove harmful in the long run.

Although well known for its anthelmintic action in the Chinese and Indian traditional medicines, frequent use of areca nut is suspected to cause oral carcinoma.

Areca Nut Plus: A Home-made Dentifrice

Burn the betel nut till it is charred. Mix in equal quantities of katha and finely powdered cloves. Bottle and use it as a tooth powder to combat bleeding gums, gum infection, halitosis etc.

In Science

Burkill, I. H. 1935. *A Dictionary of the Economic Products of the Malay Peninsula*, I: 225. (The 'nutty' nuts.)

Central Council for Research in Ayurveda and Siddha. 1996. *Pharmacological Investigations of Certain Medicinal Plants and Compound Formulations Used in Ayurveda and Siddha.* New Delhi. 470. (Anti-implantation role of the nut causing foetal loss.)

Chopra, R. N. et al. 1956. *Glossary of Indian Medicinal Plants.* New Delhi: CSIR, 23. (Medicinal properties reported: anthelmintic, aphrodisiac, astringent, cardiac depressant, convulsant, emmenagogue, hypotensive and spasmogenic. Its use in urinary trouble and as a vemifuge recorded.)

Chopra, R. N. et al. 1994. *Chopra's Indigenous Drugs of India.* Second edn. Calcutta: Academic Publishers. 280

Garg, S. K and G. P. Garg. 1970. A preliminary report on the smooth muscle stimulating property of some indigenous plants on isolated rat uterus. *Bull. P.G.I.*, Chandigarh. 4: 162.

Garg, S. K. and G. P. Garg. 1971. Anti-fertility effect of *Areca catechu* Linn. and *Carica papaya* Linn. in female albino rats. *Indian J. Pharm.* 3: 23. (Extracts of nuts, a promising anti-fertility agent.)

Lalitha Kumari, H. et al. 1964. Observations on the effect of Areca tannins on the rat uterus. *Indian J. Pharm* 26:268.

Lalitha Kumari, H. et al. 1965. Antibacterial and antifungal activities of *Areca catechu* Linn. *Indian J. Exptl Biol.* 3:66. (Water extract of the nut was found effective against *S. aureus* and *Trichophyton rubrum*; alcoholic extract inhibited the growth of *C. albicans*, *C. tropicalis*, *E. coli* and and *T. interdigitale*.)

Library of Tibetan Works and Archives, 1994. *Tibetan Medicine,* Dharamsala, 40. (Arecoline and its effects.)

Sairam, T. V. 2000. Medicinal Uses of Areca Nut. *Heritage Healing.* Feb. 33

Sirsi, M. et al. 1963. Influence of Areca nut extract on capillary circulation Part I. Pharmacology of *Areca catechu* Linn. *The Lacenciaie.* 13:22.

Sirsi, M. et al. 1963. On the pharmacology of *Areca catechu* Linn. *Curr. Sci.* 32: 455.

Sirsi, M. et al. 1966. Peripheral and central actions of *Areca catechu.* New Delhi: CSIR, Symposium on CNS drugs. 249. (Sedative effect of Arecoline, the active principle in the drug.)

Sirsi, M. 1967. The effect of Arecoline and some CNS drugs on 'motor learning' in rats. *Curr. Sci.* 36: 234.

7

Cabbage

Brassica oleracea var. capitata. Linn.

Cabbage will heal wounds full of pus and tumours when all other remedies fail . . .
—Cato, the Censor
(234-149 BC)

A Source of Patents

Cabbage, the popular vegetable, is also found therapeutically effective in many home-remedies. White cabbage leaves have an affinity for pus and hence draw out toxins from the body. They also reduce swelling. Certain chemicals in cabbage, called anti-oxidants, can prevent cancer. They achieve this by capturing roaming 'free radical' oxygen molecules, which otherwise promote cellular damage and cancer. They neutralize agents that activate cancer-causing carcinogens; they stimulate enzymes to flush out carcinogens.

In ancient times, the Egyptians and Romans used to drink cabbage juice before dinner to prevent intoxication. According to folklore, the ancient Romans started eating cabbage so intensely that their physicians ran out of a job.

A modern scientist, Jim Duke, Ph.D, chief of the medicinal plants section, United States Department of Agriculture is reported to eat cabbage every day – usually a big bowl of coleslaw for lunch which he believes will prevent colon cancer, prevalent in his family.

Cabbage seeds are also reported to prevent hangovers.

Apart from cabbage, the other cruciferous plants that crusade against cancer are: broccoli, brussels sprouts, cauliflower, cress, horseradish, kale, kohlrabi, mustard, radish, rutabaga, and turnips.

The cabbage, which is classified as a 'desmutagen', a chemical cancer antagonist, has been a source of patents. In 1980, Japanese scientists patented two techniques for isolating cancer-fighting amino acid from cabbage juice.

To make cabbage juice more palatable one may add celery juice from both stalks and leaves (3:1). For extra flavour, one can add some carrots, tomatoes, pineapple or citrus juice.

The Profile

Botanical Name	:	*Brassica oleracea* var. *capitata* Linn.		
English Name	:	Cabbage		
Indian Names	:	Hindi	:	*Bandh gobi*
		Tamil	:	*Muttakose*
Family	:	Cruciferae		
Appearance	:	Small shrub with large leaves, prominent inflorescence		
Distribution	:	Throughout India.		
Medicinal Part	:	Leaves		

In Tradition

Abscess, boils, infected cuts, sores and wounds	:	Remove the ridges of a leaf. Dip it in hot water and apply it as a poultice in a loose bandage. Replace the leaf frequently.
Asthma, bronchitis, chronic headache, cystitis, gastric ulcers, psoriasis	:	Drink fresh cabbage juice (½ cup) every day.
Bruises, swelling	:	Apply macerated cabbage leaves and bandage, if necessary.
Cough	:	Boil shredded red cabbage leaves in a little water. Filter. Add some honey and drink.
Eye inflammation	:	Apply the soft pulp of cabbage leaves on closed eyes. (*Note*: Avoid infection.)
Headache, certain types of neuralgia	:	Soften the leaves in warm water and apply on the affected areas.
Mastitis	:	Place crushed cabbage leaves directly on the breasts.
Mouth ulcers	:	Dab with white cabbage juice frequently using a piece of cottonwool.
Obesity	:	Make a salad with cabbage shreddings and tomato slices, sprinkled with a very little rocksalt and garlic juice. Take this in place of dinner.
Sore throat	:	Gargle with white cabbage juice 2 or 3 times a day.
To prevent cancer	:	Include cabbage regularly in the diet.
Warts	:	Apply the juice of a white cabbage.

A Word of Caution

Some advise eating red cabbage raw may cause constipation and irritation of the colon due to the high level of iron content therein.

Those who suffer from goitre should avoid cabbage.

Cabbage's ulcer-fighting capability varies greatly depending on the season and soil conditions; cabbages cultivated in the tropics are believed to be medicinally more useful than those produced in cold climates. Their healing factors are also reported to be more pronounced only when taken in raw form.

A controversial report appeared in a 1985 Japanese study that suggested that cabbage consumption incurred a relatively higher risk of colon and stomach cancer. On the other hand, certain other studies indicate that the cabbage-eating Japanese have less incidence of colon cancer than other groups! In certain other studies, cabbage-fed mice and hamsters are reported to have developed cancer when simultaneously given a carcinogen.

In Science

Alberto-Puelo, M. 1983. Physiological effects of cabbage with reference to its potential as a dietary cancer-inhibitor and its use in ancient medicine. *J. Ethnopharmacol.* 9(2): 261-272.

Ansher, S. S. et al. 1986. Bio-chemical effects of Dithiolthiones. *Food Chem.Toxicol.* 24(5): 405-415. (A dose of cabbage-type dithiolithione works wonder as an anti-cancer agent.)

Barker, D. J. P. et al. 1986. Vegetable consumption and acute appendicitis in 59 areas in England and Wales. *Brit. Med. J.* 292:927-930.

Boyd, J. N. et al. 1982. Modification of beet and cabbage diets of aflatoxin B1-induced rat plasma alpha-foetoprotein elevation, hepatic tumorigenesis and mutagenicity of urine. *Food Chem.Toxicol.* 20(1): 47-52. (Aflatoxin, the world's most virulent carcinogen, a fungal mould linked to high rates of cancer, was detoxified by the vegetables; brussels sprout was the most potent, twice as protective as next in line, cabbage.)

Buchman, D. D. 1996. *Herbal Medicine—The Natural Way to Get*

Well and Stay Well. Wing Books.

Carper, J. 1993. *The Food Pharmacy.* Simon & Schuster, Reprinted. 56-63.

Cheney, G. et al. 1950. Anti-peptic ulcer dietary factor (Vitamin 'U') in the treatment of peptic ulcer. *J. Amer. Dietet. Assn.* 26:668-672. (Eye-dropper amounts of fresh cabbage juice fed to guinea pigs every day helped prevention of cancer.)

Graham, S. et al. 1979. Diet and colon cancer. *Amer. J. Epidemiol.* 109(1): 120. ('Dose-response') of cabbage: at least one serving a week could cut colon cancer by 60%.)

Haenszel, W. et al. 1980. A case control study of large bowel cancer in Japan. *J. Nat. Cancer Inst.* 64(1):17-22.

Hoff, G. *et al* 1986. Epidemiology of polyps in the rectum and sigmoid colon. Evaluation of nutritional factors. *Scandinavian J. Gastroenterol.* 21:199-204. (Consumption of cruciferous vegetables—cabbage, broccoli, cauliflower and brussels sprout—and an emphasis on high fibre diet in general could prevent cancer.)

Manouso, O. et al. 1983. Diet and colo-rectal cancer: A case-control study in Greece. *International J. Cancer,* 32(1): 1-5.

Shealy, C. N. 1998. *The Illustrated Encyclopaedia of Healing Remedies.* Element Books, 85.

Singh, G. B. et al. 1962. Effect of *Brassica oleracea* var. *capitata* in the prevention and healing of experimental peptic ulceration. *Indian J. Med. Res.* 50: 741-749.

Spector, H. et al. 1959. Reduction of x-radiation mortality by cabbage and broccoli. *Proc. Soc. Exptl. Biol. & Med.* 100: 405-407. (Guinea pigs fed with cabbage and broccoli before 400 rads of deadly whole body x-radiation managed to survive the death-blow.)

Tajima, K. et al. 1985. Dietary habits and gastro-intestinal cancers: A comparative case-control study of stomach and large intestinal cancers in Nagoya, Japan. *Japanese J. Cancer Res.* 76(8):705-716. (Those who ate cabbage had the lowest death-rate from all causes, placing cabbage on a high pedestal along with the other 'old faithfuls' viz., olive oil and yogurt.)

Wattenberg, L.W. 1983. Inhibition of Neoplasia by minor dietary constituents. *Cancer Res.* (Suppl.) 43: 2488s-2453s. (Mechanisms by which chemicals in simple foods like cabbage and broccoli could reach into the living cells and stop cancer.)

8

Indravalli

Cardiospermum halicacabum

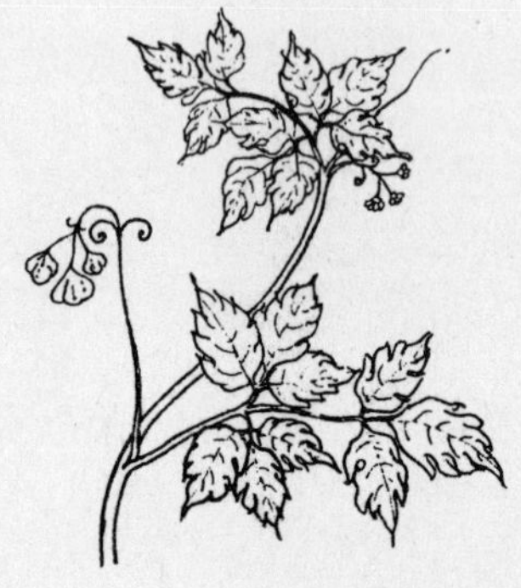

Karnasphota, the fever-killer . . .
—Hridayapriya

Considered as one of the Ten Auspicious Flowers (*Dasapushpam*) in ancient Hindu texts, indravalli finds a significant place in Indian ethno-medicine.

The Spiritual Facilitator

In the Tamil mystic tradition, a Siddha (also referred to as *sitthar* or *chitthar*) is a person who has achieved a state of spiritual enlightenment or self realization. Writers on alchemy, astrology, astronomy, medicine, tantra or yoga were all rated in common parlance, as Siddhas. Some prominent Siddhas not only hailed from Tamil Nadu but from all parts of India and even from outside its geographical or, for that matter, linguistic boundaries as there were Arabs and Chinese among them.

Saint Tirumular never restricts a Siddha by geographical boundaries. For him, any person whose mind is 'serene and clear like an ocean' is an eligible candidate to be referred to as a Siddha.

Through rigorous physical and mental practices, which involve various techniques such as the control of the breath (pranayama), the control of the mind (meditation), the regulation of postures (asana) and gestures (mudra), a Siddha seeks to attain what is known as siddhi (achievement), which is classified into eight types:

anima, the ability to become as tiny as an atom;
mahima, the ability to expand oneself infinitely;
laghima, levitation or ability to remain afloat;
garima, the ability to reach anywhere and everywhere;
prakamya, the ability to overcome natural obstacles;
ishitva, the ability to create or control;
vashitva, control over the entire creation; and
kamavasayitva, the ability to attain everything desired (which includes achieving the state of desirelessness!).

It is for achieving *laghima* that a Siddha is reported to use indravalli as a facilitator.

In Folk Medicine

Traditionally, indravalli is associated with *vayu* (wind), one of the Five Elements that plays a role in balancing *tridosha.* Several tribal pockets in Kerala employ the plant for alleviating arthritic pain. They have even found that the soil in which indravalli grows can be medicinal. They add some milk to such soil to make a paste and apply it on affected limbs. In Tamil Nadu, a chutney made of this plant (See below) forms an essential ingredient in the daily diet of those who suffer from excess *vata.* It induces heat which helps in the elimination of the phlegm accumulated in lungs and the wind accumulated in limbs. Besides balancing *vata*, the chutney helps in promoting appetite, expelling urine and blocked stools.

Ethno-medicine finds the drug useful in the treatment of a number of ailments: amenorrhoea, bronchitis, fevers, hydrocele, nervous disorders, oedema, piles, rheumatism, sprains, urine retention etc.

Profile

Botanical Name	:	*Cardiospermum halicacabum* Linn.
English Names	:	Balloon vine, Heartseed, Heart's pea
Indian Names	:	Bengali : *Lata phatkari, Sibjhul*
		Gujarati : *Karolio*
		Hindi : *Kanphuti, Kapalphoti*
		Kannada : *Kanakayya*
		Malayalam : *Ulinna*
		Marathi : *Kapalphodi*
		Sanskrit : *Indravalli, Karnasphota, Sakralata*
		Tamil : *Mudakathan, Mudakaruthan, Mudukottan, Modikottan*
		Telugu : *Buddakakra, Vekkudutiga*
Family	:	Sapindaceae
Appearance	:	A hairy or shiny annual or perennial with slender branches, climbing by means of hook-like tendrils. Leaves, teethed, pointing at the apex. Flowers, small, white. Fruits, an inflated, 3-valved winged capsule. Seeds, black with a large heart-shaped aril.
Distribution	:	Throughout India, found frequently in waste places in the Deccan, the Coromandel and West Coast.
Medicinal Parts	:	Leaves, root, seeds, the whole plant.
Ayurvedic Preparations	:	*Arukaladi tailam, Neelibhringadi tailam.*

In Tradition

Cough, piles :	Soak a few leaves in drinking water stored in a mud pot and drink it frequently.
Fistula, piles :	Grind 1 tsp seeds, 2 peppers and 2 tbsp durva grass with 2 tbsp butter. Mix this paste in 1 glass butter-milk and drink on an empty stomach every morning. Bandage the affected portion with leaves fried in ghee.
Arthritis, diseases caused by *vata*-aggravation :	Take ½ cup each of both cleaned leaves and roots of indravalli along with ½ tsp cumin and 2 black pepper, ½ inch piece of ginger (crushed) in an earthern pot. Add 3 glasses of water and boil the contents thoroughly till the volume is reduced to 1 glass. Take ½ glass of this decoction twice a day.
Asthma, cough, phlegm-accumulation, wheezing :	Take 6 tbsp each of indravalli leaves, climbing brinjal and one inch piece of galangal root (crushed) and 1 tsp cumin, 4 black peppers and 1 tsp dried ginger powder in a mud pot. Add 3 glasses of water. Boil thoroughly till the volume is reduced to 1 glass. Take 1 or 2 tbsp twice daily.
Menoschesis (suppression of menstruation) :	Fry indravalli leaves in coconut oil and tie on the lower abdomen for a few hours. Repeat 2 or 3 times a day.
Psoriasis, scabies, skin diseases :	Grind 1 cup indravalli leaves into a fine paste along with ½ cup coconut oil. Keep it in the sun and apply over the affected areas.
Ear ache, pus-formation in ears :	Squeeze a few drops of the leaf juice into the ears. Plug the ear with cotton wool.
Joint pain :	Fry a handful of indravalli leaves in 1 cup gingelly oil. Cool. Apply the oil over the affected areas. Grind a handful of indravalli leaves and add to idli batter. Eat idlis made out of this batter at least once a week.

Problems in women after child-birth :	Fry some leaves in castor oil and use them to foment the abdominal region. (*Note*: They can be tied to the abdomen overnight.)
Vata/pitta-aggravation	Clean and crush the whole plant into a fine paste. Take 1 tsp along with a little castor oil. (*Caution*: This treatment may cause severe loose motions.)

A Word of Caution

The consumption of indravalli leaves may cause severe loose motions. The plant has a sedative action on the central nervous system.

Some controversies exist with regard to the correct identification and nomenclature of this drug as referred to in the ancient ayurvedic texts. The Bengal school identifies the drug as Jyotishmati or Lataphatkari, while others refer to it as Kakadani. For some, it is Karnasphota or Krishnagunja.

Indravalli Chutney: The Recipe

Clean, dry and fry a handful of leaves in 2 tbsp ghee, preferably in a new earthern pot. Add urad dal, coriander leaves, curry leaves, ginger, tamarind paste (all 1 tbsp each) and a little asafoetida and continue frying till the whole mixture turns coppery. Now grind this mixture with salt (to taste) and the chutney is ready. This can be eaten with rice or chapati or bread.

Frequent intake of this chutney is reported to cure *vata*-aggravations, particularly arthritic swellings, joint pain etc.

In Science

Central Council for Research in Ayurveda and Siddha. 1990. *Phytochemical Investigations of Certain Medicinal Plants Used in*

Ayurveda. New Delhi. 304. (The plant chemistry.)

Central Council for Research in Ayurveda and Siddha. 1996. *Pharmacological Investigations of Certain Medicinal Plants and Compound Formulations used in Ayurveda and Siddha.* New Delhi, 147-158. (The decoction of roots exhibited analgesic, anti-inflammatory and diuretic effects in rats and mice; essential oil extracted from the seeds produced long-lasting hypotension in anaesthetized dogs and the action remained unaffected by atropine.)

Chopra, R. N. 1933. *Indigenous Drugs of India.* Calcutta: The Art Press. 570.

Council for Scientific and Industrial Research. *The Wealth of India.* Raw Materials, Vol. II. New Delhi, 75.

Covello, M. 1951. *Ann.Chim.*(Rome), 41:780. (The seed chemistry.)

Dass, A. K. 1966. *Bull. Bot. Surv. India*, 8:357. (Steroids from dried plants.)

Desai, K. B. and S. Sethna. 1954. *J. Maharaja Syajirao Univ.* Baroda, 3:33 (Steroids in the roots.)

Gedeon, J. and F. A. Kincl. 1956. *Arch. Pharm.* 289:162. (Chemistry of the seed oil.)

Hopkins, C. Y. et al. 1968. *Phytochemistry*, 7:619. (Chemistry of the seed oil.)

Kirtikar, K. R. and B. D. Basu. 1935. *Indian Medicinal Plants.* Vol I. 623.

Mikolajczak, K. L. et al. 1970. *Lipids.* 5(10): 812. (Chemistry of the seed oil.)

Modi, N. T. and B. S. Desillnankar, 1972. Some preliminary pharmacological investigations on *Cardiospermum halicacabum* (*Jyotismati*) *Indian J.Pharm.* 34:76. (Lowering hypertension.)

Pillai, N. R. and N.Vijayamma. 1985. Some pharmacological

studies on *Cardiospermum halicacabum* Linn. *Anc.Sci.Life.* 5(1): 32-36. (Significant sedative effect on central nervous system.)

Santhakumari G. et al. 1981. Diuretic activity of *Cardiospermum halicacabum* Linn. in rats. *Jour. Sci. Res. Pl. Med.* 2: 32-34. (Diuretic and smooth muscle relaxing effects of the drug.)

Watt, G. 1889-99. *A Dictionary of the Économic Products of India.* Vol II. 155.

9

Aavarai

Cassia auriculata

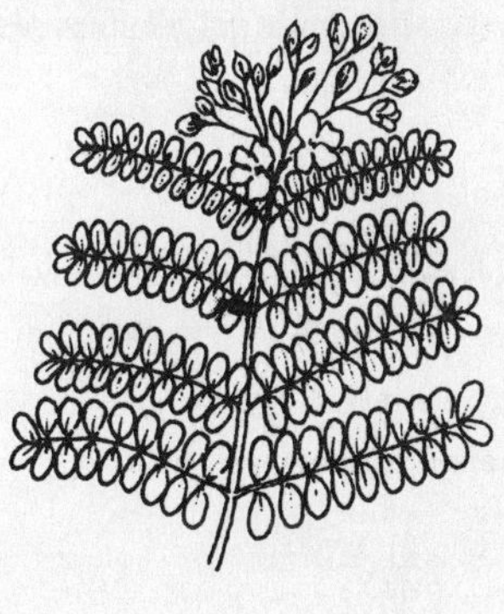

Can you see any dead body, when the aavarai is in full bloom?
—A Tamil saying

The Green Umbrella

Villagers in Tamil Nadu who walk long distances on foot in the hot summer months are often found plucking a handful of aavarai branches and placing them on their head before turbaning their head with a piece of cloth. This is a natural way of keeping one's head cool!

Aavarai tends to retain water in the body. It strengthens the nervous system and improves health. It helps in the reduction of sugar in blood and urine. According to Agathiar Gunapadal, a Tamil text, the flowers are useful in brightening the body and make it shine like gold.

In folk medicine, the flowers are used in the treatment of gonorrhoea. They also cool the body, eliminate fatigue and body odour and improve the complexion by eliminating dryness.

The villagers in Tamil Nadu use the flowers as a vegetable. The flowers are often dried and powdered and stored and used in place of tea leaves. Sometimes the bark, flowers, leaves and fruits are dried and powdered and mixed in equal amounts and the resultant *panchanga churanam* is used as a ready-to-serve home remedy.

The bark, popularly known as aavarai bark is the principal indigenous material used in South Indian tanneries. While the bark is astringent, the leaves and flowers are anthelmintic. The aavarai root is used in the treatment of skin afflictions.

The Profile

Botanical Name	:	*Cassia auriculata* L.		
English Names	:	Avaram, Tanner's cassia		
Indian Names	:	Gujarati	:	*Awal*
		Hindi	:	*Tarwar*
		Kannada	:	*Tangedu*
		Malayalam	:	*Avara*
		Marathi	:	*Tarwad*
		Tamil	:	*Aavaarai, Aaguli, Meghari, Thalapodam*
		Telugu	:	*Tangedu*
Family	:	Caesalpineaceae		
Appearance	:	A bush or shrub, 3 to 5 feet tall with large bright yellow flowers growing wild in central India and the Western Peninsula. Cultivated in other places.		
Distribution	:	Madhya Pradesh, Rajasthan, Tamil Nadu, Western Peninsula.		
Medicinal Parts	:	Bark, gum, flowers, fruits, leaves, root.		

In Tradition

Burning sensation in the body, diabetes, excessive hunger, thirst and urination, eye problems due to diabetes, giddiness, physical weakness, insomnia	Take ½ tsp *panchanga churanam* with some hot water, 2 or 3 times a day for 40 days or 80 days continuously.
Blood pressure, constipation, diabetes, dryness of skin, giddiness, joint pain, nervous weakness	Powder the dried seeds and bottle. Before retiring every day, soak ½ cup kala chana (black gram) and a sliced fig in 2 glasses of water kept in a new mud pot. Next morning boil them till the volume of water is reduced to half. Filter and remove the solids. Now add ½ tsp powdered seeds of aavarai to the filtrate and drink. Use for 40 days continuously.
Body odour	Wash the body with a paste made of zedoary and aavarai leaves. (*Note*: Avoid the consumption of meat and other proteinaceous foodstuffs.)
Constipation	Grind 1 tbsp each of curry leaves and leaves of aavarai into a fine paste. Add 1 tsp honey and take immediately after a meal.
Diabetes	Grind ½ tsp each of the following ingredients (fully dried) into a coarse powder: leaves, flowers, fruits, bark and root. Boil with 2 glasses of water till the volume is reduced to ½ glass. Dosage: 1 tbsp.
Diabetes, burning sensation in male sex organ	Soak some cleaned flowers in drinking water kept in an earthernware pot. Drink it frequently.
Diabetes, to improve the complexion and eyesight	Soak 2 tbsp fresh flowers in water for a few hours and drink.
Burning sensation during urination, diabetes, leucorrhoea	Mix ¼ tsp gum in 1 cup water and drink twice a day for a few days.

Eye diseases	:	Fry some leaves in a little ghee. Cool and place them on the closed eyelids and tie a bandage for 10 minutes.
Leucorrhoea, spermatorrhoea, urinary diseases, burning sensation in male reproductive organ	:	Mix some flowers with gulkand and take twice daily for a few days.
Body ache, burning sensation in the body, dry skin conditions	:	Heat ½ litre gingelly oil. Mix ½ cup each aavarai bark and zedoary with 1 red chilly and 1 tsp camphor and boil well. Cool, filter and bottle the resultant oil. Apply and massage the affected parts.
Menorrhagia	:	Place some cleaned flowers into the vagina for 10-15 minutes. Repeat frequently.
Itching	:	Mix a handful of leaves with ½ cup green gram and grind into a fine paste. Use it as a substitute for soap during baths.
Swelling in hands and legs	:	Take 1 tbsp each of aavarai bark and dried ginger and boil well in ½ cup water till the volume is reduced to 2 tbsp. Filter and take.

Note: Individual results may vary.

In Science

Aida, K. et al. 1987. Inhibition of aldose reductase activities by Kampo medicines. *Planta Med.* 53(2): 131-135. (Traditional oriental herb prescriptions containing cassia, cinnamon, liquorice, paeonia etc. exhibited potent enzyme inhibitory activity confirming the efficacy of these medicines in some chronic diabetic complications.)

Benjamin, T. and A. Lamikarna. 1981. Investigation of *Cassia alata*, a plant used in the Nilgiris in the treatment of skin diseases. *Quart. J. Crude Drug Res.* 9(2-3): 93-96. (Antibacterial properties of *Cassia* spp.)

Brenan, J. P. M. 1958. New and noteworthy cassias from tropical Africa. *Kew Bull.* 13:231-252.

Herrera, C. L. et al. 1984. Philippines plant as possible source of anti-fertility agents. *Philipp. J. Sci.* 113(1-2): 91-129. (Strong decoction of leaves of *Cassia* spp. exhibited anti-fertility effect.)

Linsen, T. 1987. Treatment of 200 cases of constipation with *Cassia angustifolia.* Yurman *J. Tradl. Chinese Med.* 8(1):38-39. (Dose of 10 gm leaves of senna (*C.angustifolia* or *C. acutifolia*) soaked in boiled water for drinking. In 99% cases, bowel movements started after 3-4 doses. 20% cases were treated with Tab. Phenolphthaleinum or together with enema served as control and its effective rate was only 75%.)

Mital, S. P. and B. Singh. 1986. Introduction of genetic resources of some important medicinal and aromatic plants in India. *Indian J. Genet.* 46(1): 209216.

Nair, B. K. H. et al. 1977. Cassia fistula in pyoderma—a clinical trial. *J. Res. Indian Med. Yoga and Homoeo.* 12(4):16-21.

Pandey, Y. N. 1974. Identification of certain Cassia seeds in the indigenous systems of medicine. *Quart. J. Crude Drug Res.* 12:20-22.

Pandey, Y. N. 1975. Cassia seeds used as drug in the indigenous medical systems of India. *Quart. J. Crude Drug Res.* 13:61-64.

Prakash D. and S. Prasad. 1971. Pharmacognostical studies on *Cassia tora* L. *J. Res. Indian Med.* 6(3):270-280.

Radhakrisna, N. et al. 1986. Antifungal activity of medicinal plants. *J. Res. Indian Med. Yoga and Homoeo.*

Rai, K. N. and R. A. Dasaundhi, 1990. A new flavone glycoside from the roots of *Cassia auriculata* Linn. *J. Bangladesh Acad. Sci.* 14(1): 57-61. (Chemistry of roots.)

10

Camphor

Cinnamomum camphora

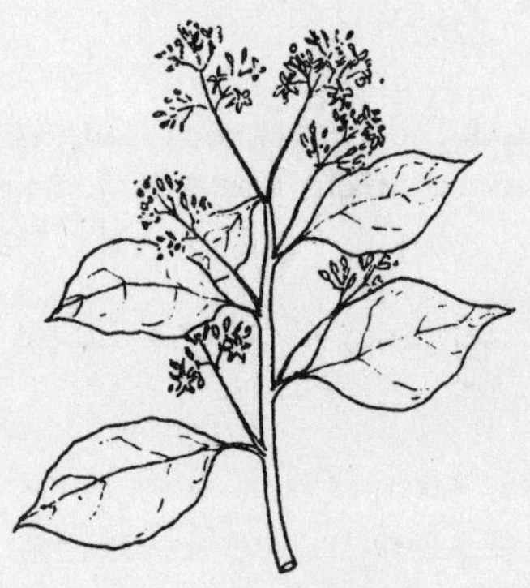

Karpurah . . . a remover of toxins
—Gunapathan

The Prayer Crystals

Camphor is a white, crystalline solid obtained from a tree which is native to China and Japan. It is formed in oil-cells dotted all over the tree. Generally the leaves are used for extracting the aromatic oil.

On steam-distillation, blue, brown and white fractions of camphor are obtained. It is the white camphor which possesses medicinal properties and finds its application in traditional medicine. The blue camphor is the weakest and heaviest fraction, which finds its use in perfumeries. As the brown camphor is reported to contain carcinogens, it is better to avoid it, particularly as a medicine.

Camphor possesses analgesic and antiseptic qualities. It has a pungent aromatic taste, which is followed by a sensation of coldness. It is also a heating substance and is helpful in problems such as joint and muscle pain. It is extensively used in the treatment of inflammation. It is externally applied in the treatment of open wounds, rheumatism and sprains. In conjunction with menthol or phenol, it relieves itching of the skin. It is used as a bronchial dilator, decongestant and expectorant as it decongests nasal and sinus congestions, clears the mind and cures headache. It acts on both the nervous and respiratory systems.

Camphor burns with a bright smoky flame and is an important constituent in Hindu prayers, particularly in performing arti. It volatilizes at ordinary room temperature and sublimes when heated.

The Profile

Botanical Name	:	*Cinnamomum camphora* (L) T. Nees & Eberm		
English Name	:	Camphor		
Indian Names	:	Hindi	:	*Kapur, Karpur, Mushkapur*
		Sanskrit	:	*Karpuram*
		Tamil	:	*Karpuram*
Family	:	Lauraceae		
Appearance	:	A large, handsome, evergreen tree, often grown on the edges by cultivators. Leaves, aromatic, leathery, shining. Fruits, dark green, dry and globose, turning black on maturity.		
Distribution	:	South India		
Medicinal Parts	:	Leaves and twigs.		
Medicinal Uses	:	Compress, massage oil, salve, steam inhalation.		

In Tradition

Abdominal pain due to urine retention	:	Warm 1 tbsp mustard oil. Add a piece of camphor and ¼ tsp sandal powder. Massage the lower abdomen.
Asthma, breathing problems	:	Mix 1 tbsp camphor powder in ½ cup coconut oil and apply on the chest.
Bed sores	:	Dissolve 1 tbsp camphor powder in ½ cup olive oil and warm the mixture. Apply on the affected parts. (*Note*: This is also a preventive treatment).
Bronchitis, cold	:	Take ½ litre steaming water in a pan. Add a few drops of camphor oil. Inhale the vapours. (*Caution*: Stop if you feel dizzy.)
Bronchitis, common cold, fevers, headache	:	Burn the camphor and use it as a sudorific to increase sweating. (*Caution*: Stop if you feel dizzy.)
Common cold, fatigue, headache, aching limbs		Mix 2 tsp each of camphor and menthol and apply the resultant liquid on the affected parts.
Gum infection, halitosis, pyorrhoea	:	Mix bark of neem, cloves, haritaki, aerial roots of banyan tree and camphor (l:l:l:3:6). Powder and use as tooth powder.
Nose bleed	:	Add a pinch of camphor powder in 1 tsp coriander leaf juice. Soak a piece of cotton wool and squeeze 2 or 3 drops into both the nostrils.
Rheumatic pain	:	Dissolve 2 tbsp camphor powder in ½ cup coconut oil. Warm and massage the affected parts.
Ringworm infection on children's heads resulting in falling and greying of hair	:	Mix 1 tsp camphor in 2 tbsp coconut oil and apply regularly on the affected portion of the head. After 30 minutes wash off with lukewarm water.
Halitosis, pyorrhoea	:	Mix the following in powder form: neem bark (½ cup), haritaki (½ cup), aerial roots of banyan (1 cup), cloves (1 tbsp) and camphor (1 tbsp).Use this mixture as a

		tooth powder cum gum-paint thrice a day after every meal.
☙ Toothache	:	Crush a tiny bit of camphor with 3 or 4 black peppers or cloves into a fine powder and apply on the affected area.
☙ Vaginal itching	:	Grind 1 tsp camphor in 4 tbsp rosewater. Soak a tampon in the solution and apply to vagina for 15 to 20 minutes. Repeat 2 to 3 times, if necessary.

Note: Individual results may vary.

A Word of Caution

Use camphor only in small doses and once in a while. Internal consumption of camphor may lead to toxicity, resulting in convulsions, delirium, coma or even, in rare cases, death due to respiratory failure.

The brown fraction of the camphor is reported to contain some carcinogens.

In excess, camphor induces *pitta.*

Make sure that the camphor purchased by you is steam-distilled from natural sources.

In Science

Agarwal, S. G. et al. 1987. Some industrially important aromatic plants of Sikkim. *Indian Perfum.* 31(2): 113-115.

Baruah, A. K. S. et al. 1975. Examination of volatile oil of *Cinnamomum camphora* grown at Jorhat (Assam) *Indian J. Pharm.* 37: 39- 41.

Burkill, I. H. 1935. *A Dictionary of Economic Products of the Malay Peninsula.* London: Crown Agents of the Colonies. Vol. I.

Howard, A. L. 1948. *A Manual of the Timbers of the World.* London:

Macmillan. 106.

Khien, P. V. et al. 1988. Contribution to the study of essential oils of *Cinnamomum camphora* leaves. *J. Pharmacy*, 28(4/5): 13-16. (Oil content and the chemical component.)

Kimura, Y. et al. 1987. Effects of Japanese and Chinese traditional medicine 'Hachimi-gan' ('Ba-Wei-Wan') on lipid metabolism in rats fed high sugar diet. *Planta Med.* 53(2): 128-131. (The drug containing *cassia, cinnamomum* etc. inhibited the elevation of serum triglycerides.)

Macmillan, H. F. 1946. *Tropical Planting and Gardening.* London: Macmillan. 395.

Mital, S. P. and B. Singh. 1986. Introduction of genetic resources of some important medicinal and aromatic plants in India. *Indian J. Genet.* 46(1): 209-216.

Raghavan, M. S. 1940. *A Note on the Possibility of Camphor Cultivation in South India.* Madras: Government Press. 8.

Ramachandra Rao, Y. et al. 1988. Major constituents of essential oils of *Cinnamomum zeylanicum. Indian Perfum.* 32(1): 86-89.

Sensarma, P. 1989. *Plants in the Indian Puranas: An Ethnobotanical Investigation.* Calcutta: Nayoprakash. 171.

Shealy, C. N. 1998. *The Illustrated Encyclopaedia of Healing Remedies.* Element Books. 33.

11

Cucumber

Cucumis sativus

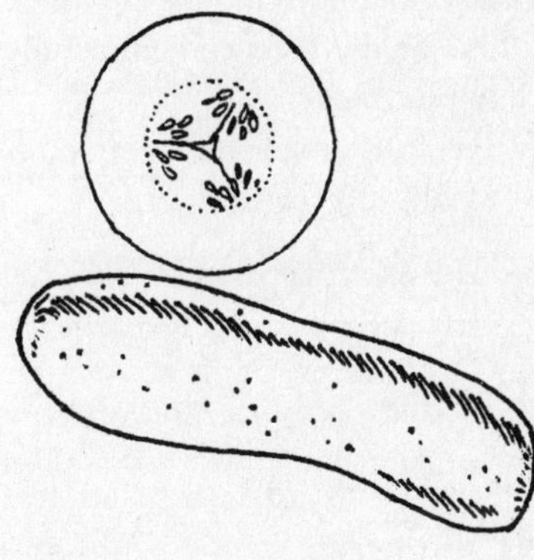

Cucumber seeds, an ideal remedy for water retention and urinary stones . . .
—Kumbha Muni

Nature's Water Bottle

The cucumber is a gift of Nature to those who are weary and thirsty in the hot summer months. The fruit, which is a rich source of vitamin C, contains an enormous quantity of water (as high as 96%), which explains why Indian villagers carry cucumbers with them in the summer months rather than bottles of mineral water.

The small fruits are often preferred for pickling and the large ones for making salads and chutneys. Fresh or pickled, the cucumber is helpful in many ways: in regaining normality after heat-stroke, in overcoming heat-induced symptoms such as dizziness, headache, nausea etc. In the tropics, it is often consumed with a little jaggery, which helps in controlling the aggravation of *pitta*. Dryness caused by heat, boils that arise due to excessive heat and pimples are also cured by the intake of ripe cucumbers.

Cucumber seeds are cooling, diuretic and tonic and hence are used in popular home remedies. As the seeds are capable of flushing out excess water from the body, it is used by those who suffer from heart and kidney ailments. They are also found useful in the dissolution of uric acid from the kidneys and urinary tract. The seed kernel, which forms 75% of the seed contains crude proteins and fats. The ash is rich in phosphates.

An easy method to identify the most medicinally effective cucumber fruit is that it should be yellow in colour.

The Profile

Botanical Name	:	*Cucumis sativus* Linn.		
English Name	:	Cucumber		
Indian Names	:	Bengali	:	*Khira*
		Hindi	:	*Khira*
		Marathi	:	*Khira*
		Tamil	:	*Vellarikai, Kakrikai*
		Telugu	:	*Dosakaya*
Family	:	Cucurbitaceae		
Appearance	:	A fleshy, bristly, creeping or climbing vine with long-petioled leaves, incised to make 5 points. The climber attaches itself to objects with the help of tendrils. Flowers, yellow in colour and bell-shaped. Fruits cylindrical, elongated, thick, of varying shapes and sizes. Colour of the fruit also varies from whitish green to dark green, turning to yellow or brown, when fully ripe.		

Distribution	:	Indigenous to North India, but widely cultivated all over the country.
Medicinal Parts	:	Fruits (both tender and ripe), leaves, seeds.

In Tradition

Arthritis, biliousness, colic, constipation, eczema, jaundice, fever, gout, intestinal worms	:	Regular intake of fruits.
Chronic constipation	:	Take cucumber salad with every meal.
Throat-swelling	:	Roast 1 tsp crushed cucumber leaves with 2 tsp cumin. Grind into a fine powder. Take tsp in 1 tsp honey.
Excessive thirst, diabetes, jaundice, burning sensation in the body	:	Eat slices of 1 medium-sized cucumber with a little salt and pepper with every meal regularly.
Difficulties in passing urine	:	Grind 1 piece each cucumber and carrot, ¼ inch ginger, ¼ tsp vetiver. Add 1 glass buttermilk and take every day for 10 days.
Burning sensation during urination, kidney stones	:	Grind 1 tsp cucumber seeds into a fine paste. Add ½ cup of juice of banana stem (i.e. the white inner stem, after peeling off the green sheaths). Mix thoroughly and filter. Add sugar to taste and drink.
	:	Chew ½ tsp cucumber seeds and drink 1 glass water.
Headache	:	Grind the following into a very fine paste: durva grass, leaves of cucumber, white garlic and rice. Warm the mixture slightly and plaster on the forehead.
Heart burn	:	Drink cucumber juice regularly.
Pimples	:	Apply a paste of cucumber pulp.

✤ Redness in eyes, burning sensation thereof, eye inflammation	:	Lie down for half-an-hour and place transversely cut thin cucumber slices on both the eyelids.
✤ Skin problems	:	Massage the affected area with juice of cucumber fruits.
✤ To gain weight	:	Eat cucumber with dates frequently.
✤ Tongue, heavily coated with fuzz		Clean the tongue with a freshly cut cucumber slice.
✤ Sexual debility	:	Extract pulp from ripe neem fruits. To 1 cup of this pulp add 2 tbsp each of the following in fine powder form: seeds of lauki, seeds of cucumber, pista, almond, coriander seeds, seeds of water melon, saunf, liquorice, seeds of grapes. Add 2 cups ghee and 2 cups powdered mishri and heat the mixture till the moisture is eliminated fully. Cool and bottle. Dosage: 1 tsp twice daily.
✤ Sunburn	:	Apply fresh cucumber paste or juice all over the affected areas.
✤ Acidity, arthritis, chest diseases, duo-denalor gastric ulcers, eczema, gout, heart burn, kidney infections, lung diseases, skin disorders, swellings, urine retention	:	Take cucumber fruits or juice with every meal.
✤ Wrinkles	:	Apply a paste of cucumber paste every day on the face at bed-time.
✤ Leucorrhoea	:	Grind ½ cup cucumber seeds into a fine paste. Add 1 cup juice of banana stem (white portion inside the stem.) Mix thoroughly and filter. Add ½ cup coconut water and drink every day for a few days.

Note: Individual results may vary.

A Word of Caution

Cucumbers are not recommended for those who suffer from asthma, convulsions, epilepsy etc. Pregnant women and women who have suckling infants are also sometimes advised to avoid cucumbers.

As the plant imparts coolness, it may aggravate *kapha*. To overcome this, it is prudent to consume cucumber with a little pepper powder.

In Science

Bailey, L. H. 1947. *Standard Cyclopaedia of Horticulture*. New York: Macmillan. I, 907. (Cucumber cultivation.)

Baruah, J. N. et al. 1963. Fungitoxicity of different polyphenolic fractions of *Acacia arabica* bark. *J. Inst. Chem. India*, 35(6): 308.

Bodding, P. O. Rev. 1986. *Studies in Santal Medicine and Connected Folklore*. Calcutta: The Asiatic Society. Reprinted. 163 (Nasal drops of leaf juice cures headache.)

CSIR, *The Wealth of India*, Raw Materials, II: 391-392. (Wealth in cucumber.)

Mital, S. P. and B. Singh, 1986. Introduction of genetic resources of some important medicinal and aromatic plants in India, *Indian J. Genet.* 46(1): 209-216.

Jurdi, M. and A. Acra, 1987. The concurrent growth of plants and chemical purification of wastewater used as a hydroponic unit. *Acta Biol. Hung.* 38(1): 161-183. (Cucumber seedlings were successfully grown hydroponically on raw wastewater obtained from one of the main sewer outfalls in Beirut. Other plants grown: chillies, tomatoes etc.)

Ng, T. B. et al. 1992. Proteins with abortifacient, ribosome inactivating, immuno-modulatory, anti-tumour and anti-AaS activities from *Cucurbitaceae* plants, *Gen. Pharmacol.* 23(4): 579-590. (Medicine in cucumber.)

Lust, J. B. 1974. *The Herb Book*, Bantam Books. 115.

Purewal, S. S. 1944. *Vegetable Gardening in the Punjab*. Govt. of Punjab, 69. (Growing cucumber.)

Shealy, C. N. 1998. *The Illustrated Encyclopaedia of Healing Remedies*. Element Books. 89. (Cure from cucumber.)

12

Zedoary

Curcuma zedoaria

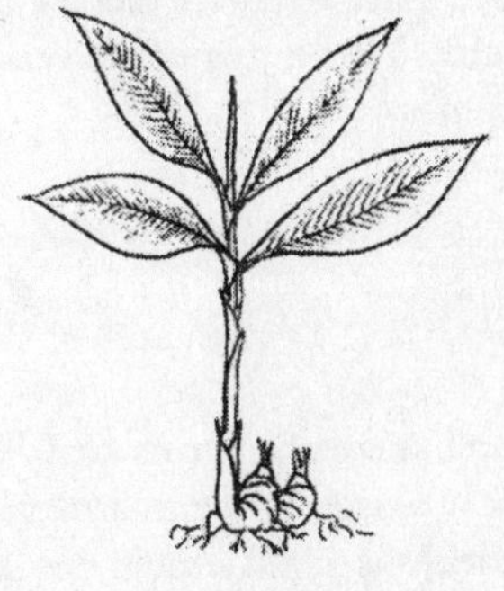

Aranya-haridra fights leprosy.
—Bhaavaprakasam

In Indian *Hamams*

Much before soap cakes started invading Indian *hamams*, the traditional household had employed herbal bath powders such as besan, green gram, turmeric and zedoary.

The enchanting aroma of zedoary had made it an ideal bath powder. A native of north east India, zedoary has since spread its roots into many parts of China and Sri Lanka. On the West Coast, it is usually grown under the shade of areca nut trees.

Now that chemical soap is very often being replaced with

herbal gels and shampoo, zedoary is slowly making a come-back into the world of women's toiletries.

Apart from its natural fragrance, zedoary's capacity both in retaining the moisture of the skin and in flushing out pathogens and bacteria from its pores has made zedoary very popular.

Zedoary consists of large and fleshy tubers, which are, after harvesting, cleaned and cut into thin transverse slices and then dried in the sun. When fully dried, the slices turn into a greyish buff colour, possessing an agreeable musky aroma, characteristic of zedoary.

Rural industries in Bengal utilize the tubers of zedoary for extracting Shoti starch, a product which is highly valued as a dietary imput for infants as well as the elderly and it is used as a substitute for arrow root or barley. Apart from its dietary use, zedoary is also a sought-after material by the manufacturers of bitters, liqueurs, cosmetics and perfumes.

In Folk Medicine

Zedoary occupies pride of place in folk medicine for its stimulant and carminative properties. It is specially used in the treatment of respiratory disorders like asthma, bronchitis, cold, cough, etc. The drug is also reported to be an effective cure in skin ailments thanks to its antibacterial and antifungal properties. It promotes digestion and as a stomachic, it is gentler than ginger. Hence, it is used as a gastro-intestinal stimulant in flatulent colic. It is also reported to cure splenic disorders, besides halitosis. As a tonic, it is often prescribed for women after child-birth.

The Profile

Botanical name	:	*Curcuma zedoaria* Roxb. non Rosc.
	:	*Amomum zedoaria* Christm.

	:	*Curcuma zerumbet* Roxb.		
	:	*Curcuma aromatica* Salisb.		
English Name	:	Zedoary		
Indian Names	:	Bengali	:	*Ekangi, Kachura*
		Gujarati	:	*Kachura*
		Hindi	:	*Kachura, Kali haldi, Jangli haldi*
		Kannada	:	*Kachura*
		Malayalam	:	*Kacholam, Pula kizhanna*
		Marathi	:	*Kachura*
		Sanskrit	:	*Karchura*
		Tamil	:	*Kichali Kizhangu, Kichili*
		Telugu	:	*Kachoram*
Ayurvedic Name	:	*Karchura*		
Unani Name	:	*Zedoary*		
Family	:	Zingiberaceae		
Appearance	:	Large perennial herb with yellowish white rhizomes with a sharp pungent taste. Leaves, large lance-like, shiny. Flowers, yellow in the axils of pouched bracts.		
Distribution	:	Grows wild in the eastern Himalayas and in the moist deciduous forests of coastal Karnataka and Kerala.		
Medicinal Part	:	Dried rhizomes.		
Ayurvedic Preparations	:	*Asana eladi tailam, Bratityadi kwatha, Dasamul arishtam, Kachoradi churnam, Valiya Narayana tailam, Valiya Rasnadi kashayam.*		

In Tradition

- Body ache : Boil a piece of zedoary in 1 cup gingelly oil. When lukewarm, massage the whole body.
- Body odour, ringworm Mix equal quantities of fine powders of turmeric and zedoary and use it for washing the body frequently. (Note: It may also be necessary for the internal cleansing of the body to use enema or panchakarma treatments; eating meat and other

	food-stuffs with a high protein content may have to be avoided.)
Cold	: Boil 2-3 pinches of zedoary, cinnamon and long pepper in 1 glass water. Take it with 1 tsp honey.
Enlargement of spleen, spermatorrhoea, stomach problems	: Take 2 or 3 pinches of zedoary with honey.
Heaviness in head	: Burn zedoary and inhale the smoke.
Itch, leucoderma, scabies, skin diseases	: Boil 1 tbsp each of zedoary and babchi seeds in 1 cup neem oil. Allow it to cool, filter and bottle. Apply this oil frequently over the affected areas. Grind a piece of zedoary with leaves of adhatoda into a fine paste and apply over the affected areas.
Leech bite	: Apply the juice extracted from zedoary or turmeric.
Wounds	: Dust a fine powder of zedoary over the wounds.

Note: Individual results may vary.

A Note on the Ayurvedic Drug 'Karchura'

The identity of the plant source of the ayurvedic drug 'karchura' is yet unsettled. While some authors consider *Hedychium spicatum*, a plant found in the Himalayas as the drug, Kerala physicians use zedoary, which is locally available in their formulations with considerable success. *Kaempferia galanga* is yet another plant source.

Zedoary Herbal Powder: A Soap Substitute

Grind zedoary, chana dal, vetiver and soap pod (1:1:1:2) into a very fine powder and bottle. Use it as a soap substitute. Whilst bathing, take 1 or 2 tbsp of this powder and make a paste with a little milk or rice gruel. Apply on the body and allow it to remain for about 10 minutes before washing it off with water.

In Science

Aiyer, K. N. and M. Kolammal, 1964. *Pharmacognosy of Ayurvedic Drugs*, Trivandrum. 8:91 (Zedoary destroys pathogenic organisms.)

Banerjee, A. and S. S. Nigam, 1977. Antibacterial activity of the essential oils derived from the various species of genus *Curcuma* Linn. *J. Res. Indian Med. Yoga & Homoeo.* 12: 89. (Activity against pathogenic organisms: *B. subtilis, E. coli, Kl. aerogenes, P. solanacearum, S. aureus, S. paratyphi, S. typhi* etc. The activity observed even in greater dilutions was more intense than that exhibited by other species of *Curcuma* like turmeric.)

Bhatia, A. et al. 1964. Effect of curcumin, its alkali salts and *Curcuma longa* oil in histamine induced gastric ulceration. *Indian J. Exp. Biol.* 2: 158-160.

Central Council for Research in Ayurveda and Siddha, 1996. *Pharmacological Investigations of Certain Medicinal Plants and Compound Formulations used in Ayurveda and Siddha.* New Delhi. 179-181. (Extract of zedoary rhizome showed significant antibacterial effect against *Salmonella paratyphi* and inhibited the growth of dermatophytes, viz. *C. albicans, E. floccosum, M. canis, M. gypseum, T. mentagrophytes, T. rubrum, T. tonsurans etc.)*

Gupta, S. K. et al 1976. Isolation of ethyl-p-methoxycinnamate, the major antifungal principle of *Curcuma zedoaria. Lloydia*, 39:218. (The antifungal principle isolated.)

Janaki, N. and T. R. Ingle, 1967. An improved method for the isolation of curcumin from turmeric (*Curcuma longa* L.) *J. Indian Chem. Soc.* 44: 985.

Mitra, R. and L. D. Kapoor, 1973. Pharmacognostic study on 'Amargandhi' (*Curcuma amada* L.) *J. Res. Indian Med.* 8:25-33.

Pachauri, S. P. and S. K. Mukherjee, 1970. Effect of *Curcuma longa* (Haridra) and *Curcuma amada* (Amragandhi) on the cholesterol level in experimental hypercholesterolaemia of rabbits. *J. Res. Indian Med.* 5: 27-31.

Sanjiva Rao, B. et al. 1928. Constituents of Indian essential oils. XXIV. Essential oil from rhizomes of *Curcuma zedoaria* Rosc. *J. Soc. Chem. Ind.* 47:171; *Chem. Abstr.* 1929: 23, 1717.

Sivarajan, V. V. and I. Balachandran. 1994 *Ayurvedic Drugs and Their Plant Sources.* New Delhi. Oxford & IBH 229.

Venkitaraman, S. et al 1977. Antifungal activity of single and compound indigenous medicinal preparations – an experimental study (in vitro) and clinical evaluations. *J. Res. Indian Med. Yoga & Homoeo.* 12(1): 25. (Marked antifungal activity of the extracts of *Curcuma zedoaria. The organisms were C. albicans, E. floccosum, M. canis, M. gypseum, T. mentagophytes, T. tonsurans etc.)*

13

Horsegram

Dolichos biflorus

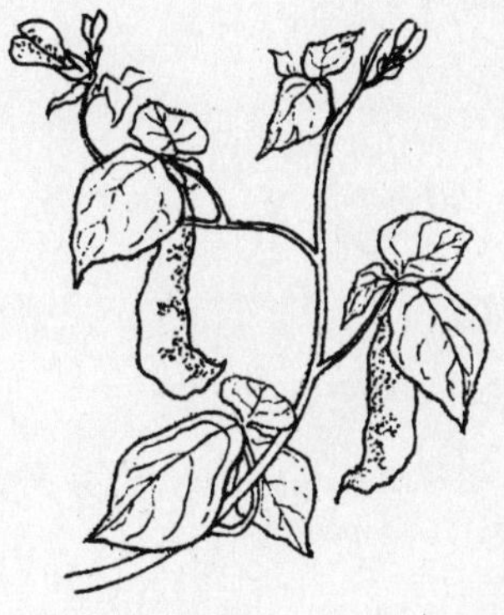

Ellu (sesame) for weaklings and kollu (horsegram) for the obese.
—A Tamil proverb

The Horse Feed

Indigenous to India, horsegram derives its name evidently from its popular use as a feed for horses.

The seeds of horsegram, which are either black or brown, and which are rich in crude proteins, carbohydrates, fats, minerals, iron, calcium, phosphorous, carotenes, nicotinic acid etc., form a valuable nutritive supplement to bulky straw fodders. They are often cooked and then fed to horses. The drought-struck rural poor and hard working but poorly paid labourers in India also find the seeds a cost-effective protein source.

Medically speaking, the seeds are astringent, diuretic and tonic. Apart from the seeds, stems, leaves and split husks of the plant also find their use as cattle feed.

The Profile

Botanical name	:	*Dolichos biflorus* Linn.
English Name	:	Horsegram
Indian Names	:	Bengali : *Kurti Kalai*
		Gujarati : *Kalathi, Kulit*
		Hindi : *Kulthi*
		Kannada : *Hurali*
		Malayalam : *Muthera, Muthiva*
		Marathi : *Kulith, Kulthi*
		Sanskrit : *Kulathi, Kulattha, Kulaththika*
		Tamil : *Kollu*
		Telugu : *Ulavalu*
Family	:	Papilionaecea
Appearance	:	A branched, trailing annual with small trifoliate leaves. Pods, curved, containing 5-6 flattened, ellipsoidal seeds.
Distribution	:	Distributed in tropical parts upto an elevation of 5000 feet.
Medicinal Parts	:	Plant, seeds.
Ayurvedic Preparations	:	*Kulatthayusha, Kulatthadipralepa, Kulaththadyghrata.*

In Tradition

❧ Elephantiasis : Grind a handful each of horsegram and

		fine sand obtained from ant-hills with the white of an egg. Apply.
Impotency	:	Mix equal quantities of horsegram and rice and make a porridge. Eat with milk everyday for a few weeks regularly. (*Note*: Avoid constipation.)
Painful swelling in hands and legs	:	Roast a handful of horsegram and tie in a cloth. Heat the area with this.
Ulcers	:	Boil ¼ cup horsegram with a pinch of asafoetida, ¼ tsp dried ginger and 2-3 pinches of liquorice. Add 1 tsp honey and take daily for a month.

Note: Individual results may vary.

In Science

Banerjee, B. 1957. Seeds of *Dolichos biflorus* as diuretic. *Bull.Calcutta School Trop. Med.* 5(2):71. (Clinical experiments conducted with water extract of seeds in a dose of 8 oz daily in divided doses for 2 weeks on patients with splenomegaly, with cirrhosis, nutritional oedema and chronic diarrhoea exhibited much increase in urine output and reduction in body weight suggesting direct action of the extract.)

Central Council for Research in Ayurveda and Siddha. 1990. *Phytochemical Investigations of Certain Medicinal Plants used in Ayurveda.* New Delhi. 73-74. (Beta-sitosterol and reducing sugars isolated from the seeds.)

Central Council for Research in Ayurveda and Siddha. 1996. *Pharmacological Investigations of Certain Medicinal Plants and Compound Formulations used in Ayurveda and Siddha.* 205-207. (Horsegram is reported to be a myocardial stimulant. Being non-toxic, it is capable of bringing down cholesterol and increasing urine output.)

Chopra, R. N. et al. 1956. *Glossary of Indian Medicinal Plants.* New Delhi: CSIR, 100. (Known for its diuretic activity, horsegram is also administered as a treatment for leucorrhoea and menstrual disorders in women.)

Chandrasekhar, M. and S. Chitra. 1978. Evaluation of the protein quality of sprouted horsegram and greengram on albino rats. *Indian J. Nutr. Dietet.* 15(7): 223-227. (Sprouted horsegram and greengram with supplement of skimmed milk and methionine proved to be the best growth promoters.)

Dhar, M. L. et al. 1968. Screening of Indian plants for biological activity (Part V) *Indian J. Exptl. Biol.* 6(4): 232-247. (Hypotensive and antispasmodic activity of horsegram.)

Garg, S. K. 1976. Anti-fertility screening of plants: Effect of four indigenous plants on early pregnancy in female albino rats. *Indian J. Med. Res.* 64(8): 1133-1135. (Experiment could not prove any anti-fertility effect.)

Font, J. et al. 1971. *Biochim. Biophys. Acta.* 243:434. (Haemaglutinins from the seeds.)

Hemadri, K. and S. S. Rao. 1983. Anti-fertility, abortifacient and fertility promoting drugs from Dandakaranya, *Ancient Sci. Life* 3(2): 103-107. (Abortifacient activity of *Dolichos biflorus.*)

Ingham, J. L. et al. 1981. *Phytochemistry.* 20: 807. (Isoflavanoids isolated from the leaves.)

Keen, N. T. and J. L. Ingham. 1980. *Z. Naturforsch. C. Biosci.* 35C:923. (Coumestrol and psoralidin in the leaves and stems.)

Meyer, D. and R. Bourrillon. 1973. *Biochimie,* 55:5. (Beta-glucosides reported in the seeds.)

Mitra, J. et al. 1983. *Phytochemistry.* 22:1063. (Chemical constituents of seeds.)

Mital, S. P and B. Singh. 1986. Introduction of genetic resources of some important medicinal and aromatic plants in India. *Indian J. Genet.* 46(1): 209-216.

Peshin, A. et al. 1994. Anti-calcifying properties of *Dolichos biflorus* (horsegram) seeds. *Indian J. Exptl Biol.* 32(12): 889-891.

Satyavati, G. V. 1984. Indian plants and plant products with anti-fertility effect. *Ancient Sci. Life* 3(4): 193-202. (Decoction of *Dolichos biflorus* administered daily for three days was believed to terminate pregnancy.)

Singh, G. and G. W. G. Bird. 1956. Studies on the nature of the haemoglutinating present in *Dolichos biflorus*, *J. Sci. Industr. Res.* 15C(8): 182-183. (Water extracts of seeds exhibited haemoglutinating activity.)

Singh, J. et al. 1985. Diuretic principles of *Dolichos biflorus.* Indian Pharmaceutical Congress, Bangalore.

14

Trailing Eclipta

Eclipta alba

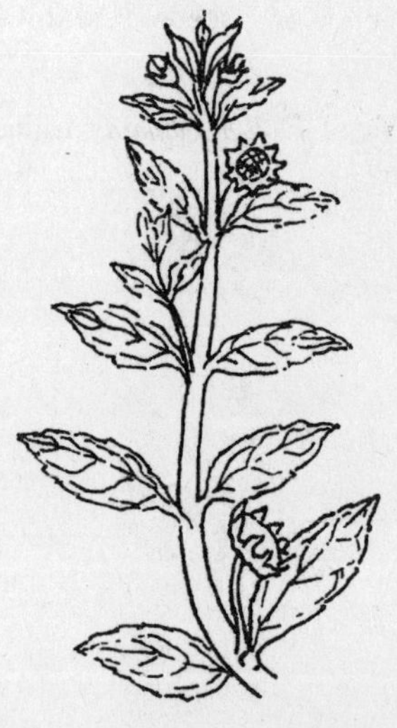

Bhringarajah conquers kapha *and* pitta.
—Gunapaatham

For the Care of Hairs

Trailing eclipta, commonly referred to as bhringaraja, is a very common weed native to India growing on waste land, and dunghills.

One of the Ten Auspicious Flowers (*Dasapushpam*), its synonyms in Sanskrit, 'kesaranjanah' and 'kundalavardhanah' refer to its hair-blackening and hair-strengthening properties respectively. As it is good for hair and skin, it has been in use for many a cosmetic preparation from ancient times. It is also credited with qualities that impart a so-called 'golden complexion' to the skin and brightness to the eyes besides endowing one with a sharp intellect and a strong body.

The fresh plants and leaves are used as a tonic.The plant juice is often administered in combination with aromatics for catarrhal jaundice. The drug improves digestion and also induces secretion of bile. The seeds are believed to be an aphrodisiac.

In folk medicine, it is used in the treatment of anorexia, asthma, cough, elephantiasis, eye ailments, gastritis, headache, inflammation, jaundice, intestinal worms, leprosy, liver problems, loss of hair, night blindness, pyorrhoea, throat problems etc.

Experiments have revealed that the shoot extract shows antibiotic activity against *E. coli* and *S. aureus.*

The Profile

Botanical Names	:	*Eclipta alba (*Linn.) Hassk. *Eclipta prostrata (linn.)* Linn.		
English Name	:	Trailing eclipta		
Indian Names	:	Bengali	:	*Keshori, Kesuti, Keshukti*
		Gujarati	:	*Bhangra, Dodhak Kaluganthi*
		Hindi	:	*Babri, Bhangra, Mochkand*
		Kannada	:	*Garagada soppu*
		Malayalam	:	*Kayoni, Kayunni*
		Marathi	:	*Bhringaraja, Maka*
		Oriya	:	*Kesarda*
		Sanskrit	:	*Bhringarajah, Tekarajah*
		Tamil	:	*Karisilankanni, Kayyanthagarai, Kaikesi*
		Telugu	:	*Galagara, Guntagalijeru, Guntaga*
Family	:	Asteraceae (Compositae)		
Appearance	:	Erect or prostrate herb with a delicate stem covered with coarse hairs. Leaves, simple, hairy and eclyptic. Flowers, small, white, in heads. Seeds, small, black, somewhat resembling mustard seeds.		

Distribution	:	All over the plains in moist and waste places and on road sides.
Medicinal Parts	:	Whole plant, leaves and root.
Ayurvedic Preparations	:	*Kayyanyadi tailam, Mahatraiphala ghritam, Narasimha rasayanam, Neelibhringadi tailam.*

In Tradition

Anaemia, jaundice	:	Grind a handful of leaves with 5 or 6 black pepper corns into a fine paste. Take ¼ tsp of this paste with butter milk.
Baldness	:	Rub fresh leaf juice into the scalp. (*Note*: Hereditary baldness may not be cured.)
Blood in urine	:	Mix ½ tsp leaf juice in 1 glass butter milk and drink twice a day for 3 days.
Cough	:	Heat juice of bhringaraja and gingelly oil (1:3) on a low flame till the moisture in the boiling mixture is thoroughly evaporated. Cool, filter and bottle. Take 1 tsp twice daily for 3 days only.
Catarrh	:	Add ½ tsp leaf juice in 1 tsp honey and take.
Catarrh, jaundice	:	Grind the leaves into a fine paste with a little pepper. Mix ½ tsp of this paste in 1 cup butter milk and take twice daily for a few days.
Cataract	:	Heat in a low flame a mixture of bhringaraja, amla and gingelly oil (2:2:1) with a small piece of liquorice till all traces of moisture are eliminated. Cool, filter and bottle. Massage the head with this oil 2 or 3 times a week.
Cirrhosis	:	Take ½ tsp juice of the plant with 1 tsp honey thrice daily. (*Note*: Intoxicating substances and tea, coffee, etc. are strictly to be avoided.)
Ear ache	:	Expel a little juice from the leaves and use as ear drops.

Elephantiasis, glandular swellings	:	Grind 2 cups leaves in ½ cup gingelly oil into a very fine paste and apply over the affected areas.
Fever	:	Take ½ tsp leaf juice with 1-2 pinches of powdered cinnamon twice daily for 2 days.
Flatulence	:	Grind 1 tsp leaves with a little garlic and pepper into a fine paste. Eat with a little cooked rice.
Gum problems	:	Chew a few leaves for 10 minutes and wash the mouth in warm water, two or three times daily.
Hair loss	:	Heat the leaf juice in coconut oil (1:1) on a slow fire till all moisture is eliminated. Cool, filter and bottle. Massage the scalp everyday for a month. (*Note*: Avoid using shampoo or soap.)
Hair, sparse growth of	:	Massage the scalp everyday with freshly expelled leaf juice. Continue for 45 days. (*Note*: Hereditary factors may hinder the treatment.)
Headache	:	Apply a mixture of the plant paste and gingelly oil (1:1) on the affected area.
Jaundice, liver disorders	:	Mix ½ tsp leaf juice with 1 powdered cardamom and take twice daily for a few days. Boil 1 tsp each of the following in ½ litre water till the volume is reduced to half: bhringaraja leaves, white radish, chinese hibiscus flowers, neem flowers and neem leaves. Take the resultant decoction in 3 doses, with 1 tsp palm sugar.
Liver diseases, skin ailments	:	Take 1 or 2 pinches of powdered root twice daily with butter milk for 2 weeks.
Premature greying of hair	:	Powder a mixture of amla, bhringaraja and black seeds of sesame (1:1:2). Bottle. Take 1 tsp of this mixture with honey twice a day for 30 days. (*Note*: Avoid anxiety and worrying.) Grind equal quantities of bhringaraja and gokhru into a fine powder and bottle. Dosage: ½ tsp with 1 tsp honey, thrice daily.

Home Remedies

❧ Scorpion sting	:	Grind the leaves into a very fine paste and apply.
❧ Snake bite	:	Mix ½ tsp leaf juice in butter milk and drink.
❧ Tooth ache	:	Rub the fresh (crushed) plant on the gums.
❧ Wounds	:	Wash the wounds with leaf juice. Apply a paste of leaves.
❧ Wounds and ulcers in cattle	:	Grind the roots into a very fine paste and apply.

In Science

Chandra, Satish. 1969. The Ayurvedic drug –'Bhringaraj'. *Quart. J. Crude Drug Res.* 9:1961-1968.

Chandra, T. *et al.* 1987. Effect of *Eclipta alba* on inflammation and liver injury. *Filoterapia* 58(1): 23-32. (Effective against liver injury and inflammation.)

Dixit S. P. and M. P. Achar, 1979. Bhringaraja in the treatment of infective hepatitis. *Curr. Med. Pract.* 23(6): 237-242. (Effective in the treatment of infective hepatitis.)

Dixit, S. P. and M. P. Achar, 1980. Study of Bhringaraja (*Eclipta alba*) therapy in jaundice in children. *J. Sci. Res. Plants Med.* 2(4): 96-100. (50 mg/kg of body weight with honey in 3 divided doses administered showed 80% complete clinical and biochemical recovery from hepatitis in 1- 5 week's time.)

Dube, C. B. et al. 1982. A trial of bhringaraja ghanasatwavati on the patients of hepatocellular jaundice. *J. Natl. Integ. Med. Assoc.* 24(9): 265-269.

Gupta, S. C. et al. 1976. Cardio-vascular effects of *Eclipta alba* Hassk (Bhringaraja) *J. Res. Indian Med. Yoga & Homoeo.* 11(3): 91-93. (Found to possess myocardial depressant and hypotensive capabilities.)

Nadkarni, K. M. 1914. *Indian Plants and Drugs*. Madras: Norton & company .

Saxena, A. K. et al. 1993. Hepato-protective effect of *Eclipta alba* on subcellular levels in rats. *J. Ethnopharmacol.* 40(3): 155-167.

15

Vidanga

Embelia ribes

Vaivilangam . . . drives away every minute worm . . .
—Agathiyar Gunapaadal

The Expeller of Worms

The dried fruits, which are used as an of adulterant of black pepper, have also certain noteworthy medicinal uses as they have been traditionally used in Ayurveda and unani systems of Indian medicine as anthelmintic. They are often administered prior to a purgative.

A clinical trial conducted recently in the Calcutta School of Tropical Medicine, however, indicates that the drug had no effect whatsoever on worms such as hookworm and tapeworm. It was, however, quite effective in the treatment of ascariasis.

A recent clinical trial conducted by Paul et al. (1980) reveals that a single dose of 8 gm of the drug was quite sufficient as it could effectively expel worms and parasites within 6-24 hours of administration.

In Java, the plant is used as a vegetable; the leaves and fruits are cooked and eaten. Sometimes, the leaves are also used in salads without cooking.

The Profile

Botanical Name	:	*Embelia ribes* Burm. f.		
Indian Names	:	Bengali	:	*Biranga, Baibirang*
		Gujarati	:	*Vavading, Vyvirang*
		Hindi	:	*Bidang, Baberang, Baibrang, Vidang, Wawrung*
		Malayalam	:	*Tiruvitikanni, Vaivilangam, Vishalam*
		Marathi	:	*Kakannie, Karkanni, Vavdinga, Waiwarang*
		Oriya	:	*Bidango*
		Sanskrit	:	*Vidanga*
		Tamil	:	*Vaayuvidangam, Vaayuvilangam*
		Telugu	:	*Vidangamu, Vilangamu, Vaayuvilangamu*
Ayurvedic Name	:	*Vidanga*		
Unani Name	:	*Baibarang*		
Appearance	:	A large shrub with shiny, lance-like leaves. The leaves, though shiny above, look somewhat paler or silvery beneath. The whole leaf is covered with minute red glands, which are more conspicuous in tender leaves. Flowers, greenish yellow. Fruit, globose, black when ripe with persistent style attached. They look wrinkled and warty when dried.		

HOME REMEDIES

Distribution	:	Throughout India upto 1500 m.
Medicinal parts	:	Fruits (dried), root.
Other Species	:	*Embelia robusta.*
Ayurvedic Preparations	:	*Vidangadi lauoh, Vidangarishta, Vidangasava.* etc.
Unani Preparations	:	*Hab ashkar, Ma'jun kalkalanj, Sufuf chutaki,* etc.

In Tradition

Chest diseases, fevers	:	Boil ½ tsp dried fruits in 1 glass water and drink.
Cough, diarrhoea	:	Soak ½ tsp root powder in 1 glass of water and drink.
Headache	:	Grind the fruits with very little butter into a paste. Apply over the affected area and sleep for some time.
Indigestion, stomach upset, stomach ache	:	Add ¼ tsp fruit powder to a glass of milk and take.
Intestinal worms	:	Pound ¼ tsp each of the following and boil in 1 glass of water till the volume is reduced to half: aniseed, ajwain, black cumin, Indian senna, katki, root of nisoth, seeds of palash, fruits of vidanga. Dose: 2 to 3 tbsp to be followed by a purgative pill or castor oil. Take at bed time. Take ¼ tsp fruit powder with 1 tsp honey for 2 consecutive days in the morning: to be followed by a purgative or castor oil on the 3rd day.
Scorpion sting, swellings	:	Grind the fruits into a fine paste and apply.
Skin diseases	:	Grind the fruits into a fine paste and apply on the affected areas.

Note: Individual results may vary.

A Word of Caution

The drug is a strong purgative.

In Science

Gopal, R. H. and K. K. Purushothaman. 1988. Effect of a few plant isolates and extracts on bacteria. *Bull. Med. Ethnobot. Res.* 7(1-2): 78-83. (*E. ribes* shows inhibitory activity.)

Kholkute, S. D. et al. 1978. Anti-fertility effects of *Embelia ribes* Burm. *Indian J. Exptl. Biol.* 16:1035. (Remarkable anti-implantation activity in female rats.)

Khurana, S. K. et al. 1972. Mass spectral analysis of the pigments from *Embelia ribes* and *Connarus monocarpus. Curr. Sci.* 41: 331. (Predominant constituent, embelin, isolated and its structure elucidated.)

Krishnaswamy, M. and K. K. Purushothaman. 1980. Anti-fertility properties of *Embelia ribes*: Embelin. *Indian J. Exptl. Biol.* 18:1359. (Oestrogenic activity in immature female albino rats.)

Mital, S. P. and B. Singh. 1986. Introduction of genetic resources of some important medicinal and aromatic plants in India. *Indian J. Genet.* 46(1): 209-216.

Paul, R. and S. R. Vatsa. 1980. Clinical trial of an Ayurvedic herb on worm infestation. *Nagarjun*, 23: 234. ('Good results and marked improvement' in the cases of tapeworm and Giardia; no such results in cases of hookworm and roundworm.)

Prakash, A. O. 1979. Effect of *Embelia ribes* on uterine weight of normal and ovariectomized rats. *Planta Med.* 35:370. (Prevention of pregnancy by powdered berries.)

Prakash, A. O. 1981. Anti-fertility investigation on embelin: An oral contraceptive of plant origin. Part I. Biological properties.

Planta Med. 41: 259. (Pure embelin did not show anti-fertility activity.)

Sarin, J. P. S. and G. K. Ray. 1961. Estimation of embelin from *Embelia ribes* Burm. f. *Indian J. Pharm.* 23:330. (A standard procedure of assay of embelin.)

16

Dugdhika

Euphorbia hirta

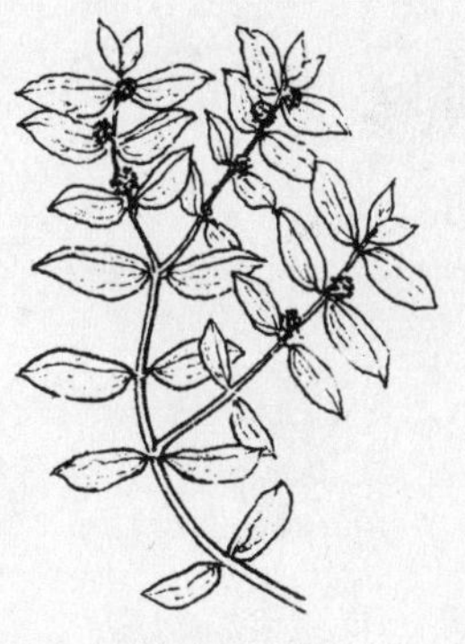

Ammanpacharisi . . . the solution for all female problems!
—From an old Tamil folk-song

The Milky Herb

The presence of a milky fluid inside this plant has given rise to many of its Sanskrit names: dugdhika, kshira, vikshirini etc.

As in the case of the famous Doctrine of Signatures, where the resemblance of a plant part to a human organ seems to have a co-relation with the effect of that plant on a human organ (e.g., liverwort and the liver, mandukaparni and the brain etc.), the presence of milky fluid in the plant here shows a strange co-relation with its capability of increasing lactation in women.

The ayurvedic drug dugdhika is actually derived from different plant sources, all belonging to the genus *Euphorbia : E. hirta, E. hypericfolia, E. microphylla* and *E. thymifolia*. Generally these plants are harvested for medicine at the time of flowering and fruiting as they show peak efficiency only then.

The dried herb, which constitutes the drug is acrid, bitter, diuretic, and hot in action. It has a depressant action on the heart and respiration. It is believed to be an aphrodisiac. It is used in the treatment of diseases due to the morbidity of *kapha* and *vata*. Asthma, cough, poisonous affections, respiratory disorders, skin diseases etc. are also treated by the drug with satisfactory results.

The Profile

Botanical Names	:	*Euphorbia hirta* Linn. *Euphorbia pilulifera auct.* Non Linn. *Chamaesyce hirta* (Linn.) Millsp.
Indian Names	:	Bengali : *Barakeru* Gujarati : *Dudheli* Hindi : *Lal dudhi* Malayalam : *Nilapala, Nelapalai* Marathi : *Moti dudhi* Sanskrit : *Dugdhika, Kshira, Nagarjuni, Pusitoa, Vikshirini,* Tamil : *Ammanpacharisi* Telugu : *Nanabala*
Family	:	Euphorbiaceae
Appearance	:	Erect, herb with yellowish hair. Leaves in opposite pairs, darker on the upper side, 3-nerved, margins faintly toothed. Flowers, minute, white in clusters ('Cyathium'). Fruit small and hairy. Seeds, 3-angled, wrinkled, brown in colour.
Distribution	:	In the plains across the country, particularly on wasteland and on roadsides.
Medicinal Parts	:	The whole plant.

In Tradition

Blood in urine, gonorrhoea	:	Take ¼ tsp leaf paste with 1 glass of cow's milk.
Digestive disorders, intestinal worms	:	Take ¼ tsp paste obtained from leaves and seeds with some warm water.
Dysentery in children	:	SEE 'Ammanpacharisi Kudineer'.
Gonorrhoea	:	Soak ¼ tsp each of dugdhika, the root bark of tamarind, and leaves of keezhanelli (*Phyllanthus amarus*) in 1 glass of milk for ½ hr. Filter. Add sugar and drink.
Jaundice	:	SEE 'Ammanpacharisi Syrup'.
Pimples	:	Grind equal quantities of dugdhika and tulsi leaves into a fine paste and apply on the affected areas.
Pitta-aggravation	:	Take ¼ tsp leaf paste with 1 glass of milk and 1 tsp palm sugar.
To increase lactation in women	:	Add a few cooked leaves to the daily diet.
Warts, wounds of cattle and animals	:	Apply the fresh milky latex of the plant on the affected area frequently.

Ammanpacharisi Kudineer : Where Drinking Water Turns Medicinal

Boil ¼ tsp dugdhika leaves with a pinch of powdered masikai (*Quercus infectoria*) in 1 glass water till the volume is reduced to ¼. Drink.

Ammanpacharisi Syrup : A Home Remedy for Jaundice

Collect ¼ tsp each of the leaves of dugdhika, trailing eclipta and dronapushpi. Clean them thoroughly in running water and grind them into a very fine paste with a little water and 2-3 pinches of black pepper. Take 1 glass milk and stir in the paste with 1 tsp sugar and drink.

In Science

Anonymous, 1978a. *The Ayurvedic Formulary of India*. Delhi. 249. (*E. thymifolia* as an accepted source for the drug 'dugdhika.')

Central Council for Research in Ayurveda and Siddha. 1991. *A Handbook of Common Remedies in Siddha System of Medicine*. 2nd Revised Edition. New Delhi. 17. (Simple remedy in the treatment of dysentery in children.)

Chunekar, K. C. 1982. *Bhavaprakasanighantu of Sri Bhavamisra*. Commentary. Varanasi. 459. (Identification of dugdhika.)

Jain, S. K. 1994. *Medicinal Plants*. New Delhi: National Book Trust. 5th edition. 81-86. (On Euphorbias.)

Mital, S. P and B. Singh, 1986. Introduction of genetic resources of some important medicinal and aromatic plants in India. *Indian J. Genet.* 46(1): 209-216.

Nadkarni, A. K. 1954. *Indian Materia Medica*. Bombay. 529. (Medicinal use of the weed from the wastelands.)

Sharma, P. V. 1983. *Dravyaguna Vijnana*. Varanasi. 302.

Sharma, G. D. et al. 1982. A clinical trial of *Euphorbia prostrata* W. Ait. and *E. thymifolia* L. in the treatment of bronchial asthma (tamakaswasa). *J. Res. Ayur. Siddha* 3(3&4): 109-118. (Efficacy in the treatment of bronchial asthma.)

Sharma, G. P. and P. V. Sharma. 1972. Experimental studies on antispasmodic and bronchodilator actions of dugdhika (*Euphorbia thymifolia* L. and *E. prostrata* W. Ait.) *J. Res. Indian Med.* 7(4): 24-28. (Clinical proof for the antispasmodic and bronchodilatory activity of *E. thymifolia* in guinea pigs.)

Sinha, P. et al, 1984. Pharmacognostical studies in *Euphorbia thymifolia* L. *Bull. Med. Ethnobot. Res.* 5(3-4): 159-170.

Sivarajan, V.V. 1994. *Ayurvedic Drugs and their Plant Sources.* New Delhi: Oxford & IBH. 141-143. (A detailed account of the plant source of 'dugdhika'.)

Vaidya Bapalal, 1982. *Some controversial drugs in Indian medicine.* Varanasi. 188. (*E. hypericifolia* and *E. microphylla* are also considered as the smaller variety or 'laghudugdhika'.)

17

Indigo

Indigofera tinctoria

Aviri can fight eighteen types of posion . . .
—From a Tamil song by Agathiar

Roses are Red, Indigo's Blue

In Indian medicine, indigo is considered as a reputed drug for the promotion of hair growth. It is a good remedy for poisonous affections, thanks to its anti-toxic property. It also cures abdominal enlargement (ascites), excessive urination, enlargement of spleen, giddiness, gout etc.

It is also reported to possess anti-tubercular properties.

A large number of medicinal plants including indigo are being used in the treatment of snake bites. With a view to finding out whether the claims put forward by some indigenous medical systems have any basis of truth Caius and Mhaskar (Indian Medical Research Memoirs No. 19, January, 1931) carried out extensive pharmacological and toxicological investigations on dogs. The opinion of these workers is that most of these plants, including indigo, have a preventive, antidotal or therapeutic effect.

The Profile

Botanical Name	:	*Indigofera tinctoria* Linn.
English Name	:	Dyer's indigo, True indigo
Indian Names	:	Bengal : *Nil*
		Gujarati : *Nil*
		Hindi : *Nil*
		Kannada : *Nili*
		Marathi : *Nili*
		Malayalam : *Neelam, Amari, Avari*
		Sanskrit : *Neelika, Ranjani*
		Tamil : *Neelam. Avari, Aviri*
		Telugu : *Nili, Avari, Neelichettu, Neli*
Family	:	Papilionaceae
Appearance	:	Erect shrub, stems and branches green, leaves pale green or bluish. Flowers small, rose-coloured.
Distribution	:	Cultivated in many parts of India.
Medicinal Parts	:	Leaves, root, whole plant.
Ayurvedic Preparation	:	*Nilibhringadi tailam.*

In Tradition

Asthma, palpitation of heart, hydrophobia (rabies), kidney disorders, lung diseases, whooping cough	Take ¼ tsp indigo leaf juice with 1 cup milk.

HOME REMEDIES

- Bladder stones, epilepsy : Take 2-3 pinches of root-powder with a glass of warm water.
- Bronchitis, epilepsy, nervous disorders : Take ¼ tsp extract of the plant with 1 glass water.
- Haemorrhoids, sores, ulcers : Apply a fine paste of the plant on the affected areas.
- Mouth ulcers : Apply the juice of the young branch mixed with honey.
- Paleness or whiteness in the lips : Rub a seed of *Abrus precatorius* in a little indigo leaf juice and apply on the lips. Use a few times.
- Scabies, ulcers, wounds Apply a poultice made of the leaves.

Note: Individual results may vary.

In Science

Anand, K. K. et al. 1979. Protective effect of alcoholic extract of *Indigofera tinctoria* Linn. in experimental liver injury. *Indian J. Exptl. Biol.* 17:685. (Alcoholic extract of aerial parts showed marked protection.)

Anand, K. K. et al. 1981. Histological evidence of protection by *Indigofera tinctoria* Linn. against carbon tetrachloride induced hepatotoxicity—an experimental study. *Indian J. Exptl. Biol.* 19:298. (The protective effect confirmed.)

Bhatnagar, S. S. et al. 1961. *Biological activity of Indian medicinal plants.* Part I. Antibacterial, anti-tubercular and antifungal action. *Indian J. Med. Res.* 49: 799. (Whole plant extract exhibits anti-fungal action against *Helminthosporium sativum.*)

Dhawan, B. N. et al. 1980. Screening of Indian plants for biological activiy. Part IX. *Indian J. Exptl. Biol.* 18:594. (Extract of the whole plant excluding roots showed hypoglycaemic effect in rats; CNS depressant effects in mice.)

Mital, S. P. and B. Singh. 1986. Introduction of genetic resources of some important medicinal and aromatic plants in India. *Indian J. Genet.* 46(1): 209-216.

Satyavati, G.V. et al. 1987. *Medicinal Plants of India.* New Delhi. Vol.2. (Pharmacological studies made on the plant.)

Sen, A. K. et al. 1986. A water-soluble galactomannan from the seeds of *Indigofera tinctoria* (Leguminosae). *Carbohydrate Res.* 157:251.

18

Jangli Arandi

Jatropha curcas

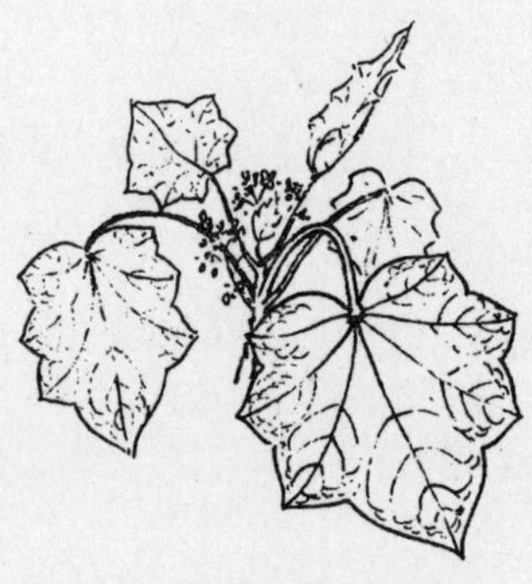

Kaataamanaku, a cure for piles...
—From a Siddha song

Beauty and the Beasts

Most of the plants of the genus *Jatropha* are handsome, with pretty foliage and brightly coloured flowers and hence a tropical gardener's delight.

But with their beauty, comes poison aplenty in their saps or seeds. In fact they are able to protect themselves from browsing animals only with this. Their defence mechanism is highly elaborate. They are covered with innumerable hairs that sting. Each hair consists of a single large cell, expanded at the base and elongated above, ending in a small knob, which is bent to one side.

The wall of the hair at the bend is extremely thin and at the slightest touch the head is broken off leaving a sharp oblique point. The sharp point penetrates the skin of any marauder who has trespassed into the plant's territory. The pressure from the expanded end of the hair injects formic acid into the skin of the intruder causing a burning sensation in the same manner as that of an ant's sting.

Santals, the ancient tribal group in India, value the plant and use it for the treatment of a number of ailments prevalent in their society: anascara, carbuncles, convulsions, cramps, dropsy, neuralgia, pleurisy, pneumonia, syphilis etc.

Medicinally, the juice of the plant is a purgative; it is haemostatic and styptic.

The leaves are lactogenic and rubefacient.

The seeds are acro-narcotic, poisonous and purgative. Oil extracted from the seeds is antiseptic and depurative. In combination with bland oil, it is used as an embrocation in chronic rheumatism.

The root bark is stomachic and astringent.

The Profile

Botanical Name	:	*Jatropha curcas* Linn.		
English Name	:	Angular-leaved physic nut		
Indian Names	:	Bengali	:	*Bagbherenda, Erandagachh*
		Gujarati	:	*Jamalgota, Jepal, Ratanjota*
		Hindi	:	*Jangli-arandi, Safed erand*
		Kannada	:	*Kaada haralu, Bettadaharalu*
		Malayalam	:	*Katamanak, Kattavanaku, Kadalvanaku*
		Marathi	:	*Mogali eranda, Ran erandi*
		Punjabi	:	*Japhrota, Rattanjot*
		Sanskrit	:	*Vyaaghrairanda*
		Tamil	:	*Kaataamanaku, Kadalaamanaku, Eliaamanaku*

	Telugu :	*Adavia amudamu, Katiyamudamu, Nepalam, Pepalam, Peddanepalamu*
Ayurvedic Name	:	*Dravanti*
Appearance	:	A glabrous shrub or small tree with an acrid latex. Leaves, simple, alternate, long-stalked, 3-5 lobed. Flowers yellowish green.
Distribution	:	A native of tropical America, the plant grows in India, and is cultivated mainly as a hedge plant in South India.
Medicinal Parts	:	Twigs, leaves, fruits, seeds, whole plant.
Other species	:	*Jatropha gossypifolia* Linn.

In Tradition

- Abscess, boils : Grind the leaves without water to a fine paste. Apply on the affected areas.
- Carbuncles, boils, eczema, itches : Apply the leaves externally.
- Piles : Apply the leaf juice externally.
- Eczema, herpes, itch, ringworm, scabies, sores, ulcers, wounds : Seed oil applied externally.
- Swollen gums : Brush the teeth with the twigs.
- Leprosy, rheumatism : Use a decoction of the bark for washing.
- To increase lactation in women : Fry the leaves and tie over the breasts.

Note: Individual results may vary.

In Science

Abrol, B. K. and I. C. Chopra. 1963. Development of indigenous vegetable insecticides and insect repellants. *Bull. Reg. Res. Lab.*

Jammu. 1: 156. (The fruit extracts were found mildly active against the common house fly and mosquito.)

Anonymous, 1978. *The Ayurvedic Formulary of India.* Delhi. 249.

Banerji, J. et al. 1984. Gadain, a lignan from *Jatropha gossypifolia. Phytochemistry.* 23:2323.

Bhatnagar, S. C. and M. K. Sinha. 1970. Chemical examination of *Jatropha curcas. Indian J. Chem.*8: 1047.

Bor, N. L. and M. B. Raizada, 1990. *Some Beautiful Indian Climbers and Shrubs,* Oxford Univ. Press. Revised Second ed. 189-195.

Bose, B. C. et al. 1961. Observations on the pharmacological actions of *Jatropha curcas. Archives Int. Pharmacodyn. Ther.* 130(1-2):28.

Bose, A. et al. 1977. Phytochemical and pharmacological study of the plant *Jatropha curcas* Linn. *Proc. IX Ann. Cong. Indian Pharmacol. Soc. Varanasi.* Dec 29-31. *Indian J. Pharmacol.* 9:81. (Fruit extract lowers the blood pressure, produces cardiac depression and spasmogenic effect on smooth and skeletal muscle.)

Chatterjee, A. et al. 1981. Crystal structure of a lignan from *Jatropha gossypifolia. Phytochemistry,* 20:2047.

Chunekar, K. C. 1982. *Bhavaprakasanighantu of Sri Bhavamisra.* Commentary. Varanasi. 399. (in Hindi.)

Chopra, R. N. et al. 1956. *Glossary of Indian Medicinal Plants.* New Delhi.

Dhawan, B. N. et al. 1977. Screening of Indian plants for biological activity. Part VI. *Indian J. Exptl. Biol.*15: 208. (Diuretic activity of the whole plant extract, excluding roots.)

Gupta, R. C. 1985. Pharmacognostic studies on 'Drawanti'. Part I *Jatropha curcas* Linn. *Proc. Indian Acad. Sci.* 94(1): 65-82.

Indian Council of Medical Research 1987. *Medicinal Plants of India.* Vol.2. New Delhi. 101-105.

Jain, S. K. 1965. Medicinal plant-lore of the tribals of Bastar. *Econ. Bot.* 19:236. (The plant—*Jatropha gossypifolia* is believed to cure toothache.)

Jain, S. K. and C. R. Tarafder. 1970. Medicinal plant-lore of the Santals (A revival of P. O. Bodding's work.) *Econ. Bot.* 24:241.

Mehta, T. N. and M. V. Gokhale. 1964. The fatty acid composition of the physic nut (*Jatropha curcas* L.) oil. *Indian J. Appl. Chem.* 27:109. (Seed oil contains arachidic, linoleic, myristic, palmitic, and stearic acids.)

Mitra, C. R. et al. 1970. Chemical examination of *Jatropha curcas. Indian J. Chem.* 8:1847.

Mooss, N. S. 1980. *Ganas of Vahata*, Kottayam.114.

Parthasarathy, M. R. and K. P. Saradhi. 1984. A coumarino-lignan from *Jatropha gossypifolia. Phytochemistry.* 23: 867.

Nadkarni, A. K. 1954. *Indian Materia Medica,* Bombay. 705.

Raghunathan, S. and R. Mitra, (Eds.) 1982. *Pharmacognosy of Indigenous Drugs.* New Delhi. 264.

Rao, A. R. and M. Malaviya. 1964. On the latex cells and latex of Jatropha. Proc. Indian Acad. Sci. 60B:95. (Latex of the younger parts are dark yellow, creamish yellow and white, whereas in the older parts, the colour is dark reddish, brownish orange and cream.)

Sengupta, P. and P. B. Das, 1964. Chemical investigation of the stem bark of *Jatropha gossypifolia* Linn. *J. Indian Chem. Soc.* 41:88. (The neutral fraction of the benzene extract yields B-sitosterol.)

Sharma, P.V. 1983. *Dravyaguna Vijnana.* Varanasi. 428. (In Hindi.)

Sinha, A. 1959. Chemical examination of the seeds of *Jatropha curcas* Linn. *J. Instn. Chem.* (India) 31:213. (Arabinose, glucose, rhamnose and xylose are reported in the seeds.)

Subramanian, S. S. et al. 1971. Flavanoids of the leaves of *Jatropha gossypifolia. Phytochemistry.* 10:1690. (The leaves yield 2 flavanoid glycosides: vitexin and isovitexin.)

19

Tomato

Lycopersicon lycopersicum

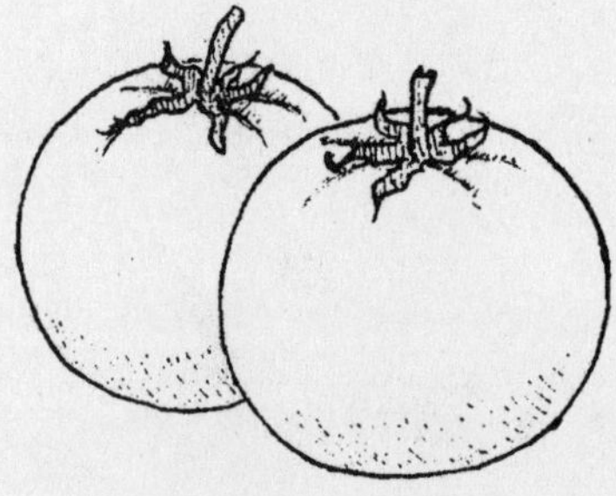

Raktamachi—a stimulant tonic . . .
—Svayamkriti

The Divine Tomato

Very recently, hundreds of muslims thronged into the small house of a young housewife, Shabana Hussain in Bradford, Northern England to see a wonder in the tomato cut open by her. On chopping a tomato, Shabana discovered the following words seemingly written in Arabic in its veins: 'There's no God but Allah'.

Long loved by weight-watchers, the tomato is found to fight cancer. Experiments conducted at Boston's Harvard Medical

School reveal that tomatoes can significantly reduce the incidence of cancer of the breast, cervix, colon, lung, oesophagus, oral cavity, prostate, rectum and stomach. In yet another study made in Wales, the tomato ranked well as a reliable guard against appendicitis.

Tomatoes are rich in lycopenes, the powerful anti-oxidants that protect our body by neutralising free radicals that damage cells, leading to cancer, eye and heart diseases.

The lower risk of prostate cancer among Americans, lung cancer among Norwegians, stomach cancer among Hawaiians—are all a gain attributed to the daily intake of tomatoes.

Some people's belief that the tomato is an aphrodisiac is due to a translator's error: The French name for tomato, 'apple of love' (*pomme d'amour*) was derived from the sound of the Italian word *pomi dei mori* and not from what the name actually meant: 'apple of the moors'!

The Profile

Botanical Names	:	*Lycopersicon lycopersicum* (Linn.) Kar *Lycopersicon esculentum* Mill. *Solanum lycopersicum* Linn.		
English Name	:	Tomato		
Indian Names	:	Bengali	:	*Belathi begoon*
		Gujarati	:	*Vilayati vengan*
		Hindi	:	*Vilayithi baingan, Tamatar*
		Kannada	:	*Chapparaba dane, Tomato*
		Konkani	:	*Tambuta*
		Marathi	:	*Velvangi, Bailwangi*
		Tamil	:	*Thakkali*
Family	:	Solanaceae		
Appearance	:	A spreading pubescent herb with a strong characteristic odour. Fruits green, red or yellow when ripe.		
Distribution	:	Throughout India		

Medicinal Part	:	Fruit.

In Tradition

❧ Acne, bad complexion, eczema, skin ailments	:	Mix ½ cup each of tomato juice, beet juice and celery juice. Take 3 times a day.
❧ Blackheads	:	Apply mashed tomato directly to face. Allow it to remain for 15 minutes and wash off. Repeat 2 or 3 times a day.
❧ Blood impurities, indigestion	:	Take the fruit juice daily.
❧ Gastric or kidney disorders, impurities in blood	:	Regular intake of the fruit juice.

A Word of Caution

Although there appears no concrete evidence so far for an association between tomato consumption, its oxalic acid content and urolithiasis, moderate consumption is recommended.

In Science

Amin, K. M. Y. et al. 1982. Central effects of alcoholic extract of *Lycopersicon esculentum* (Tomato) leaves: a preliminary study. Abstract XIV *Ann. Conf. Indian Pharmaco. Soc.* Bombay Dec. 29-31. *Indian J. Pharmacol.* 14:72. (The leaf extract revealed CNS-depressant activity in experimental rats.)

Aswal, B. S. et al. 1984. Screening of Indian plants for biological activity. Part X. *Indian J. Exp. Biol.* 22:312. (The whole plant extract did not show any pharmacological properties such as antibacterial, antifungal, antiprotozoal, antiviral, hypoglycaemic, anti-cancer, diuretic etc.)

Banerjee, N. C. et al. 1972. Screening of *Lycopersicon esculentum* tomato as a local anaesthetic agent. *Indian Vet. J.* 49: 503. (While the leaf-extract revealed local anaesthetic activity comparable to that of procaine hydrochloride, the fruit-extract did not show any local anaesthetic activity at all.)

Buttery, R. G. et al. 1987. Tomato leaf volatile aroma components. *J. Agric. Food Chem.* 35(6):1039-1042. (Chemistry of odour.)

Carper, J. 1988. *The Food Pharmacy*. London: Simon & Schuster. 297-298.

Coates, R. M. et al. 1988. Identification of alpha-santalenoic and endo-beta-bergamotenoic acids as moth oviposition stimulants from wild tomato leaves. *J. Org. Chem.* 53(10): 2186-2192. (The presence of oviposition-stimulating chemicals found in leaves.)

Datta, S. C. 1963. Free amino acids of Indian fruits. *Bull. Bot. Soc.* Bengal, 17:8.

Dixit, S. N. and S. C. Tripathi, 1975. Fungistatic properties of some seedling extracts. *Curr. Sci.* 44: 279. (Juice of the tomato seedlings exhibited fungistatic activity against *Fusarium nivale* but not against *Cephalosporium sacahari*.)

Gopalan, C. et al. 1984. *Nutritive Value of Indian Foods*. Hyderabad: National Institute of Nutrition. New Delhi: ICMR. 81, 93,128 & 130.

Indian Council of Medical Research. 1987. *Medicinal Plants of India*. New Delhi. 1987. 189.

Jurdi, M. and A. Acra. 1987. The concurrent growth of plants and chemical purification of waste waters used as a hydroponic unit. *Acta Biol. Hung.* 38(1): 161-183. (Tomatoes successfully grown hydroponically on raw waste water in Beirut. Other plants grown are: cucumber, chillies etc.)

Kaul, S. and S. L. Verma. 1967. Oxalate contents of foods commonly used in Kashmir. *Indian J. Med. Res.* 55: 274. (59.0 mg per cent.)

Khanna, P. et al. 1980. Anti-microbial principles from tissue culture of some plant species. *Indian J. Pharmaceut. Sci.* 42:113. (Anti-microbial activity against *E.coli, Strep. faecalis, Staph. albus.*)

Lakshmiah, N. and B.V. Ramasastri. 1969. Folic acid content of some Indian foods of plant origin. *J. Nutr. Dietet.* 6:200. (In tomatoes, free and total folic acid content found to be 8.4 and 28 ug/100 g respectively.)

Lust, J. B. 1974. *The Herb Book*. Bantam Books.

Mahna, S. K. and S. C. Jain. 1975. Free amino acid composition of *Lycopersicon* species and their fruit mutants. *Sci. Cult.* 51: 511. (Identification of free amino acids.)

Mallia, A. K. et al. 1967. Carotenoids in *Lycopersicon esculentum* (tomatoes). *J. Nutr. Dietet.* 4:277. (The major carotenoid 75% was lycopene.)

Misra, S. B. 1978. Antifungal activity of vapours of some plants. *Acta Bot. Indica.* 6(Suppl):118. (Leaf-vapours found to be partially inhibitory against *A. tenuis, C. lunata, F. nivale,* and *Helminthosporium gramineum.*)

Misra, S. B. and S. N. Dixit. 1979. Antifungal activity of leaf extract of some higher plants. *Acta Bot. Indica* 7: 147. (Leaf extract totally inhibited *Ustilago tritici* and *U. hordei.*)

Misra, S. B. and S. N. Dixit, 1979. A simple method for determining fungitoxicity of vapours of plant extracts. *Indian J. Mycol. Plant Pathol.* 9:250.

Mukadam, D. S. et al. 1976. Antifungal activities in deproteinised leaf extracts of weeds and non-weeds. *Indian J. Microbiol.* 16(2): 78. (Significant inhibition of *Pestalotia* sp., *A. brassicicola* and *H. apattarnae* spore germination.)

Nanda, R. S. 1972. Fluoride content of North Indian foods. *Indian*

J. Med. Res. 60: 1470. (Fruits collected from Lucknow revealed 0.2 to 0.5 ppm fluoride content.)

Om Chandra, et al. 1968. Pharmacology of the active principles of *Lycopersicon esculentum* leaves. A preliminary report. *Indian J. Physiol. Pharmacol.* 12:31. (Acetone extract of the leaves produced prolonged fall in the blood pressure of dogs.)

Om Chandra, et al. 1969. A study of the local anaesthetic activity of tomato leaves. *Indian J. Pharmacol.* 1(2): 7. (Acetone extract of the leaves showed potent local anaesthetic activity as compared to procaine and cocaine.)

Om Chandra, et al. 1969. A study on the local anaesthetic activity of the acetone extract of *Lycopersicon esculentum* leaves. *Jap. J. Pharmacol.* 19:625.

Roy Choudhury, R. 1980. Effect of extract of certain *Solanaceous* plants on plant virus infection. *Acta Bot. Indica* 18:91. (The extract inhibited the tobacco mosaic virus.)

Taberner, P.V. 1985. *Aphrodisiacs: The Science and the Myth.* Philadelphia: University of Pennsylvania. 60.

20

Persian Lilac

Melia azedarach

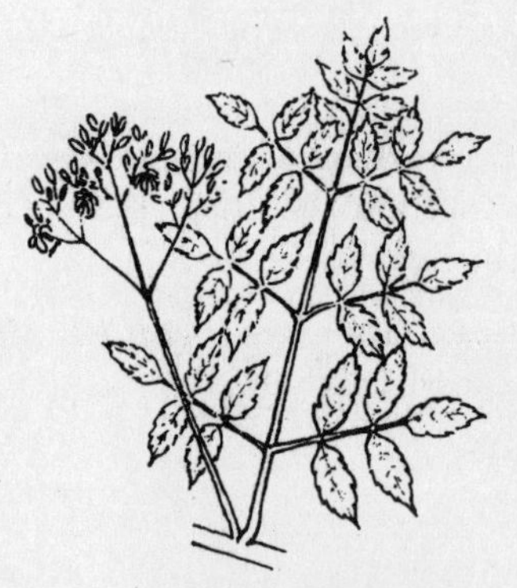

Mahanimbah fights toxins . . .
—Dhanvantri Nighantu

The Neem's Cousin

This elegant tree bears a strong resemblance to its more popular cousin, neem. The structure of the leaves and the colour of the flowers—lilac in *melia* and white in neem—however, distinguish them from each other.

A tree native to West Asia, the Persian lilac spread and enriched the Indian subcontinent hand in hand with Islam.

The tree is often cultivated in India as an avenue tree, particularly in the plains. It is also grown in tea and coffee plantations for providing the much-needed shade for the commercial crop.

Ecologically, the tree is considered ideal for afforestation attempts and in developing wastelands. Commercially, it yields a valuable timber, which is resistant to attack by white ants and at the same time tough, moderately hard, moderately heavy, durable, and lustrous with a dry feel. A gum is also obtained from the trunk, which has some commercial significance.

The leaves, unlike those of neem, are only slightly bitter and are therefore eaten by the rural poor after boiling them thoroughly with other greens and vegetables. Many small cultivators use them as a dependable green manure. In ethno-medicine, the leaf juice finds its application as a remedy to fight intestinal worms.

The fruits, which are used as a charm against certain infections, possess a bitter taste and a nauseating smell. They are reported in scientific literature as poisonous to man and livestock, although I have come across famine-hit cattle eating them hungrily without any apparent ill-effects.

Melia, the Insect-repellant

The leaves, bark and fruits of the Persian lilac possess powerful insect-repellant properties. The dried leaves are placed inside books and also between the folds of garments to protect them from the invasion of pests. A decoction made of leaves, flowers and fruits is often used in rural India as an effective insecticide in safe-guarding clothing, lentils and dry fruits. Several plants are protected from grasshoppers and locusts by a periodical spray of the leaf decoction. In Ghana, the plant extract is reported to be used for protecting cocoa beans from the attack of pests such as *Ephestia spp.*

Like neem, the Persian lilac is used in folk medicine throughout India. It is high time now to explore the pharmacology of this tree for human welfare.

The Profile

Botanical Name	:	*Melia azedarach* Linn.		
English Names	:	Bead tree, China tree, Persian lilac, Pride of India		
Indian Names	:	Assamese	:	*Thamaga*
		Bengali	:	*Ghora nim, Maha nim*
		Gujarati	:	*Bakam, Limbodo*
		Hindi	:	*Bakain, Drek*
		Kannada	:	*Are bevu, Hutechu bevu*
		Khasi	:	*Dieng-jah-rasang*
		Malayalam	:	*Karain vembu, Mala veppu, Sima veppu*
		Marathi	:	*Padrai, Pejri*
		Punjabi	:	*Drek*
		Sanskrit	:	*Mahanimba*
		Tamil	:	*Malai vembu*
		Telugu	:	*Konda vepa, Turaka vepa, Konda vepa*
		Nepali	:	*Bakaina*
Family	:	Meliaceae		
Appearance	:	A moderate-sized deciduous tree, resembling the neem tree. Flowers, lilac. Bark, dark grey with shallow, longitudinal furrows. Leaves, pinnate with toothed margin. Fruits with 4 seeds.		
Distribution	:	Cultivated in the plains.		
Medicinal Parts	:	Bark, fruits, flowers and leaves.		
Ayurvedic Preparation	:	*Kalingadi tailam.*		

In Tradition

- Eruptive skin diseases, lice infection : Apply flowers as a poultice.
- Nervous headaches : Apply flowers and leaves as a poultice.
- Intestinal worms : Take 1 tsp leaf juice.
  Dry and powder the bark. Take 2 pinches

with hot water.

- Lice, skin diseases : Apply a poultice of the flowers.

Note: Individual results may vary.

In Science

Atwal, A. S. and H. R. Pajni. 1964. Preliminary studies on the insecticidal properties of drupes of *Melia azedarach* against caterpillars of *Pieris brassicae* (*Lepidoptera: Pieridae.*) *Indian J. Ent.*26 (Pt II): 221. (Alcoholic extract showed active insecticidal properties.)

Bhakuni D. S. et al. 1969. Screening of Indian plants for biological activity. Part II. *Indian J. Exptl. Biol.* 7:250. (Stem bark extract shows anti-cancer, antispasmodic action; antiviral activity against Ranikhet disease virus.)

Burkill, 1935. *A Dictionary of the Economic Products of the Malay Peninsula.* London: Crown Agents for the Colonies. II: 1442.

Howard, A. L. 1948. *A Manual of Timbers of the World: Their Characteristics and Uses.* London: Macmillan 3rd edn. 361.

Jaipal, S. et al. 1983. Juvenile hormone-like activity in extracts of some common Indian plants. *Indian J. Agric. Sci.* 53:730

Krishnaswamy, V. S. 1956. *Sixty-six Trees of Vana Mahotsava.* Delhi: Manager of Publications. 126.

Mahato, S. B. 1987. Constituents of *Azadirachta indica* and *Melia azedarach. Sci & Cult.* 53(5): 1-29.

Mital, S. P and B. Singh, 1986. Introduction of genetic resources of some important medicinal and aromatic plants in India. *Indian J. Genet.* 46(1): 209-216.

Neogi, N. G. et al. 1963. In vitro anthelmintic activity of some indigenous drugs. *J. Indian Med. Assoc.* 41:435. (Leaf extract fights tapeworms and hookworms.)

Pearson, R. S. and H. P. Brown. 1932. *Commercial Timbers of India.* Calcutta: Central Publications Branch. I:241.

Quisumbing, E. 1951. *Medicinal Plants of the Philippines. Techl. Bull.* No.16, Dept. Agric. & Nat. Resources, Manila.

Shrivastava, A. K. and C. S. Chauhan. 1977. Preliminary pharmacological studies of unsaponifiable matter obtained from fixed oil of seeds of *Melia azedarach. Indian Drugs Pharmaceut. Ind.* 12(5): 39. (Seed oil showed antibacterial action against *B. subtilis, E.coli, Proteus* sp., *S. aureus* etc.)

Singh, R. and R. Singh. 1972. Screening of some plant extracts for antiviral properties. *Technology* (Sindri) 9: 415. (Antiviral activity against potato virus X.)

21

Bakul

Mimusops elengi

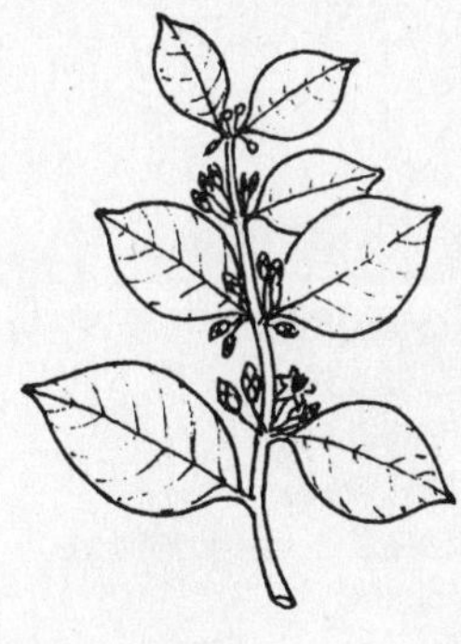

Bakula strengthens teeth . . .
—Dhanvantri Nighantu

Flower Power

The fragrant flowers are often made into garlands. They are also used in the extraction of '*maulsari attar*'. The flowers are dried and powdered. The flower-powder is often used as snuff to produce a copious discharge from the nose and in the process a headache may be cured.

Young twigs are used in villages for cleaning the teeth.

The ripe fruits are edible. They are considered quite useful in chronic dysentery.

The bark, flowers and fruits are considered to be astringent.

The bark is reported to increase fertility in women. It is also antipyretic and a tonic.

The leaves are used against snake bite by some forest-dwellers in South India.

Seeds in the form of a suppository are said to relieve constipation in children.

The Santals use the plant in the treatment of a number of ailments such as anascara, bronchitis, carbuncles, consumption, cough, dropsy, menorrhagia, small pox, sores, syphilis, ulcerated tongue etc.

The Profile

Botanical Name	:	*Mimusops elengi* Linn.		
English Name	:	Spanish cherry		
Indian Names	:	Bengali	:	*Bakul*
		Gujarati	:	*Barsoli, Bolsari*
		Hindi	:	*Bakul, Maulsari*
		Kannada	:	*Bakula, Pagade*
		Konkani	:	*Vovaliruku*
		Malayalam	:	*Bakulam, Elengi, Makura, Mukura*
		Marathi	:	*Bakul, Ovalli*
		Punjabi	:	*Maulsari*
		Sanskrit	:	*Bakula, Madhugandha, Simhakeshara, Sthirapushpa*
		Tamil	:	*Magizham, Magadam, Vagulam*
		Telugu	:	*Pogada, Vakulamu*
Family	:	Sapotaceae		
Appearance	:	A medium, evergreen, ornamental tree cultivated for its fragrant flowers. Leaves, opposite, alternate, glabrous with rounded base with a characteristic odour, brittle when dry and astringent in taste.		
Distribution	:	Andaman islands, Deccan peninsula.		

In Tradition

- Chronic dysentery : Take ½ tsp fully ripe fruit pulp with 1 cup warm water.
- Headache : Dry flowers, powder and use as 'snuff'.
- Gum infection, halitosis, mouth ulcers : Young twigs may be used as a tooth brush.

Note: Individual results may vary.

In Science

Aswal, B. S. et al. 1984. Screening of Indian plants for biological activity. Part X. *Indian J. Exptl. Biol.* 22:312. (Extract from the whole plant excluding roots showed diuretic activity in experimental rats; it did not show antiprotozoal, antiviral, hypoglycaemic activities.)

Banerjee, R. et al. 1978. Steroid and triterpenoid saponins as spermicidal agents. *Indian Drugs.* 17:6. (Saponin from the seeds exhibited spermicidal activity in human semen.)

Bahl, C. P. et al. 1968. Chemical observations of some Indian plant drugs. *Curr. Sci.* 37:1. (Chemistry of the bark, flowers and leaves.)

Bhargava, K. P. et al. 1970. Anti-inflammatory activity of saponins and other natural products. *Indian J. Med. Res.* 58:724. (Saponins from the seed had no anti-inflammatory effect in rat paw odema.)

Chopra, I. C. and L. D. Kapoor.1968. Steroid sapogenin-bearing plants of India. *Indian For.* 94:620. (Presence of saponin.)

Gopalan, C. et al. 1984. *Nutritive Value of Indian Foods.* National Institute of Nutrition, Hyderabad. New Delhi: ICMR. 90. (Presence of calcium and phosphorus.)

Gupta, G. K. et al. 1976. Chemical constituents of *Mimusops elengi. Indian J. Chem.* 14B: 818. (Chemistry of flowers.)

Misra, G. et al. 1974. Studies on *Mimusops* sp. *Planta Med.* 26: 155.(A review of literature on chemical studies of 3 species of *Mimusops.*)

Mital, S. P. and B. Singh. 1986. Introduction of genetic resources of some important medicinal and aromatic plants in India. *Indian J. Genet.* 46(1): 209-216.

Misra, G. and C. R. Mitra. 1967. Constituents of fruit and seed of *Mimusops elengi. Phytochemistry*, 6: 453. (Chemical analysis.)

Misra, G. and C. R. Mitra. 1967. Constituents of bark of *Mimusops elengi. Phytochemistry*, 6: 1309. (Chemistry of bark.)

Misra, G. and C. R. Mitra. 1968. Constituents of leaves, heartwood and root of *Mimusops elengi. Phytochemistry*, 7:501.

Mitra, R. 1981. Bakula. A reputed drug of Ayurveda, its history, uses in Indian medicine. *Indian J. Hist. Sci.* 16:169. (Pharmacognostic characteristics of various parts of the plant.)

Mitra, R. and K. C. Yadav 1980. Pharmacognostical study on Bakul—*Mimusops elengi* Linn. leaf. *Indian J. For.* 3:15. (Presence of sterols, reducing sugars, saponins and tannins reported.)

Satyanarayana, T. et al. 1977. Antibacterial activity of six medicinal plant extracts. *Indian Drugs*, 14:209. (Antibacterial role of leaf extract against a number of pathogens including *B. subtilis, Sal. paratyphi, Staph. albus, Vib. cholerae, Xanth. campestris* etc.)

Sharma, B. M. et al. 1970. Pharmacognostic study of fruits of *Mimusops elengi* L. (Bakul) *J. Res. Indian Med.* 4(2): 214. (Fruit as a medicine.)

Sharma, M. L. et al. 1978. Pharmacological screening of Indian medicinal plants. *Indian J. Exptl. Biol.* 16:228. (Hypotensive effect of ethanolic extract of fruits and leaves reported; neither anti-coagulant, anti-inflammatory, antipyretic, diuretic, hypoglycaemic activities nor any effect on CNS and isolated tissues noticed.)

Sinha, A. 1962. Chemical examination of *Mimusops elengi* Linn. Part I. Examination of the fatty oil from the seeds. *Proc. Natl. Acad. Sci.* India 32A (I): 56. (Composition of seed oil.)

Varshney, I. P. and K. M. Logani. 1969. Studies of the saponins and sapogenins from *Mimusops elengi* Linn. *Indian J. Appl. Chem.* 32:173. (Bark as a source for saponins and sapogenins.)

Vijayalakshmi, K. et al. 1979. Nematicidal properties of some indigenous plant materials against second stage juveniles of *Meloidogyne incognita* (koffoid and white) chitwood. *Indian J. Ent.* 41:326.

22

Oleander

Nerium oleander

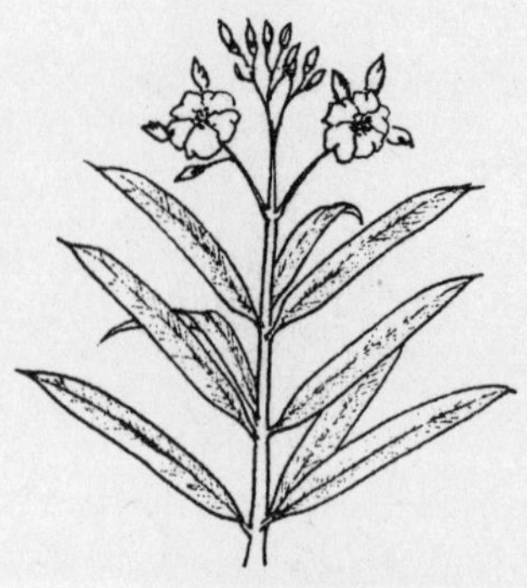

Oleander poison in combination with wine and rue is an antidote for snake poison.
—Dioscorides, the personal physician of the Emperor of Rome

The Horse Killer

Widely acknowledged as a killer of both humans and cattle, the plant's Sanskrit synonyms *ashwamarakah* and *hayamarakah* which emphasize its capability of killing the horse alone may appear rather strange. But for a student of history, it may not be so, as several war chronicles have replete references to oleander being used in ancient battles as a weapon against the enemy. Theophrastus has, in detail, referred to the ancient practice of poisoning enemy horses with oleander and the constant threat faced by the horses of Alexander the Great during his conquests (334-323 B.C.) Dioscorides and Pliny are also on record as to the toxicity of those 'handsome leaves and flowers' which give a deathblow to battle animals. One can unearth from the annals of history that not only battle animals but also soldiers have succumbed to the plant poison. In 1796, several French 'soldats' fighting in Corsica, died immediately after savouring meat skewered on an oleander branch. In Africa, many soldiers who slept on pallets made of oleander either died or were seriously poisoned with depression, fever, nausea, diarrhoea, weak heart beat and pulse, or paralysis – the typical symptoms arising in any oleander poisoning.

Oleander: A Lazy Gardener's Delight

A native of the Mediterranean region, oleander flourishes as a hedge plant throughout India. From a gardener's point of view, the plant is great. It doesn't demand much attention and it knows how to take care of itself. Armed to face the scorching North Indian summer, the plant not only retains its composure and charm but also thrives vigorously. It blooms actively, despite the north-westerly winds that attack the alluring plains like the historic Mongols. As a hedge plant, it is quite effective in keeping stray cattle at bay. It is interesting to watch how animals behave when they encounter the shrub and how submissively they avoid coming anywhere near its vicinity! Further, the plant can be easily propagated; its cuttings instantly start rooting during the monsoon months. What else can a lazy gardener expect from a plant?

The Extinct Oleander

Rajanighantu, an ayurvedic text of great antiquity refers to four varieties of *karavira*: red, white, yellow and black (blue?). Modern botanists have been able to identify only the first three varieties. Red and white are identifiable with *Nerium oleander*. The yellow-flowered variety can be equated with *pitakaravira* (*Thevetia peruviana*) of the same botanical family. The black-flowered variety is still a mystery to botanists. Years of search have borne no fruit, and in all probability, this variety could, sadly, be one of those million plants which have vanished from the face of the earth due to human depradation.

The Poison As a Medicine

The plant is a well-known folk-medicine from time immemorial. Ayurveda must have derived its knowledge of this plant, as well as others from several ancient tribal cultures in the subcontinent. Dioscorides, the personal physician of the Emperor of Rome has observed that oleander poison taken with wine and rue (*Ruta graveolans*) is a cure for snake bite.

The Santals, who constitute an important tribal group in India known for their medicinal wisdom, find oleander useful in curing asthma, bronchitis, consumption, dysentery, inflammation of the gums and menorrhagia. In the southern parts of India, the poisonous drug finds traditional use in the treatment of blood-clots, fevers, leprosy, swellings, and venereal ulcers.

Although poisonous in nature, the root if properly and carefully administered, works as a powerful cardiac tonic. Recent pharmacological experiments have confirmed this and the tincture from its leaves is found twice as potent as digitalis. One of the glycosides in the plant, plumeride is also found endowed with anti-stress properties. The anti-cancerous properties of this plant are also referred to in many recent papers.

Karaviradi taila, an oil prepared from oleander and other plants, such as *chitraka* (*Plumbago zeylanica*) and *vidanga* (*Embelia ribes*) in a curious blend with cow's urine has been a popular ayurvedic remedy in skin restoration.

In some Indian villages, the root of the plant is used to terminate unwanted pregnancies. In this process, the efficacy of the drug is such that in addition to ensuring the termination of pregnancy, it also terminates the pregnant as well! Perhaps the role of oleander in women's social history in India would be a good topic for a doctoral thesis!

The Profile

Botanical Names	:	*Nerium indicum* Mill *Nerium odorum* Soland *Nerium oleander* Blanco.		
English Names	:	Oleander, Sweet-scented oleander, Rose-berry spurge		
Indian Names	:	Bengali	:	*Karabi*
		Gujarati	:	*Kanher, Kagaer*
		Hindi	:	*Chandni, Kaber, Kaner, Karavira*
		Kannada	:	*Kanagile, Kanagilu, Paddale*
		Konkani	:	*Dhavekaneri*
		Malayalam	:	*Areli, Karaviram*
		Marathi	:	*Kanera, Kanher*
		Punjabi	:	*Kaner*
		Sanskrit	:	*Karavira*
		Tamil	:	*Arali, Kanaviram, Karaviram, Kasturipattai, Kaviram, Sevvarali, Valikkoli*
		Telugu	:	*Ganneru, Karaviramu, Kasturipatta*
Family	:	Apocynaceae		
Appearance	:	An evergreen erect, shiny and woody shrub with a whorl of 3-6 leaves at the node. The whole plant is full of white milky latex and highly poisonous. Leaves, narrow, deep-green, lance-like, tapering with a stout midrib. Flowers, pinkish red or white, fragrant, single or double, found in a cluster (cyme). Flowers and fruits, aplenty, all year.		

Distribution	:	A native of the mediterranean region, oleander is found from Persia to China and Japan. The plant growing wild in the Himalayas from Bhutan to Kashmir, upto an altitude of about 2000 m. and in the upper Gangetic plains is also found in the central and southern parts of India.
Medicinal Parts	:	Flowers, leaves, root, root bark.
Ayurvedic Preparations	:	*Karaviradi tailam Malatyadi tailam, Mustamritadi tailam.*

In Tradition

Chancres, haemorrhoids, leprosy, scorpion sting, skin diseases of a scaly nature, snake bite, ulcers	:	The root-paste is applied externally. (*Caution*: POISONOUS.)
Chancres, swelling and ulcers on penis	:	Wash the affected areas with a decoction of leaves. (*Caution*: POISONOUS.)
Ear ache, ear infection, pus in ear, ear ulcers	:	Heat 2 tsp gingelly oil with ⅛ of an inch crushed root bark. When bearably warm, use 1 or 2 drops as ear drops. (*Caution*: POISONOUS. Do not repeat the treatment frequently.)
Ophthalmic problems associated with copious lachrymation	:	Use the fresh juice of the leaves. (Caution: POISONOUS. Also avoid infection.)
Ringworm, skin complaints	:	Apply a paste of root bark and leaves. (*Caution*: POISONOUS.)
Skin diseases	:	Apply a root paste. Boil a few leaves in ¼ cup coconut oil. Cool. Use it as an ointment. (*Caution*: POISONOUS.)

Swelling	:	External application of a decoction of the leaves. (*Caution*: POISONOUS.)
Venomous bites	:	External application of leaf juice. (Caution: POISONOUS.)
Scaly condition of the skin, leprosy	:	External application of the oil of the root bark. (*Caution*: POISONOUS.)
Skin ailments	:	Boil a few leaves in adequate quantity of sesame oil. Cool and bottle. Apply on the affected areas. (*Caution*: POISONOUS.)

Note: Individual results may vary.

A Word of Caution

Every part of the plant is poisonous. It contains a glucoside akin to digitalin which acts as a heart poison. There is 2½ times as much poison in oleander leaves as there is in Digitalis.

In Science

Abe, F. and T. Yamaguchi. 1979. Oleasides—Novel carenolides with an unusual frame-work on *Nerium*. *Chem. Pharm. Bull.* 27:1604. (Chemical personality of leaves.)

Abrol, B. K. and I. C. Chopra. 1962-63. Development of indigenous vegetable insecticides and insect repellants. *Bull. Reg. Res. Lab.* Jammu. 1(2): 156. (Root extract showed moderate activity against house flies and mosquitoes.)

Basu, D. and A. Chatterjee. 1973. Occurrence of plumericin in *Nerium indicum. Indian J. Chem.*11: 297. (Chemistry of the roots.)

Bor, N. L. and M. B. Raizada. 1990. *Some Beautiful Indian Climbers and Shrubs*. Bombay Natural History Society, Oxford Univ. Press. Revised 2nd edn. 217. (The oleander parade.)

Chopra, R. N. et al. 1956. *Glossary of Indian Medicinal Plants*. New

Delhi: CSIR. 175. (A powerful cardiac poison, causing paralysis and respiratory depression.)

Chopra, R. N. and I. C. Chopra. 1955. *A review of work on Indian medicinal plants.* New Delhi: ICMR. 81. (Spasmodic and cardiotonic activity of the tincture of flowers.)

CSIR, *Pharmacological Investigations of Certain Medicinal Plants and Compound Formulations used in Ayurveda and Siddha.* New Delhi. 174, 463. (Anti-implantation activity of the root extract.)

Dev, V. and H. S. Wasir. 1985. Digitalis poisoning by an indigenous plant cardiac glycoside. (*Thevetia neriifolia*- pilakaner) *Ind. Heart J.* 37(5):321-322. (Pharmacology and clinical use of the yellow-flowered *Thevetia.*)

Dhar, M. L. et al. 1968. Screening of Indian plants for biological activity. Part I. *Indian J. Exptl. Biol.* 6:232. (The root extract showed no antifungal activity against *Candida albicans* etc; no antibacterial activity against *E. coli* etc; no anthelmintic, anti-cancer, antiprotozoal, antiviral and hypoglycaemic activity. However, it showed spasmogenic activity in the isolated guinea pig ileum and CNS-depressant effects in mice.)

Jain, P. C. and S. C. Agarwal 1976. Activity of plant-extracts against some keratinophilic species of *Nannizzia.* (The leaf extract of karaveera totally inhibited the growth of *Nannizzia* spp.)

Jain, S. K. and C. R. Tarafder. 1970. Medicinal plant lore of the Santals (A revival of P. O. Bodding's work.) *Econ. Bot.* 24:241.

Joshi, C. G. and N. G. Nagar, 1952. Antibiotic activity of some Indian medicinal plants, *J. Sci. Industr. Res.* IIB(6):261. (Antibiotic activity against *S. aureus.*)

Khalsa, H. G. et al. 1964. Insecticidal properties of *Abrus precatorius* Linn. and *Nerium odorum* Soland. *Indian J. Ent.* 29(Pt. I) : 113. (Extracts of roots, stems and fruits showed moderate insecticidal activity.)

Khanna, K. K. and S. Chandra. 1972. Antifungal activity in some plant extracts. *Proc. Natl. Acad. Sci.* (India) 42B (Pt.3): 300. (The leaf extract did not inhibit spore germination of *A. alternata* isolated from wheat.)

Kishore, N. et al. 1982. Fungitoxicity of the leaf-extracts of some higher plants against *Fusarium moniliforme*. *Natl. Acad. Sci. Lett.* 5(2): 43. (The leaf extract inhibited the spore germination.)

Kohli, R. P. et al. 1967. Some cardio-vascular effects of *Nerium indicum* IV. Scientific conf. *P. G. Instt. Ind. Med. Proc.* 5. (Cardiotonic activity.)

Kohli, R. P. et al. 1968. A study of cardiotonic activity of *Nerium indicum* on heart lung preparation of dog. Vet. Sci. Conf. *P. G. Instt. Indian Med. Proc.* 25.

Kohli, R. P. et al. 1969. A study of cardiotonic activity of *Nerium indicum* (Rakta-kaner) on heart-lung preparation of dog. *J. Res. Indian Med.* 4(1): 54. (Leaf extract produces a reversal of experimentally induced heart-failure.)

Nadkarni, A. K. 1954. *Indian Materia Medica*. Bombay.

Pal, S. et al. 1968. Search for anti-cancer drugs from Indian medicinal plants (Ayurvedic, Unani etc.) *Indian J. Med. Res.* 56: 445. (Leaf extract showed moderate inhibition against Ehrlich's ascites carcinoma.)

Rajendran, B. and M. Gopalan. 1978. Note on juvenomimetic activity of some plants. *Indian J. Agric. Sci.* 48:306. (The plant extract shows no juvenile hormone-mimicking activity against the red cotton bug.)

Sanyal, P. K. and H. K. Das. 1956. Pharmacological study of the tincture of Rakta-karabi (*Nerium odorum* Soland.) flowers. *Proc. 43 Indian Sci. Cong.* Pt.III: 350. (Cardiotonic activity and the possible use of tincture of flowers in myocardial weakness.)

Satyanarayana, T. et al. 1975. Phytochemical studies on *Nerium odorum* (root bark). *Indian J. Pharm.* 37:126. (Chemical constituents of the root bark.)

Sharma, P. C. and L. D. Kapoor. 1970. Pharmacognostic study of *Nerium indicum* Mill. *J. Res. Indian Med.* 5(1):39-47. (Pharmacognosy of oleander.)

Siddiqui, S. et al. 1986. Kaneric acid—a new triterpene from the leaves of *Nerium oleander. J. Nat. Prod.* 49:1086. (Chemical structures of kaneric acid.)

Siddiqui, S. et al. 1987. Isolation and structure of neriucoumaric and isoneriucoumaric acids from leaves of *Nerium oleander. Planta Med.* 53:424.

Siddiqui, S. et al. 1987. Isolation and structure of two cardiac glycosides from leaves of *Nerium oleander. Phytochemistry*. 26:237. (Fresh leaves had yielded two cardiac glycosides.)

Singh, R. and R. Singh. 1972. Screening of some plant extracts for antiviral properties. *Technology* (Sindri) 9:415. (The stem bark extract did not inhibit potato virus X.)

Singh, N. et al. 1970. Cardiovascular pharmacology of *Nerium indicum* (Kaner) *J. Res. Indian Med.* 5(1):32. (Emetic and hypotensive properties; as a cardiac stimulant too!)

Singh, N. et al. 1976. A glycoside from the roots of *Nerium indicum* as an adaptogen producing a state of non-specific increase in resistance in animals. *IVth Indo Soviet Symp.* Chemistry of Natural Products including Pharmacology, Lucknow. 122. (Confirmation of adaptogenic activity in rats and mice from an innovative indicator: their ability to swim.)

Singh, N. et al. 1978. Pharmacological investigation of some indigenous drugs of plant origin for evaluation of their antipyretic, analgesic and anti-inflammatory activity. *J. Res. Indian Med. Yoga. and Homoeo.* 13(2):58. (Plumieride, a chemical isolated from the root, showed analgesic, antipyretic and anti-inflammatory effects in albino mice.)

Singh, N. et al. 1978. Evaluation of toxicity and therapeutic potentialities of *Nerium indicum. J. Res. Indian Med. Yoga and Homoeo.* 13(4): 17. (The toxic oleander found to be more potent than Digitalis with a margin of safety similar to that of strophanthin.)

Thakur, R. S. et al. 1989. *Major Medicinal Plants of India*. Lucknow: CIMAP. 366-369. (A beautiful profile of the plant and its medicinal importance.)

Trease, C. E. and W. C. Evans. 1983. *Pharmacognosy*. London: Bailliere Tindall. 12th edn. 404. (The oleander glycosides, akin to those in Digitalis, have identical use.)

Trivedi, V.B. and S. M. Kazmi. 1979. Inhibitory effects of kaners on fungi. *Indian Drugs Pharmaceut. Ind.* 14(6):23. (Antifungal activity of the leaf and root extract against *Alternaria alpandi* etc.)

23

Night Jasmine

Nyctanthes arbor tristis

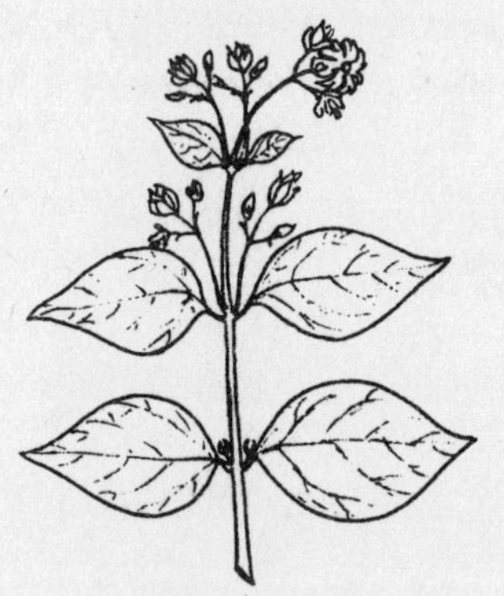

(The fragrant flowers) fuel erotic pleasures. . .
—Agathiar Gunapaadal

The Sad Tree

The flowers of this shrub bloom at night and enchant the whole world, and hence its popular name in Hindi, *'Raat-ki-Raani'*, which means 'the Queen of the Night'. At day-break the enchantment is all over and normality returns as the shrub drops its petals one by one like tear-drops. Hence the Latin name *'arbor tristis'* which means 'the sad tree'.

Hindus find these flowers fit for the worship of Lord Krishna, as it is said that He had brought this tree from the heavens with one of his favourite consorts, Satyabhama. The Hindu epic,

Vishnu Purana narrates this story. This tree, called *Parijataka*, it is said, was once a beautiful daughter of a king. She fell in love with the resplendent Sun god, who spurned her. She felt deserted, committed suicide and was cremated. From her ashes arose this shrub, which casts its flowers in the morning, unable to face the sun.

The perfume of the flowers is very similar to that of jasmine and *Cestrum nocturnum* (also known by the popular Hindi name, '*Raat-ki-Raani*').

The leaves are a reliable substitute for sand-paper: you can polish your furniture with them!

An orange-coloured dye obtained from the flowers is used for colouring silk and cotton fabrics. Patanjali, the great authority on the science of yoga, refers to the clothes dyed in this way as '*sephalika*'.

In Medicine

The leaves are antibilious and diuretic and often found useful in fevers and rheumatism.

The Profile

Botanical Name	:	*Nyctanthes arbortristis* Linn.		
English Names	:	Night queen, Night jasmine, Coral jasmine, Tree of sorrow, Weeping nyctanthes		
Indian Names	:	Bengali	:	*Harsinghar, Seoli, Sephalika, Singhar*
		Gujarati	:	*Jayaparvati*
		Hindi	:	*Harshingar, Raat-ki-Raani, Sephalika*

		Kannada	:	*Harsing, Paarijaata*
		Malayalam	:	*Mannapu, Pavizhamalli*
		Marathi	:	*Khurasli, Paajakta, Paarijaataka*
		Oriya	:	*Godokodiko*
		Punjabi	:	*Harsinghar, Kuri, Laduri*
		Sanskrit	:	*Paarijaata, Mandaara, Raagapushpi, Shephaalika*
		Tamil	:	*Manjapu, Pavazhamalli*
		Telugu	:	*Kabilanagadustu, Sepali, Pagadamalle, Shvetasurasa*
Family	:	Oleaceae (Nyctanthaceae)		
Appearance	:	A small tree or a large shrub, hardy with rough grey bark. Leaves rough, entire. Flowers small, fragrant. Petals white with a ring of orange where the corolla spreads out from its tube. Capsules more or less roundish in outline and compressed.		
Distribution	:	Wild in the sub-Himalayan and central Indian forests. Often grown as an ornamental in gardens almost all over India.		
Medicinal Parts	:	Leaves, flowers, bark, seeds.		

In Tradition

- Chronic fevers : Mix ¼ tsp leaf juice with 1 tsp honey and take with warm water.
- Dandruff, scalp conditions : Apply powdered seeds.
- Intestinal worms : Mix ¼ tsp leaf juice with honey (1 tsp) and a pinch of common salt and take.
- Reptile poisoning, sciatica : Boil ½ tsp leaves in a glass of water over a gentle fire. Drink.
- Chest and throat congestion, cough, phlegm accumulation : Take a few pinches of the bark powder with areca nut and betel leaf.

❧ Scurvy and scalp affections	:	Powdered seeds used as a paste with water may be used.
❧ Swelling	:	Apply the flower paste.

Note: Individual results may vary.

In Science

Anjaneyulu, A. S. R. and Y. L. N. Murty, 1981. The triterpenoid constituents of the leaves of *Nyctanthes arbortristis* Linn. *J. Indian Chem. Soc.* 58:817.

Atal, C. K. et al. 1978. Screening of Indian plants for biological activity. Part VIII. *Indian J. Exptl. Biol.* 16:330.

Basu, N. M. et al. 1947. The vitamin C and carotene contents of several herbs and flowers used in the Ayurvedic system of medicine. *J. Indian Chem. Soc.* 24:358. (Leaves contain vitamin C.)

Bhakuni, D. S. et al. 1969. Screening of Indian plants for biological activity. Part II. *Indian J. Exptl. Biol.* 7:250. (The ethanolic extract showed CNS depressing effect, hypothermia in mice.)

Bhowmick, B. N. and B. K. Choudhary. 1982. Antifungal activity of leaf extracts of medicinal plants on *Alternaria alternata* (Fr.) Keissler. *Indian Bot. Rept.* 1:164. (No antifungal action. Instead, the extract stimulated the fungal growth and sporulation.)

Bhowmick, B. N. and V. Vardhan. 1981. Antifungal activity of some leaf extracts of some medicinal plants on *Curvularia lanata. Indian Phytopathol.* 34:385. (No antifungal activity.)

Central Council for Research in Ayurveda and Siddha, 1996. *Pharmacological Investigations of Certain Medicinal Plants and Compound Formulations Used in Ayurveda and Siddha.* New Delhi, 260. (A brief account of Night Jasmine.)

Chandra, G. 1970. Chemical composition of the flower oil of

Nyctanthes arbortristis. Indian Perfumer. 14:19. (Chemistry of the flower oil.)

Chauhan, J. S. and M. Saraswat. 1978. A new glycoside from the stem of *Nyctanthes arbortristis. J. Indian Chem. Soc.* 55: 1049.

Dhingra, V. K. et al. 1976. Carotenoid glycosides of *Nyctanthes arbortristis* Linn. *Indian J. Chem.* 14B:231. (Carotenoid glycosides isolated from the orange-red corolla tubes.)

Ganguly, S. N. et al. 1972. Oleanolic acid from *Nyctanthes arbortristis.* Proc. 59th Session Indian Sci. Cong. Calcutta, 142.

Gupta, S. K. and M. M. Bokadia. 1976. Flavanoids from the flowers of *Nyctanthes arbortristis* Linn. *Vijnana Parishad Anusandhan Patrika,* 19:377. (From the orange-coloured corolla tube.)

Indian Council of Medical Research, 1987. *Medicinal Plants of India.* Vol. 2. New Delhi, 343-347. (Night Jasmine: a profile.)

Jagraj, B. L. 1936. Constituents of the colouring matter of *Nyctanthes arbortristis*—identity of nyctanthin with a-crocetin. *Proc. Nat. Inst. Sci.* India 2:57.

Lal, J. B. and S. Dutta. 1933. Chemical examination of the leaves of *Nyctanthes arbortristis. Bull. Acad. Sci. Univ. Prov. Agra,* (Oudh). 3:83.

Majumdar, D. N. and A. K. Agarwal. 1966. Investigation on the chemical constituents of *Nyctanthes arbortristis* Linn. Abstr. of the paper presented at the 18th meeting, Indian Pharmacol. Soc., Varanasi, Dec. 27-30. 1966. *Indian J. Pharm.* 28: 340.

Neogi, N. C. and S. Ahuja. 1960-61. Pharmacological studies on the bark of *Nyctanthes arbortristis* Linn. *J. Scient. Res.* Banaras Hindu Univ. 11: 196. (How a glycoside extracted from the bark acts on a frog's heart.)

Pandey, U. K. et al. 1982. Note on the use of some insecticides against *Bagrada cruciferarum. Indian J. Agric. Sci.* 52:305. (Extract shows strong insecticidal action against the painted bug.)

Purushothaman, K. K. et al. 1985. Arbortristosides A and B, two iridoid glucosides from *Nyctanthes arbortristis. Phytochemistry.* 24:773. (From the seeds.)

Qazi, G. A. et al. 1973. Compositional studies on minor seed oils from six plant families. *Oil Seeds J.* 26:5. (Chemical composition of seed oil.)

Rimpler, H. and J. U. Junghanns. 1975. Nyctanthoside—a new iridoid from *Nyctanthes arbortristis. Tetrahedron Lett.* 2423.

Sabir, M. et al. 1974. Pharmacological actions of *Nyctanthes arbortristis. Proc. Vth. Ann. Conf. Indian Pharmacol. Soc.* Hissar, Dec. 30 Jan 1. *Indian J. Pharmacol.* 6:17.(Hypotensive effect observed.)

Santapau, H. 1966. *Common Trees.* New Delhi: National Book Trust, 21-24.

Saxena, R. S. 1980. *Some pharmacological studies of Nyctanthes arbortristis* Linn. Thesis M.D., Meerut Univ., Meerut. (Mimeo.)

Saxena, R. S. et al. 1984. Study of anti-inflammatory activity in the leaves of *Nyctanthes arbortristis* Linn. An Indian medicinal plant. *J. Ethnopharmacol.* 11:319. (Confirmed.)

Sen, A. B. and S. P. Singh. 1964. Chemical examination of *Nyctanthes arbortristis. J. Indian Chem.* Soc.41: 192.

Sharma, N. et al. 1978. Pharmacological screening of Indian medicinal plants. *Indian J. Exptl. Biol.* 16:228. (Non-toxic.)

Singh, R. and R. Singh. 1972. Screening of some plant extracts for antiviral properties. *Technology* (Sindri), 9: 415. (Bark extract showed inhibition against potato virus X.)

Singh, R. B. and V. K. Jindal. 1985. Polysaccharides from *Nyctanthes arbortristis* Linn. Seeds—isolation, purification and preliminary analysis of polysaccharide. *J. Indian Chem. Soc.* 62:627.

Singh, R. C. et al. 1983. On some more pharmacological properties of *Nyctanthes arbortristis* Linn. (Harsingar)—the plant known for anti-inflammatory actions. Abstr. paper presented XVIth Ann. Conf. Ajmer, Dec. 28-30., *Indian J. Pharmacol.* 16:47. (Extract of leaves showed dose-dependent antipyretic and tranquillising effect; histamine-antagonistic and purgative activities also reported.)

Singh, S. P. et al. 1965. Flavanoids of *Nyctanthes arbortristis. Bull. Nat. Inst. Sci. India.* 41. (From the leaves.)

Thakur, R. S. et al. 1989. *Major Medicinal Plants of India.* Lucknow: CIMAP. 370-374.

Turnbull, J. H. et al. 1957. Nyctanthic acid, a constituent of *Nyctanthes arbortristis. J. Chem. Soc.* 569. (Present in the seed kernel.)

Tyagi, P. and A. K. Vasishtha. 1983. Component of glycosides in *Nyctanthes arbortristis* seeds oil. *J. Oil Technol. Assn. India.* 15:27. (Chemistry of seed oil.)

Vasishtha, S. K. 1938. Chemical examination of the fixed oil from the seeds of *Nyctanthes arbortristis* Linn. *J. Benares Hindu Univ.* 2:343.

24

Indian Jalap

Operculina turpethum

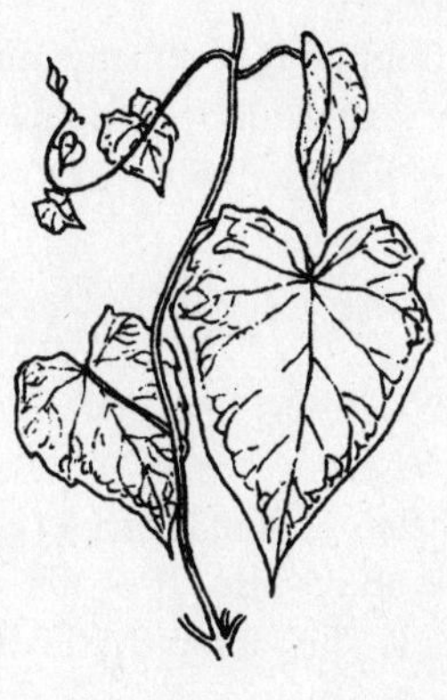

Trivrit eliminates germs and fevers.
—Nighantu Ratnakara

Better Late Than Never!

The Indian jalap, also known as turpeth, is a handsome climber yielding a purgative drug which has been much sought after in Indian systems of medicine. The drug, however, had its official recognition in the Indian pharmacopoeia only in 1946. Better late than never!

The dried root of the plant, which constitutes the drug turpeth, is a well-known cathartic, that is a drug which induces active movement of the bowels.

As elimination of *ama* is given importance in Ayurveda to kickstart healing processes, drugs such as turpeth play a vital role in the treatment of various ailments, particularly constipation, consumption, eye diseases, fevers, dropsy, anasarca, jaundice, hepatic and haemophilic disorders, kidney or liver diseases, leprosy, melancholia, oedema, piles, rheumatic and paralytic affections, and skin diseases etc.

Turpeth is often administered in combination with various other ingredients such as salt, black pepper, ginger, *haritaki, vibhitaki* and *amla,* (the last three forming *'triphala'*.)

In the Malabar region of Kerala, it is used in partnership with dried ginger, for fighting inflammation.

The root is also reported to be a popular folk remedy in many tribal belts in India, where—leave alone mosquitoes—people find themselves often stung by a scorpion or bitten by a snake.

Varieties of Turpeth

There are two varieties of Indian jalap, distinguishable by the colour of the tuberous roots: black and white. It is the white variety which is preferred by physicians. The reason for this is that the black variety is considered to be so potent a purgative that it has to be avoided at all costs.

The Profile

Botanical Names	:	*Operculina turpethum* (L.) Silva-Manso *Ipomoea turpethum* (L.) R.Br. *Convolvulus turpethum* Linn.		
English Names	:	Indian jalap, Turpeth		
Indian Names	:	Bengali	:	*Dudh kalmi, Teori*
		Gujarati	:	*Nishotar, Phutkari*

Hindi	:	*Nisoth, Pitohri*
Kannada	:	*Tigade*
Malayalam	:	*Chivakaver, Rochani*
Marathi	:	*Nishottara*
Punjabi	:	*Chitabansa, Nisot*
Sanskrit	:	*Trivrit, Triputaa, Kumbha, Saralaa, Nishotraa*
Tamil	:	*Sivadai*
Telugu	:	*Tegada, Tellategatta*

Ayurvedic Name : *Nishoth, Trivrit, Triputa*

Unani Name : *Turbud safaid*

Family : Convolvulaceae

Appearance : A climber with stout, twining, quadrangular, winged stem. Leaves, long with cordate base. Flowers, white, funnel-like on long stalk, and in bunches. Fruits, round, usually bearing 4 seeds.

Distribution : All over the Indian peninsula upto 1000 m. Also cultivated.

Medicinal Parts : The dried root of the plant; also root bark and stem.

Ayurvedic Preparations : *Avipattikar churna, Chandraprabha, Trivritadi Churna, Trivritadi leha, Trivritadi yoga.*

Unani Preparations : *Hab banafasha, Hab yarqan, Itrifal-i-zamani, Ma'ajun najab, Qurs mulayyin, Sharbat mushil.*

In Tradition

- Constipation : Mix ¼ tsp each of turpeth and powdered black pepper and take with 1 tsp honey. (*Caution*: PURGATIVE.)
- Dropsy, gout : Take ¼ tsp turpeth for a few days. (*Caution*: PURGATIVE.)
- Intestinal worms : Pound ¼ tsp each of the following and boil in 1 glass of water till the volume is reduced to half: aniseed, ajwain, black cumin, Indian senna, katki, root of nisoth, seeds of palash, seeds of vidanga. Dose: 2 to 3 tbsp

		to be followed by a purgative pill or castor oil at bed time. (*Caution*: PURGATIVE.)
❧ Jaundice	:	Grind 1 tsp each of the leaves of castor and keezhanelli to a fine paste and take for 3 consecutive days in the morning. For the 4th day, take ¼ tsp turpeth. (*Caution:* PURGATIVE.)

Note: Individual results may vary.

A Word of Caution

The drug can cause vomiting and fainting. Only experienced practitioners can administer the drug.

In Science

Aswal, B. S. et al. 1984. Screening of Indian plants for biological activity. Part XI. *Indian J. Exptl. Biol.* 22:487-504. (Absence of antibacterial, antifungal, antiviral, antiprotozoal, diuretic activities.)

Auterhoff, H. and H. Demleitner. 1955. Comparative studies on *Convolvulaceous* resins. *Arzneimittle-Forsch.*, 5:402; *Chem Abstr.* 49: 16352h. (Active principle of the root is a glycosidic resin, having laxative properties.)

Bakhru, H. K. 1995. *Herbs that Heal—Natural Remedies for Good Health.* Orient Paperbacks. 5th Printing. 166-168. (Turpeth–a profile.)

Central Council for Research in Ayurveda and Siddha, 1996. *Pharmacological Investigations of Certain Medicinal Plants and Compound Formulations used in Ayurveda and Siddha.* New Delhi. 342-344. (Positive purgative and cardiac depressant activity of root bark powder; no anti-inflammatory activity noticed.)

Chopra, R. N. et al. 1956. *Glossary of Indian Medicinal Plants.* New Delhi: CSIR, 181. (Purgative; in scorpion sting and snake bite.)

Chunekar, 1982. 398. (The black variety is more powerful and drastic in action than the white variety; it can cause vomiting and fainting.)

Joshi, S.V. 1998. *Ayurveda and Panchakarma—The Science of Healing and Rejuvenation.* Delhi: Motilal Banarsidas. 1st Indian edn. (How does elimination of *ama* contribute in the panchakarma treatment?)

Khare, A. K. et al. 1981. Preliminary study of anti-inflammatory activity of *Operculina turpethum.* (Nishoth). *Indian Drugs.* 19(6): 224-228. (Observed.)

Khare, A. K. 1982. Preliminary study of anti-inflammatory activity of *Ipomoea turpethum. Indian Drugs*, 19: 224. (Water extract of the root found to be the 'most potent anti-inflammatory fraction' in experimental animals.)

Kurup, P. A. 1956. Studies on plant antibiotics. Screening of some Indian medicinal plants. *J. Sci. Industr. Res.*15C(6): 153-154. (Extract of fresh roots exhibited antibacterial properties against *E.coli* and *S.aureus.*)

Kurup, P. N. V. et al. 1979. *Handbook of Medicinal Plants.* New Delhi. 219.

Mital, S. P and B. Singh. 1986. Introduction of genetic resources of some important medicinal and aromatic plants in India. *Indian J. Genet.* 46(1): 209-216.

Nadkarni, A. K. 1954. *Indian Materia Medica.* Bombay. 692. (Useful in rheumatic and paralytic affections.)

Nesamony, S. 1985. *Oushadhasasyangal.* 295. (In Malayalam.)

Pendse, G. S. and M. A. Iyengar 1961. Studies in Indian medicinal plants used in Ayurveda—Cathartics. *Curr. Sci.* 30(10): 399-400. (Turpeth's contribution in cleansing the system.)

Sharma, P. V. 1983. *Dravyaguna vijnana*, Varanasi. 420. (Charaka had recognized two varieties of the drug: red and black, presumably based on the root's colour.) (In Hindi.)

Shukla, S. P. 1986. Indigenous drugs and their utilization by human beings. *Nagarjun*. 29(5): 10-11. (Root-decoction eradicates intestinal worms; a deadly combination when mixed with black pepper.)

Singh, T. B. and K. C. Chunekar, 1972. *Glossary of Vegetable Drugs in Brhttrayi* , Varanasi. 197.

Vaidya, Bapalal. 1982. *Some Controversial Drugs in Indian Medicine.* Varanasi. 128.

Votcek, E. M. and J. A. Kastner. 1907. A new rhamnoside from *Ipomoea turpethum.* Z. Zuckerind Bohmen, 31, 307; *Chem. Abstr.* 1907,1: 1332. (On glycosides.)

25

Date Palm

Phoenix dactylifera

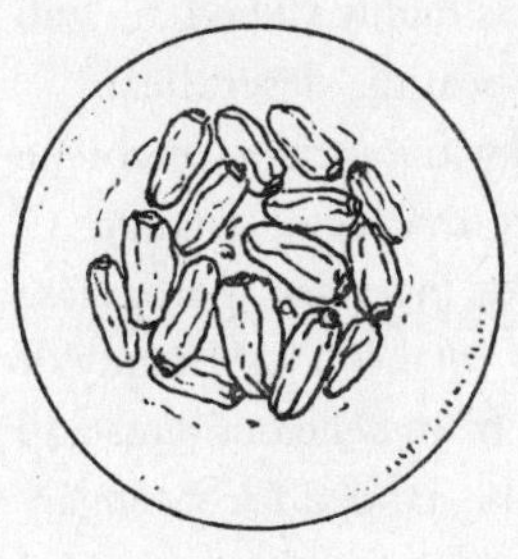

A home without dates is devoid of food.
—Prophet Muhammad (s.a.w.s.)

The Bread of the Sahara

The date palm has an age-old association with the oldest human civilization of the world: the Mesopotamian. Excavated from the Egyptian pyramids, dates are intimately related to the history of a geographical area spreading from North Africa to South Asia, including Greece, Palestine and Rome.

Iraq is the main centre of date production in the world. Date palms are quite common in Pakistan ever since the early Muhammadan invasions. There is, however, considerable scope for commercial cultivation of dates in India.

Travellers in the deserts of the Sahara are reported to put butter inside the date after removing the seed and eat it in the same way that their western counterparts would eat a bread sandwich. No wonder, the fruit is called the 'Bread of the Sahara'.

Like bananas or coconut trees, date palms find a variety of uses: the leaves for thatching and making baskets, fans, mats and ropes; the left-over leaves and fruit stalks as organic manure; branches of fruit stalks as broom-sticks; the petioles for making durable walking sticks, fishing boats etc. While the wood of the palm is durable, it is soft inside and is used for house construction. The palm yields a gum which is specific for diarrhoea. On distillation, the fresh spathes yield Tara water which is highly valued in Arab countries for making cooling sherbets to beat the desert heat.

The edible matter of the palm is loaded with nutrients: carotene as vitamin A, thiamine, riboflavin, nicotinic acid, vitamin C, tannin, pectin, sorbitol, galacturonic acid, invertase, peroxidase etc. Dates are also rich in sugars (85% of total solids). Brandy of good quality is prepared from dates apart from delicious jams and preserves. In North Africa, the date palm is tapped for its sugary sap, which is used for preparing jaggery, sugar and the fermented liquor (toddy).

Date seeds (or 'stones'), when ground or softened by soaking in water are used as camel feed. They are also used as raw material for the manufacture of oxalic acid. In addition, the seeds contain sterols and fatty acids such as caprylic, linolic, myristic, oleic, palmitic, stearic etc.

Dates are demulcent, expectorant and laxative. They are used in respiratory diseases and fevers. In Yemen, they are used as a cure for memory disturbances.

In Nigeria, dates are added to beer together with chillies to make it less intoxicating. In India, date seeds are roasted and added to coffee seeds to make coffee less caffeinated and also to bring down its cost.

The Profile

Botanical Name	:	*Phoenix dactylifera* Linn.
English Name	:	Date palm
Indian Names	:	Bengali, Gujarati, Hindi,
		Marathi : *Khajuri*
		Kannada : *Khajura*
		Malayalam : *Ittapazham, Tenitta*
		Oriya : *Khorjjuri*
		Sanskrit : *Duraroha, Pindakhajur, Pindaphala, Skandhaphala, Svaadvi*
		Tamil : *Karchura, Pericham*
		Telugu : *Ita, Kharjuramu*
Family	:	Palmaceae
Appearance	:	A tall palm tree with pinnate leaves in an open crown. Flowers, small, in branched spadices. Fruit, an oblong berry, reddish when ripe. Seed, hard, cylindrical with a longitudinal furrow.
Distribution	:	Found in arid and irrigated regions of North West India.
Medicinal Parts	:	Fruits, seeds.
Ayurvedic Preparations	:	*Drakshadi churna, Siva ghutika (Laghu).*

In Tradition

- Constipation, indigestion : Take 4 dates at bedtime and drink a glass of warm water every day. (*Note*: This is believed to prevent all stomach-related ailments such as amoebiasis, loose motions etc.)
- Cough, throat disorder Make a paste by grinding equal parts of dates, raisins, black pepper, vibhitaki, long pepper. Take 1 tsp of this paste and mix in 1 tsp honey. Take 2 or 3 times a day.
- General weakness : Add 4 dates to a glass of hot milk. Add a pinch of saffron, cardamom powder and 1

		tsp honey. Drink daily at bedtime.
❧ Sexual debility	:	Mix 4 dates and 1 tbsp palm sugar in a cup of goat's milk and drink every day.
❧ Sty	:	Rub the stone of a date on a rough surface with water and apply the paste obtained over the eyelid. (*Note:* Avoid infection.)

Note: Individual results may vary.

In Science

Abdul Wahab, A. S. and Z. Al Obeidy. 1973. *Z. Bull. Coll. Sci. Univ. Baghdad.* 14:239. (Presence of chlorogenic and isochlorogenic acids in dates.)

Al Shakir, S. H. et al. 1968. *Bull. Ga. Acad. Sci.* 26(4): 176. (Presence of amino acids, glucose and fructose in the fruits.)

Al-Wahibi, M. H. et al. 1985. *J. Coll. Sci. King Saud. Univ.* 16(1):23. (Presence of soluble sugars in seeds.)

Al-Wahibi, M. H. and M. O. Basalh. 1986. *J. Coll. Sci. King Saud. Univ.*17(1):27. (Various fatty acids in the seeds.)

Amin, A. 1980. *Nahrung*, 24(8): 705 (Occurrence of organic acids such as citric, glutaric, lactic, malonic, succinic, tartaric etc.)

Amin, E. S. et al. 1969. *Phytochemistry*. 8:295. (Chemistry of pollen.)

Amin, E. S. and K. M. Kandeel. 1972. *Carbohyd. Res.* 25(1):261. (Arabinose, galactose, rhamnose, uronic acid and xylose from hemicellulose.)

Ashmawi, H. et al. 1955. *Bull. Fac. Sci.* Cairo Univ. 61:12. (The plant chemistry.)

Central Council for Research in Ayurveda and Siddha. 1990.

Phytochemical Investigations of Certain Medicinal Plants used in Ayurveda, New Delhi. 172-175 (Glucose, fructose and free amino acids viz., alanin, aspartic acid and glycine found in the fruits.)

Council for Scientific and Industrial Research. 1969. *The Wealth of India.* Raw Materials. New Delhi. VIII: 18. (Cholesterol and estrone identified in the pollen.)

El-Shurafa, M. Y. 1978. *Libyan J. Agric.* 7:89. (Reducing and non-reducing sugars, starch, alcohol and insoluble solids in the fruits.)

Fernandez, M. I. et al. 1983. *Phytochemistry.* 22:2087. (Chemical analysis of the stems.)

Hasegawa, S. et al 1969. *J. Food Sci.* 34(6): 527. (Presence of polygalacturonase.)

Haq, O. N. and J. Gomes. 1977. *Bangladesh J. Sci. Industr. Res.* 12 (1-2): 76. (Presence of xylan.)

Hussein, F. and A. A. Elzeid. 1975. *Egypt J. Hortic.* 2(2):209. (Amino acids in the palm.)

Ismail, A. A. et al. 1978. *Egypt J. Hortic.* 5(2):83. (Presence of cholesterol.)

Jaddoou, H. and M. Al-Hakim. 1980. *J. Agric. Food Chem.* 28(6):1208. (Presence of sorbitol and sorbose.)

Jindal, V. K. and S. Mukherjee. 1970. *Indian J. Chem.* 8:417. (A polysaccharide in the seeds.)

Kikuchi, N. and T. Miki. 1974. *Nippon Nogei Kagaku Kaishi.* 48(2):137. (Fatty acids of the date palm.)

Kikuchi, N. and T. Miki. 1978. *Mikrochim. Acta.* 1(1-2):89. (Presence of cholesterol, stigmasterol, campesterol etc. in the leaves.)

Kikuchi, N. and T. Miki. 1981. *Mikrochim. Acta.* 1(3-4): 249. (Chemistry of the fruit aroma.)

Koro, S. et al. 1969. *Nippon Nogei Kagaku Kaishi.* 43(7): 457. (Sugars in the dates.)

Lust, J. B. 1974. *The Herb Book*, Bantam Books.

Koro, S. and W. Tanimura. 1976. *Nippon Nogei Kagaku Kaishi.* 50(11): 539. (Presence of a water-soluble polysaccharide.)

Luz Cordonna, M. et al. 1985. *An. Quim. Ser. C.*81(3): 208 (Chemistry of the stems.)

Mahran, G. H. et al. 1976. *Planta Med.* 29:171. (The pollen chemistry.)

Maier, V. P and F. H. Schiller. 1959. Date Growers Instt. Coachella Valley, Calif. *Rept.* 36: 8. (Mesoinositol found in green dates.)

Nezam El-Din, A. M. M. et al. 1983. *Date Palm J.* 2(2):211. (Tannins of the dates.)

Rajendran, S. and M. Muthu. 1981. *Bull. Environ. Contam. Toxicol.*27(3): 426. (Chemical composition.)

Salem, S. A. and S. M. Hegazi. 1971. *J. Sci. Food Agric.* 22 (12): 632. (Sugars in dates.)

Takahashi, D. M. 1977. *Edro Sarap. Res.Tech. Rep.* 2:199. (Chemistry of the date palm.)

Uddin, M. and M. A. Khalil. 1976. *Pak. J. Sci. Industr. Res.* 19(5-6):211. (Celluloses as cell wall polysaccharides.)

Van Rompuy, L.L.L. and J. A. D. Zeevaart. 1979. *Phytochemistry.*

18:863. (Seeds showed the presence of estrogens.)

Williams, C. A. et al. 1971. *Phytochemistry*. 10:1059. (Chemical constituents of the leaves.)

Yousif, A. K. et al. 1982. *Date Palm J*. 1(2):285. (Folic acid and biotin from the dates.)

26

Betel Leaf

Piper Betle

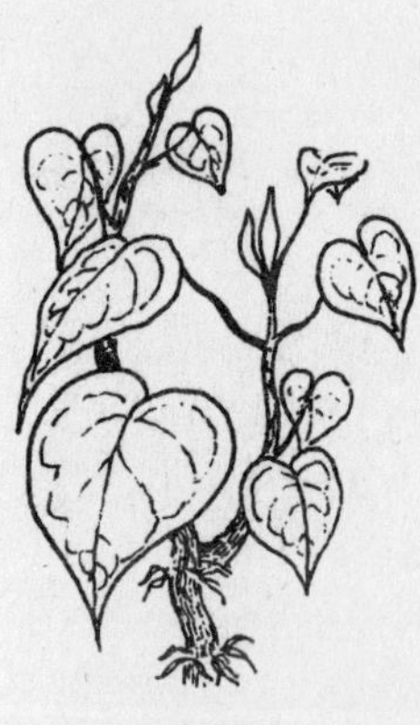

The betel leaf drives away throat irritation, stomach ache . . .
—From a Tamil song by Agathiar

Chewing Etiquette

The betel leaf is heavily linked to Indian traditions. It is considered highly auspicious and hence often exchanged in social and religious ceremonies.

The plant is a climber and the snake-like look of the stem has given rise to many a Sanskrit name such as *Nagavalli, Nagavallari, Nagini* etc. *Kamajanani*, yet another name in Sanskrit, recalls its role in marital bliss, which has given rise to the ancient social custom of its being forbidden to children, celibates, widows and ascetics.

The betel leaf combines well with a pinch of slaked lime and a few pieces of areca nut. A true connoisseur from South India would consume more nuts in the morning. While he prefers more lime during the day, he would consume more leaves at night. The reason given for this 'chewing etiquette' seems to have some sense behind it. It is believed that by the addition of more nuts in the morning, bowel movements are taken care of; and the emphasis on slaked lime during the day enhances the appetite and that leaves eaten at night prevent halitosis.

The connoisseur never eats the nuts first; he prefers the leaves instead. After carefully removing the stalk, the tip and the central vein of the leaf blade (in that order) he would first chew the plain leaves thoroughly. Then he would introduce areca nut and repeat the process. At last, using his right index finger tip, he will carry a pinch of slaked lime to the tip of his tongue to culminate the process.

There is yet another method of chewing a digestive paan after a heavy meal. Add to the leaves the required quantity of areca nut and slaked lime and also add 1 cardamom, 1 clove, 2 cubeb peppers, and a pinch of camphor. Fold and pop into the mouth.

As with several traditional practices, although originating in an empirically sound manner for the welfare of individuals and society, betel chewing has degenerated with the arrival of tobacco on the scene.

Tobacco has polluted the chew, the chewer and his surroundings and spoiled an otherwise laudable tradition.

Betel chewing is a unique ayurvedic concept, as the full potential of the leaf is made available for the health and nutrition of the chewer.

The betel leaf is known for its acrid, antiseptic, aphrodisiac, aromatic, astringent, bitter, carminative, hot and stimulant properties. In combination with lime, areca nut and one's own saliva, the emerging concoction helps in the clearance of the throat, improving the digestion, and expelling worms and other parasites that harbour in the digestive tract.

A chemical analysis of betel leaves reveals the presence of several 'goodies': vitamin A, thiamine, riboflavin, nicotinic acid, vitamin C, glucose, fructose, maltose, sucrose, malic acid, oxalic acid, amino acids, minerals, tannins, diastase and a light yellow-coloured essential oil. Chavicol, a phenolic constituent found in the essential oil is reported to have shown antibacterial activity. Arakene, the alkaloidal constituent in the leaves, which is akin to cocaine, may be the cause of their stimulant effect.

The Profile

Botanical Names	:	*Piper betle* Linn.		
English Name	:	Betel leaf.		
Indian Names	:	Gujarati	:	*Vida*
		Hindi	:	*Paan*
		Kannada	:	*Villithele*
		Malayalam	:	*Vetrilla*
		Sanskrit	:	*Nagavallari, Nagavalli, Nagini, Saptashira, Tambuli*
	:	Telugu	:	*Akku*
Family	:	Piperaceae		
Appearance	:	A root climber with simple long-stalked leaves.		
Distribution	:	Extensively cultivated in hotter and damper parts of India.		
Medicinal Parts	:	Chiefly leaves and occasionally fruits, root and stem; essential oil of leaves.		
Ayurvedic Preparations	:	*Akarakarbhadi gulika, Aranyatulasiyadi tailam, Tambula leha, Tambulasava.*		

In Tradition

Arthritis, orchitis and other types of local inflammation	:	Smear a little castor oil and warm the leaves. Apply on the affected parts.

Boils	:	Warm the leaf, apply a little castor oil and wrap.
Burns	:	Bandage with betel leaf.
Cold, cough	:	Mix 1 tsp each of the juices of betel leaf, fresh ginger and tulsi (10-15 leaves) in 1 tsp honey and take.
Cough, bronchitis, difficulty in breathing in the case of children	:	Smear a little mustard oil on leaves and warm them. Apply over the chest when bearably hot.
Cough, dyspnoea, deranged phlegm, indigestion	:	Take ½ to 2 tsp leaf juice.
Filariasis	:	Grind 5 to 6 leaves into a fine paste. Mix in 1 glass hot water and take.
Headache	:	Put 2 or 3 drops of leaf juice into the nostrils and take rest.
Insect bite, bee sting, rat bite, spider bite	:	Fold in 2-3 peppercorns with 1 tsp honey in a betel leaf and chew.
Nervous weakness	:	Mix 2 tsp betel leaf juice in 1 tsp honey and take.
Scorpion sting	:	Keep 8 to 10 peppercorns in a large betel leaf, fold and eat.
Stomach ache in children	:	Smear a little castor oil on betel leaf, warm it over a flame and keep it on the navel.
Stomach ache	:	Fold ½ tsp ajwain into a betel leaf and take.
Swelling in breasts of nursing mothers	:	Warm a betel leaf over a flame and tie it onto the affected spot.
Vata-aggravation	:	Chew a betel leaf every day.
Urine retention	:	Add 2 tsp fresh juice from leaves into ½ cup milk diluted with water and sweetened with a little sugar. Drink.
Wounds	:	Wash the wounds with leaf juice and wrap with a single leaf and bandage.

Note: Individual results may vary.

A Word of Caution

Gums, tooth enamel and the general health of the teeth are affected by the abuse of betel leaves.

Frequent chewing of the leaves can cause a taste deficiency, thickening of the tongue and even tumours.

Traditionally, the stalk of the leaf is never chewed as it is believed to cause indigestion, bad memory and dullness of the intellect.

Those who suffer from eye diseases, hypertension and tuberculosis are advised to avoid chewing betel leaf.

Adding tobacco to betel leaf may prove fatal.

In Science

Aiyer, K. N. and M. Kolammal. 1966. *Pharmacognosy of Ayurvedic Drugs* Trivandrum. 9:77.

Ali, S. M. and R. K. Mehta. 1970. Preliminary pharmacological studies of the essential oil of *Piper betle* Linn. *Indian J. Pharm.* 32(5): 132-135. (Essential oil produced anthelmintic effect on earthworms.)

Arcilla, L. et al. 1986. In-vitro sensitivity testing of Mycobacterium tuberculosis using bawang, duhat, granada, latundan, acacia and betel. *B. S. P. H.* Public Health Thesis, Univ. of the Philippines, Manila. 49. (Extract of garlic, leaves of Java plum, seeds of pomegranates, red banana peelings, acacia and betel tested. Of these, pomegranate seeds showed significant inhibitory effects.)

Baby, P. et al. 1993. *Leaf oil of Piper betle* L. The in-vitro anti-microbial studies.

Bakhru, H. K. 1995. *Herbs that Heal.* Orient Paperbacks, 5th printing. 40-43.

Bhatnagar, S. S. et al. 1961. Biological activity of Indian Medicinal

Plants. Antibacterial, anti-tubercular, antifungal action. *Indian J. Med. Res.* 49(5): 779-813. (Battle of betel against a platoon of bacteria and pathogens: *B. subtilis, D. pneumonae, E. coli, M. pyogenes var. aureus, Sh. Dysenteriae, Strep. pyogenes, S. typhosa and Vib. coma.*)

Central Council for Research in Ayurveda and Siddha. 1990. *Phytochemical Investigations of Certain Medicinal Plants used in Ayurveda.* New Delhi. 110-111. (Beta-sitosterol and 3 hydrocarbons isolated from the leaves.)

Central Council for Research in Ayurveda and Siddha. 1996. *Pharmacological Investigations of Certain Medicinal Plants and Compound Formulations used in Ayurveda and Siddha.* New Delhi, 335-337.

Bangar, G. P. et al. 1966. Anti-microbial activity of leaves and oil of *Piper betle. Indian J. Pharm.* 28(12): 327-328.

Bhaduri, B. et al. 1968. Anti-fertility activity of some medicinal plants. *Indian J. Exptl. Biol.* 6:252.

Chopra, R. N. et al. 1956. *Glossary of Indian Medicinal Plants.* New Delhi: CSIR, 194. (Antiseptic, aromatic, carminative, stimulant properties of betel leaf; folk use in the treatment of cough, excessive thirst, night blindness, painful eyes, respiratory catarrh and to prevent child-bearing.)

De, M. S. and S. C. Lahiri. 1971. Studies on leaves of *Piper betle. Bull. Calcutta Trop. Med.* 19(3): 69. (Muscle relaxant effect of petroleum ether extract of leaves in guinea pigs.)

Evans, P. H. et al. 1984. *J. Agric. Food Chem.* 32(6):1254. (Chemistry of the leaves.)

Deshpande, S. M. et al. 1970. Chemical study of *Piper betle* leaves (Letters to editor) *Curr. Sci.* 39:372. (Stearic acid in the leaves.)

Ganguly, P. and M. Choudhury. 1975. *Indian Agric.* 19(1): 199. (Stigmasterol in the leaves.)

Garg, S. C. and R. Jain. 1992. Biological activity of the essential oils of *Piper betle*, *J. Ess. Oil Res.* 4(6): 601-606.

Huang, S. L. and W. H. Chung. 1986. *Chung-Kuo Nung Yeh Hua Hsueh Huichih.* 24(2): 199. (Presence of eugenol, hydroxychavicol, tocopherol and other compounds in the plant.)

Kamboj, V. P. and B. N. Dhawan. 1982. Research on plants for fertility regulation in India. *J. Ethno-Pharmacol.* 6(2): 191-226.

Karnik, C. R. 1990. A clinical trial of a composite herbal drug in the treatment of diabetes. *Aryavaidyan.* 5(1): 36-46.

Khosa, R. L. and S. N. Dixit. 1971. *Indian J. Pharmacy.* 33:118. (Beta-sitosterol in the roots.)

Khosa, R. L. and R. H. Singh. 1972. Betel roots—an anti-fertility agent. *J. Res. Indian Med.* 7(4): 65-66. (Mild anti-fertility effect in rats.)

Lakshmanan, P. and S. Mohan. 1991. Antifungal properties of some plant extracts against collar rot of *Phaseolus aureus. Madras Agri. J.* 76(5): 266-270.

Nadkarni, A. K. 1954. *Indian Materia Medica.,* Bombay. 1961.

Misra, S. B. and S. N. Dixit. 1979. Antifungal activity of leaf extracts of some higher plants. *Acta Bot. Indica* 7:147. (Leaf extract inhibited the growth of the fungus, *Ustilago tristi.*)

Pai, M. N. and R. J. Irani. 1950. Antibacterial principle of the betel leaf. A preliminary report. *Indian Med. Gaz.* 85(7): 302.

Rathore, J. S. and S. K. Misra. 1970. Indication of antimitotic activity of *Piper betle. East.Pharmacist.* 13 (150): 49-50.

Santhanam, G. and S. Nagarajan. 1990. Wound healing activity of *Curcuma longa* and *Piper betle*, *Filoterapia*, 61(5): 458-459.

Sharma, P.V. 1983. *Dravyaguna vijnana*, Varanasi. 210 (In Hindi.) 1970. Anti-fertility effect of betel leaf stalk – A preliminary experimental study. *J. Res. Indian Med.* 4(2): 143-151.

Shilaskar, D.V. and G.C.Parashar. 1985. Studies on effect of

Psoralea *corylefolia* and *Piper betle* on cholinesterase and succinic dehydrogenase enzymes as possible targets of their anthelmintic action. *Indian Vet. J.* 62(7): 557-562. (Anthelmintic activity of betel leaf.)

Shivpurkar, N. M. et al. 1980. Tumorigenic effect of aqueous and polyphenolic fractions of betel nut in Swiss strain mice. *Indian J. Exptl. Biol.* 18(10): 1159-1161. (A study of tumour-inhibitory principles in betel leaf.)

27

Chitraka

Plumbago zeylanica

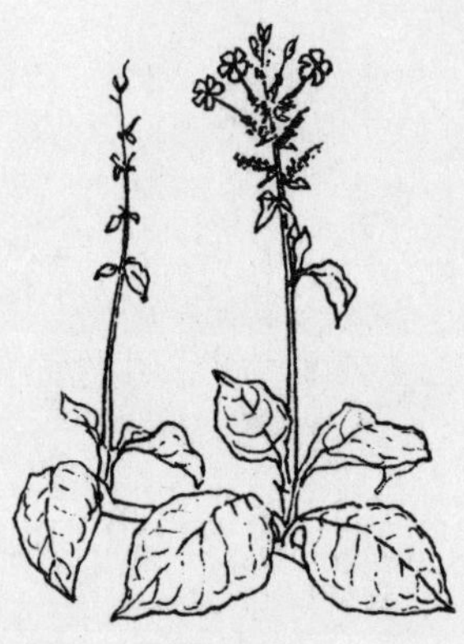

Chitraka is thermogenic . . .
—Abhidhaanmanjari

The Gardener's Delight

Chitraka or leadwort is a gardener's delight. In India, many gardeners cultivate this plant for its bright flowers borne in long spikes. They merge beautifully with the bright green leaves and striated semi-woody stems of the plant.

There are two species: the rosy flowered leadwort, *Plumbago indica* and the white flowered leadwort, *Plumbago zeylanica*. The roots of both these plants are medicinal. They are used in dyspepsia, bronchitis, cough, colic, elephantiasis, fevers, haemorrhoids, helminthiasis, inflammation, leucoderma, leprosy, rheumatism, ringworm, scabies etc.

The root is a well known abortifacient. It is also used as an appetizer. It is used as a caustic, diuretic, and expectorant. The tincture of the root bark is a powerful anti-periodic and sudorific.

The Profile

Botanical Name	:	*Plumbago zeylanica* Linn.
English Names	:	Ceylon leadwort, White-flowered leadwort.
Indian Names	:	Bengali : *Chitra, Chitrak*
		Gujarati : *Chitaro, Chitrak*
		Hindi : *Chita, Chitra, Chitrak*
		Malayalam : *Vella koduveli, Tumba koduvedi*
		Marathi : *Chitraka, Chitramula*
		Punjabi : *Chitrak*
		Sanskrit : *Chiraka*
		Tamil : *Chitramulam, Sitragam, Sitramular*
		Telugu : *Chitramulam,*
Chitramulamu		
Family	:	Plumbaginaceae
Appearance	:	A pretty shrub with semi-woody striate stems and flexible branches. Leaves simple, alternate. Leaf-stalk, reddish. Flowers, bright red in long, terminal spikes. The stout roots are cylindrical, irregularly bent, light yellowish brown with smooth surface having short transverse, shallow fissures at the regions of the bends. A light yellowish juice exudes from the fresh cut surface.
Distribution	:	Found wild in peninsular India and West Bengal, the plant is cultivated in gardens throughout India.
Medicinal Part	:	Root.
Other Species	:	*Plumbago indica* syn. *P. rosea*

In Tradition

Diarrohea, dyspepsia	:	Take ¼ finely powders root in 1 glass warm water.
Piles, leprotic lesions, skin diseases	:	Dust finely powdered root on the affected parts.
Scabies, ulcers	:	Apply the milky juice.

Note: Individual results may vary.

A Word of Caution

The plant is claimed to lead to permanent sterilization.

In Science

Bhargava, S. K. 1984. Effects of plumbagin on reproductive function of male dogs. *Indian J. Exptl. Biol.* 22:153.

Chopra, R. N. et al. 1956. *Glossary of Indian Medicinal Plants.* New Delhi.

Dhawan, B. N. and P. N. Saxena. 1958. Evaluation of some individual drugs for stimulant effect on the rat uterus: a preliminary report. *Indian J. Med. Res.* 46: 808.

Gopal, R. H. and K. K. Purushothaman. 1988. Effect of a few plant isolates and extracts on bacteria. *Bull. Med. Ethnobot. Res.* 7(1-2): 78-83. (*P. zeylanica* shows inhibitory activity.)

Gupta, M. L. et al. 1971. A study of anti-fertility effects of some indigenous drugs. *J. Res. Indian Med.* 6(2): 112.

Iyengar, M. A. and G. S. Pendse. 1962. *Pharmacognosy of the Root of*

Plumbago zeylanica.

Iyengar, M. A. and G. S. Pendse. 1966. *Plumbago zeylanica* L. (Chitrak) – A gastro-intestinal flora normaliser. *Planta Med.* 14:337. (Plumbagin's distribution inside the plant body; root found to be devoid of alkaloids and saponins.)

Jain, S. K. and C. R. Tarafder. 1970. Medicinal plant lore of the Santals. (A revival of P. O. Bodding's work.) *Econ. Bot.* 24:241.

Karnick, C. R. et al. 1982. Cultivation trials, pharmacognosy and ethno-botanical investigations of *Plumbago zeylanica* L. (Chitraka) of the Indian system of medicine. *Int. J. Crude Drug Res.* 20(4): 193. (A review.)

Krishnaswamy, M. and K. K. Purushothaman. 1980. Plumbagin: A study of its anti-cancer, antibacterial and antifungal properties. *Indian J. Exptl. Biol.* 18:876.

Lal, R. et al. 1983. Anti-fertility and uterine activity of *Plumbago rosea* in rats. *Indian J. Med. Res.* 78:287.

Misra, M. B. et al. 1966. A preliminary pharmacological screening of *Plumbago rosea* Linn. Labdev *J. Sci. and Tech.* 4:55.

Mital, S. P and B. Singh. 1986. Introduction of genetic resources of some important medicinal and aromatic plants in India. *Indian J. Genet.* 46(1): 209-216.

Nadkarni, A. K. 1954. *Indian Materia Medica.* Bombay.

Padhye, S. B. and B. A. Kulkarni. 1973. Studies on the root constituents of *Plumbago zeylanica. J. Univ. Poona* 44: 27. (Presence of plumbagin, as the major constituent and two other pigments.)

Pillai, N. G. K. et al. 1981. Effect of plumbagin in charmakeela (common warts)—a case report. *J. Res. Ayur. Siddha* 2(2): 122.

Prakash, A. O. et al. 1978. Effect of oral administration of forty-two indigenous plant extracts on early and late pregnancy in albino rats. *Probe*, 17: 315.

Prakash, A. O. and R. Mathur. 1976. Screening of Indian plants for anti-fertility activity. *Indian J. Exptl. Biol.* 14: 623.

Prasad, S. et al. 1969. *Pharmacognostical studies on roots of Plumbago zeylanica and Plumbago rosea.* Recent advances in the anatomy of tropical seed plants. Hindustan Publishing Corpn. (India) Delhi. 196. (Distinguishing characteristics.)

Premkumari, P. and G. Santhakumari, 1975. Antifungal and antibacterial activity of plumbagin. VII Ann. Conf. Indian Pharmacol. Soc. Ahmedabad, Dec. 22-29, 1974. *Indian J. Pharmacol.* 7:91.

Roy, A. K. 1960. Toxicological chemistry of *Plumbago rosea* Linn. *J. Instn. Chem. India* 32(Pt.10): 70. (Synthesis of plumbagin and other toxic substances in the roots.)

Saksena, S. K. et al. 1970. Anti-fertility screening of plants. Part V. Effect of six indigenous plants on early pregnancy in albino rats. *Indian J. Med. Res.*58: 253.

Sankaram, A. V. B. and G. S. Sidhu. 1974. Synthesis of 3, 3'-biplumbagin. *Indian J. Chem.* 12:519.

Sharma, A. P. 1972. Pharmacognostic studies on the identity of certain plants and plant parts used as drugs in the Ayurvedic and Unani systems of medicine, found in Saharanpur, Dehra Dun and Tehri-Garhwal districts. Ph.D. Thesis, Agra Univ., Agra.

Sidhu, G. S. and A. V. B. Sankaram. 1971. A new biplumbagin and 3-chloroplumbagin from *Plumbago zeylanica. Tetrahedron Lett.* No. 26: 2385.

Tewari, P.V. et al. 1966. Preliminary studies on uterine activity of some Indian medicinal plants. *J. Res. Indian Med.* 1(1): 68.

Tiwari, K. C. et al. 1982. Folklore information from Assam for family planning and birth control. *Int. J. Crude Drug Res.* 20:133.

Vaidya, B. G. 1972. Some controversial drugs of Indian medicine. V. *J. Res. Indian Med.* 7(2): 45.

Vohora, S. B. et al. 1969. Anti-fertility screening of plants. Part III. Effect of six indigenous plants on early pregnancy in albino rats. *Indian J. Med. Res.* 57:893.

28

Radish

Raphanus sativus

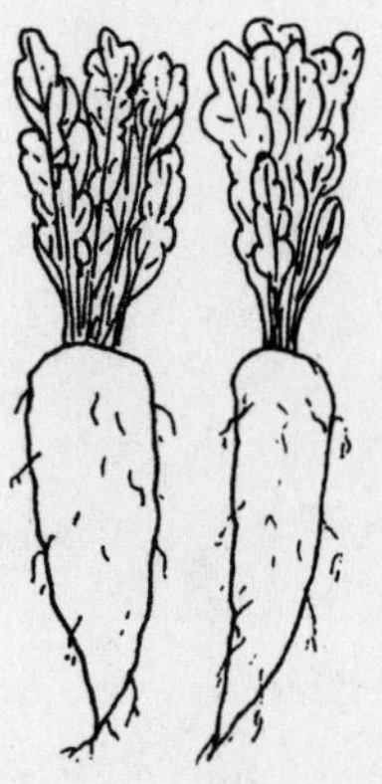

Mulika . . . conquers cephalagia . . .
—Svayamkriti

The Pungent Tuber

The roots, young leaves and fruits of the radish are commonly used in India as a vegetable. Despite their pungency, which is attributed to the presence of iso-thiocyanates, the roots are eaten raw as salads or cooked as vegetables. The leaves are often steamed before consumption.

Fresh leaf juice is considered as a highly nutritious source of vitamins and minerals, which is diuretic and laxative. Some nutrition experts recommend the intake of leaves with cooked rice as it is reported that phytin, a chemical in rice can help in bone calcification.

In Siddha medicine, the roots and seeds of radish occupy a significant place in the treatment of urinary diseases.

The roots, flowers, leaves and seed pods of the radish, are all found to be active against Gram-positive bacteria. The roots have been traditionally used in amenorrhoea, biliary disorders, cephalagia, chronic diarrhoea, colic, cough, dyspepsia, flatulence, gall bladder problems, haemorrhoids, inflammation, insomnia, leprosy, liver problems, nausea, neuralgia, paralysis, piles, skin diseases, splenopathy, strangury, urinary diseases and vitiated conditions of *kapha* etc.

Credited with refreshing carminative, diuretic, expectorant and depurative properties, the roots are a good source of ascorbic acid, minerals and trace elements such as barium, lithium, manganese, silica, titanium, fluorine, iodine and a host of useful enzymes.

In homoeopathy, radish finds its application in the treatment of chronic diarrhoea, neuralgic headache and insomnia.

The Profile

Botanical Name	:	*Raphanus sativus* L.		
English Name	:	Radish		
Indian Names	:	Bengali	:	*Mula, Muli, Mura, Muri*
		Gujarati	:	*Mula, Muli, Mura, Muri*
		Hindi	:	*Mula, Muli, Mura, Muri*
		Marathi	:	*Mula, Muli, Mura, Muri*
		Kannada	:	*Mullangi*
		Malayalam	:	*Mullangi*
		Tamil	:	*Mullangi*
		Telugu	:	*Mullangi*
		Sanskrit	:	*Mulika, Muli*
Family	:	Cruciferae		

Appearance	:	Bristly herb with fleshy tap root of different sizes and shapes. Basal leaves, coarsely toothed, long and pinnate. Cauline leaves, simple. Seeds brownish yellow.
Distribution	:	Throughout India, particularly in Gujarat, Maharashtra, Punjab and Uttar Pradesh.
Medicinal Parts	:	Roots, seeds.

In Tradition

Cough, gall bladder problems, rheumatism	:	Take 1 or 2 tsp fresh juice of radish. (*Note*: Honey can be added for improving the taste. For gall bladder problems, prolonged treatment may be necessary.)
Ear ache	:	Extract some fresh juice of radish, warm it slightly and use it as ear drops.
Jaundice	:	Boil 1 tbsp each of the following in ½ litre water till the volume is reduced to half: radish, Chinese hibiscus, leaves of bhringaraja, and leaves and flowers of neem. Take the decoction in 3 doses a day with 1 tsp powdered palm sugar.
Jaundice, to hasten recovery from	:	Take 1 glass of sugar cane juice with 1 tsp lime juice or radish juice. Piles: Fry equal quantities of radish and white onions in a little castor oil. Grind with equal quantities of palm sugar. Dose: A lemon-size twice daily.
Ringworm	:	Grind 1 tbsp seeds of sickle senna, and 2 tbsp fresh juice of radish into a fine paste and apply.
Kidney stones, urine retention	:	Extract ¼ cup juice from radish and drink as such or with 1 tsp honey every day for 2 to 3 months. (*Note:* On alternate days, the inner white portion of the banana stem can substitute radish. A minimum intake of 10 glasses of clean drinking water every day

can also help.)

- Body heat, intestinal worms, heart or liver problems : Fry a cupful of radish leaves in a little oil and include it in the daily diet for a few days continuously.

A Word of Caution

The intake of the raw juice of radish may be avoided particularly when the stomach and intestines are inflamed.

Chinese herbalists do not recommend any prolonged treatment with radish, as it is believed to cause the consumption of 'qi' (vital energy). It is, therefore, often used, only in combination with other drugs in the treatment of debilitated patients with deficiency of 'qi'.

There is a practice of avoiding the consumption of radish either as a food or medicine at the time of flowering.

In Science

Chunmo, L. 1987. Treatment of mild and moderate cases of Diabetes Mellitus with juice of *Raphanus sativus*. *J. New Chinese Med.* 19(8): 35. (Out of 23 cases of Diabetes Mellitus treated with 100-150 ml of red cortex variety of radish root juice twice daily for 14 to 21 days, 14 were cured, 6 improved with lowering of blood and urine sugar and alleviation of symptoms, and 3 were unaffected.)

Guenther, E. 1952. *The Essential Oils*. New York: D. Van Nostrand Co. VI: 62.

Lust, J. B. 1974. *The Herb Book*. Bantam Books, 365.

Mital, S. P. and Singh. 1986. Introduction of genetic resources of some important medicinal and aromatic plants in India *Indian J.*

Genet. 46(1): 209-216.

Sakoda, M. et al. 1993. Structure-activity relationships of raphanusanins and their analogues. *Phytochemistry* 32.(6): 1371-1373. (A study of plant growth inhibitors.)

Wang, W. 1987. Studies on the hypotensive constituents of seed of *Raphanus sativus. Chinese Tradl. and Herbal Drugs*, 18(3): 101-103. (Sinapine bisulfate isolated from the radish seeds showed 'strong' hypotensive activity.)

Zhang, Z. 1987. Clinical application of the seed of *Raphanus sativus. J. New Tradl. Chinese Med.* 19(5):51.

29

Sugar Cane

Saccharum officinarum

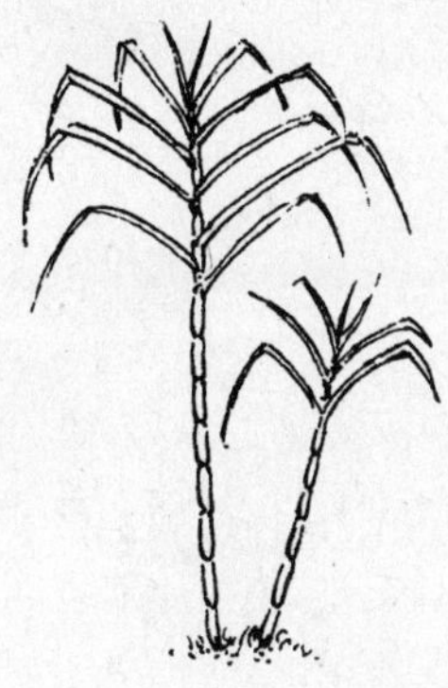

Iksuh . . . a coolant . . .
—Sushruta Samhita
Sutrasthanam

A Sweet Medicine

Sugar cane is a cash crop. Its juice has been a popular ingredient in folk remedies from time immemorial. As a substitute for honey, sugar cane juice has been used as a 'vehicle' to carry many a home medicine for its effective digestion and absorption.

The juice is not only sweet but also possesses medicinal properties as a cardiotonic, diuretic, expectorant, galactagogue, haemostatic, laxative and tonic and also for its value in cooling, emaciation and general debility. Hence it is found useful in treating a host of ailments: anaemia, bronchitis, cardiac disability, cough, erysipelas, fatigue, gastropathy, jaundice, spermatorrhoea, skin ulcers and urinary diseases, etc. It is also believed to be an aphrodisiac.

The root of sugar cane, which is cooling and diuretic is found useful in the treatment of ailments such as uropathy.

The Profile

Botanical Name	:	*Saccharum officinarum* L.
English Names	:	Noble cane, Sugar cane.
Indian Names	:	Hindi : *Ganna, Paunda, Pundiya*
		Kannada : *Iksu, Kabbu*
		Malayalam : *Karimpu*
		Sanskrit : *Iksuh, Pundrakah*
		Tamil : *Karumbu, Pundaram*
		Telugu : *Cheruku*
Family	:	Poaceae
Appearance	:	A thick, tall grass growing upto 6 meters with stems which vary in colour and in thickness. Leaves, lance-like, erect or drooping. Flower-stalk, pyramidal with large silky hairs.
Distribution	:	Cultivated in hotter parts of India.
Medicinal Parts	:	Stem, root.
Ayurvedic Preparations	:	*Amritaprasa ghritam, Balajirkadi kashayam, Balatailam, Dhatryadi ghritam, Kushmanda ghritam*

In Tradition

Anal fissure, ulcer	:	Boil 1 fig and mash it. Mix in 1 glass sugar cane juice and drink twice daily for a few days.

Body heat, *pitta*-aggravation	:	Mix in a glassful of sugar cane juice, juices from ½" ginger and one lemon and drink. (*Note*: This may also help in the prevention of bleeding piles, leucorrhoea and other diseases caused by excessive heat in the body.)
Bleeding, to stop	:	As an emergency measure, sprinkle some sugar crystals on the wound.
Bleeding piles, nausea, lack of taste, ulcers	:	Take a glass of sugar cane juice thrice daily for a few days.
Burning sensation during urination	:	Boil ½ tsp cleaned roots of sugar cane in 1 glass water and drink the decoction.
Burning sensation in the body	:	Mix 2 tbsp yoghurt in 1 glass sugar cane juice. Sprinkle 1 or 2 pinches of fenugreek powder and drink three times a day.
Cough, excessive thirst, stomach ache	:	Mix 1 tsp each of finely ground powders of cardamom, dried amla, dried ginger, liquorice and cubebs with 1 cup sugar. Bottle. Dose: ¼ tsp with 1 glass hot water.
Diarrhoea	:	Powder 5 seeds of tamarind (after completely removing the sticky pulp around them) with ¼ tsp cumin. Add 1 tsp jaggery and ½ cup water, mix thoroughly and take.
Hiccups	:	Chew 2 tsp sugar.
Jaundice, to hasten recovery from	:	Take 1 glass of sugar cane juice with 1 tsp lime juice or radish juice.
Male sterility, spermatorrhoea	:	Boil 1 tsp each flowers of moringa and mishri in 1 glass of water and take every day for a few days. Boil 2 or 3 dates and 1 tsp mishri in 1 glass milk and drink every day for a few days.
To disinfect the surroundings	:	Mix 1 tsp sugar with 2 tbsp Indian frankincense and burn the mixture. (*Note*: The smoke can drive away cockroaches, mosquitoes and other insects.)

- Spermatorrhoea : Boil ¼ tsp seeds of *Tal makhana* in 1 cup water and filter. To the decoction add 1 tsp powdered jaggery or sugar. Drink.

Note: Individual results may vary.

A Word of Caution

Excessive intake of sugar cane juice and its products may result in common cold, catarrh, diabetes etc.

As refined sugar is found to be toxic in the long run, it can be substituted by honey or jaggery.

Diabetics should be careful about using sugar cane juice or its products.

In Science

Bollenback, G. N. 1986. The sweet story of sugar's amazing healing powers. *Nutrition Today*. Jan-Feb. 25-27.

Kurup, P. N.V. et al. 1979. *Handbook of Medicinal Plants*. New Delhi. 82.

Mital, S. P and B. Singh. 1986. Introduction of genetic resources of some important medicinal and aromatic plants in India *Indian J. Genet.* 46(1): 209-216.

Moos, N. S. 1980. Ganas of *vahata*, Kottayam. 114. (Cures anorexia, disorders of *kapha*, dysuria, effect of poisons etc.)

Sharma, P.V. 1983. *Dravyaguna Vijnana* 639. (In Hindi.)

Sivarajan, V. V. and I. Balachandran. 1994. *Ayurvedic Drugs and Their Plant Sources*. Oxford & IBH, 174-175.

Takahashi, M. et al. 1985. Isolation and hypoglycaemic activity of saccharans A.B.C.D.E. and F. glycans of *Saccharum officinarum* stalks. *Planta Med.* 3: 258-260.

30

Agasti

Sesbania grandiflora

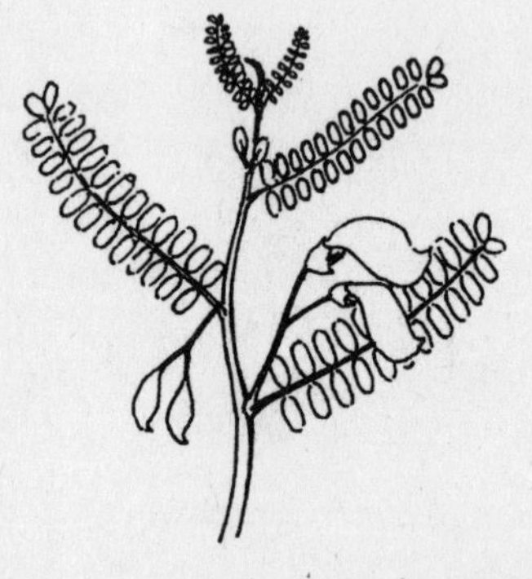

Those who consume agathi avoid the aggravation of pitta.
—From a Tamil Song by Agathiar

The Indian Sage

The flowers, fruits and leaves of agasti, a quick-growing soft-wood tree, are popularly consumed as a vegetable in many parts of India. Named after the legendary sage, Agastya Muni, folk medicine finds them effective in the treatment of catarrh, cough, discolouration of the skin, intermittent fevers, etc.

The leaf, which is acrid, aperient, anthelmintic, bitter, coolant, diuretic, laxative and tonic, is capable of overpowering the aggravating *pitta*. It is reported to be used to cure haematemesis, toxicosis, itching and also diseases caused by the excess of *kapha.*

The flower is acrid, astringent and bitter. It is used to cure catarrh, consumption, cough, fevers and night blindness. The flower juice as well as the root juice are regarded as an ideal expectorant.

The bark of agasti is astringent, febrifuge and tonic. Its infusion is reported beneficial in the treatment of smallpox.

The pods are bitter and laxative. They are believed to enhance memory power. They are also used in the treatment of anaemia, consumption, glandular enlargements etc.

The Profile

Botanical Names	:	*Sesbania grandiflora* (Linn.) Poiret *Agati grandiflora* (Linn.) Desv. *Robinia grandiflora* Linn.
English Names	:	Agasti sesbania, Swamp pea.
Indian Names	:	Bengali : *Bak* Hindi : *Bak, Basna, Agastoya* Sanskrit : *Agasti* Tamil : *Agati, Kariram, Muni*
Family	:	Papilionaceae (Fabaceae)
Appearance	:	A small, short-lived, quick-growing, soft-wood tree with pinnate leaves, about 20 to 25 leaflets in pairs. Flowers, large, showy, clawed, fleshy white, crimson or pink petals. Pods, linear, hanging. Seeds, many, pale-coloured. Flowers throughout the year and fruits in winter.
Distribution	:	Cultivated widely in South India. Also grown in Assam, Gujarat and Bengal.
Medicinal Parts	:	Leaves, flowers, bark, root.

In Tradition

Arthritic swellings, swellings in joints	:	Grind equal quantities of the root bark of agathi and roots of dhatura into a very fine paste. Apply over the affected parts.
Body heat, *pitta*-aggravation due to heat or tobacco	:	Cook 1 tbsp flowers with a little rice or dal and take 2 or 3 times a day.
Burning sensation in the body, esp. in the hands, male sex organ, etc., excessive thirst, venereal diseases	:	Crush a few pieces of the root bark and soak them in drinking water contained in an earthern pot. Use this for drinking purposes.
Dropsy	:	Mix the leaf juice and honey (5:1) thoroughly and apply a little on a finger over the top of the head.
Fever	:	Apply leaf juice all over the body to bring down the temperature.
Mental agitation	:	Massage the leaf juice over the head before a shower.
Nasal catarrh, headache	:	Juice of flowers and leaves used as nasal drops (1 or 2 drops). Mix leaf juice and honey (1:5). Use as nasal drops (1 or 2 drops).
To improve vision	:	Use flower juice as eye-drops. (*Caution*: Avoid infection.)
Wounds and ulcers	:	Apply a paste of the seeds over the affected areas. Steam the leaves and wrap on the wounds. Bandage.

A Word of Caution

The intake of agasti is to be avoided when any other drug or medicine is used. Agasti can neutralize the drug's efficacy.

Excess or frequent consumption of agasti is not recommended, as it may aggravate *vata*. It may in the long run cause toxification of the blood causing itching, psoriasis and skin rashes. It may also upset the stomach.

In Science

Aiyer, K. N. and M. Kolammal. 1964. *Pharmacognosy of Ayurvedic Drugs*. Trivandrum. 8:5.

Fojas, F. R. et al. 1982. Preliminary phytochemical and pharmacological studies of *Sesbania grandiflora* (L.) Pers. *Philippines J. Sci.* 111(3-4): 157-181. (Contains 'plenty of' sterols, saponins, tannins etc; its toxic effect could be attributed to its saponin and histamine-like compound or histamine-releasing content.)

Kalyanagurunathan, P. et al. 1985. In vitro haemolytic effect of the flowers of *Sesbania grandiflora*. *Filotrerapia*. 56(3): 188-189. (Haemolytic effect of the water extract of the flowers.)

Mital, S. P. and B. Singh. 1986. Introduction of genetic resources of some important medicinal and aromatic plants in India. *Indian J. Genet.* 46(1): 209-216.

Natarajan, T. Mooligai Kalanjiam, 1995. Chennai: Poongodi *Pathipagam*. 33-36. (Folk remedies from agati.) (*In Tamil*)

Nesamony, S. 1985. *Oushadhasasyangal*. Trivandrum. 3 (In Malayalam)

Sivarajan, V.V. and I. Balachandran. 1994. Ayurvedic drugs and their *Plant Sources*. Oxford & IBH. 17-18.

Bhattacharya, S. B. et al. 1982. A water-soluble galactomannan from *Sesbania aegyptiaca* seeds. *Phytochemistry*, 22: 161.

31

Eggplant

Solanum melongena

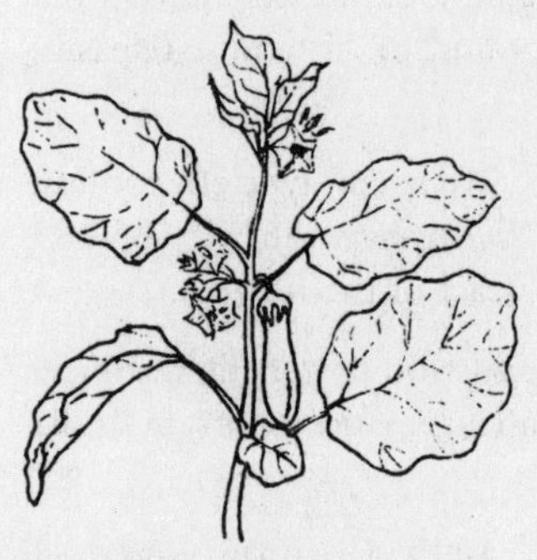

'Kathirikai may induce skin ailments such as itching, psoriasis etc.'
—Fom a Tamil verse

The Dieter's Delight

'Pathiyakari'—A Tamil name for the eggplant denoting its usage in a restrictive diet.

The unripe fruit of the eggplant is used commonly as a vegetable all over the tropics. As the fruit is quite low in calories, it is regarded as an ideal food for weïght watchers. It is reported to impart heat to the body, balancing *pitta* and *kapha* aggravations and to impart strength to the body. Some believe it to be an aphrodisiac, particularly when it is cooked and consumed with drumsticks, potatoes, onions etc.

In Nigeria, the eggplant is highly regarded as an anti-convulsant and an anti-rheumatic agent. In the folk medicines of Korea, the whole dried plant along with the fruits is consumed to treat alcoholism, lumbago, measles, pain and stomach cancer. It is also applied externally to cure burns and rheumatism.

Some western nutritionists have glorified the combination of eggplant with cheese, as the former is found to neutralize the blood cholesterol induced by the latter. A series of tests on animals conducted at the University of Graz have confirmed this finding. Even in small doses, the eggplant has been found to reduce dramatically the development of fatty plaques and atherosclerosis.

Some Japanese scientists report that the eggplant suppresses damage to animal cells (chromosomal aberrations) foreshadowing cancer. It is interesting to note that the eggplant contains protease (trypsin) inhibitors, compounds believed to help resist cancer-causing agents as well as certain viruses.

In yet another study, the eggplant surfaces as a vegetable most consumed by those with a low rate of stomach cancer.

The roots of this plant are used in the preparation of certain oils used for the massage of the head before bathing.

While the unripe fruit is reported to induce appetite and enrich the blood-content, besides functioning as a cardio-tonic, the ripe fruit is not consumed as it is laxative and can cause biliousness.

The ayurvedic drug *brihati* is derived from two varieties of *Solanum melongena*, the wild and the cultivated.

The Profile

Botanical Name	:	*Solanum melongena* Lab.		
English Names	:	Aubergine, Brinjal, Eggplant		
Indian Names	:	Hindi	:	*Baingan*
		Malayalam	:	*Valutina, Cheruvalutina, Veluttachunda,Karuttachunda*

Tamil	:	*Kathirikai*
Ayurvedic Name	:	*Brihati*
Family	:	Solanaceae
Appearance	:	A plant cultivated for its edible fruits: violet, pink or white.
Another variety	:	*Solanum melongena* var. *insanum* (L.) Prain.
Medicinal Parts	:	Fruits, leaves, root.
Ayurvedic Preparations	:	*Brihatyadikashayam, Dasamul rishtam, Indukantaghritam.*

In Tradition

Dysuria	:	Boil 1 or 2 leaves in 1 cup water, till the volume is reduced to half. Drink the concentrate.
Flatulence, stomach ache	:	Roast a brinjal in the fire. Add ¼ tsp asafoetida powder and take.
Freckles	:	Place fresh eggplant slice on the freckles for 10 to 15 minutes three times a day.
Swelling, whitlow	:	Roast an eggplant in the fire, cool and apply the pulp. Tie a bandage if necessary.
Syphilic sores	:	Apply a fine paste of the leaves on the affected parts. Boil 2–3 pinches of the root powder in 1 cup water and drink the decoction.

A Word of Caution

Those who suffer from skin ailments, ulcers etc., are advised not to include the eggplant in their diet, as certain chemicals contained therein are believed to aggravate these diseases. The ripe fruits may cause biliousness and loose motions.

In Science

Aiyer, K. N. and M. Kolammal. 1960. 1960-66. *Pharmacognosy of Ayurvedic Drugs*. Trivandrum, 4:81. (Cures dyspepsia, cardiac and respiratory disorders, fever, vomiting, ulcers etc.)

Bezbaruah, H. P. and B. Bezbaruah. 1963. Chromosome survey of some species of *Solanum* of medicinal value. *J. Proc. Indian Acad. Sci.*

Carper, J. 1988. *The Food Pharmacy*. London: Simon & Schuster, 186-187.

Chakravarty, A. K. et al. 1980. Studies on Indian Medicinal Plants. Part 57. Constitution of some *Solanum* species. Mass spectra of nuatigenin and isonuatigenin. *Indian J. Chem.* 19B: 468.

Chandra, V. 1967-68. Production of *Solanum* spp. for steroidal hormones, *Indian Drugs*, 5:57-67.

Deb, D. B. 1989. *Solanum melongena, S. incanum* versus *S. insanum* (Solanaceae). *Taxon.* 38:138-139. (Morphological variability of eggplants.)

Ibuki, F. et al. 1977. An improved method for the purification of Eggplant Trypsin Inhibitor. *J. Nutri. Sci. and Vitaminology.* 23(2): 133-143.

Mahato, S. B. 1975. An assay method for estimation of solasodine from *Solanum* spp. *J. Instn. Chem. India.* 47:237.

Mital, S. P. and B. Singh. 1986. Introduction of genetic resources of some important medicinal and aromatic plants in India, *Indian J. Genet.* 46(1): 209-216.

Mitschek, G. H. 1975. Effect of *Solanum melongena* on experimental atheromatosis. VI. Enzyme histochemical , physiopathological and chemical studies on cholesterol-induced atheromatosis in rabbits. Conclusions. (Author's translation) *Experimentelle Pathelogie.* 10 (3-4): 167-179.

Moos, N. S. 1980. *Ganas* of *Vahata.* Kottayam, 13. (On white and black fruits of eggplants.)

Sivarajan, V. V. and I. Balachandran. 1994. *Ayurvedic Drugs and their Plant Sources*, New Delhi: Oxford & IBH, 100-101.

Sastry, K. S. et al. 1974. A mosaic disease of eggplant, *Phytopathol. Mediterr.* 13: 176-178.

Vishwapaul, et al. 1958. Indian *Solanum* spp. as possible starting material for the synthesis of cortisone and steroid sex hormones. *Indian J. Pharm.* 20: 247.

32

Black Nightshade

Solanum nigrum

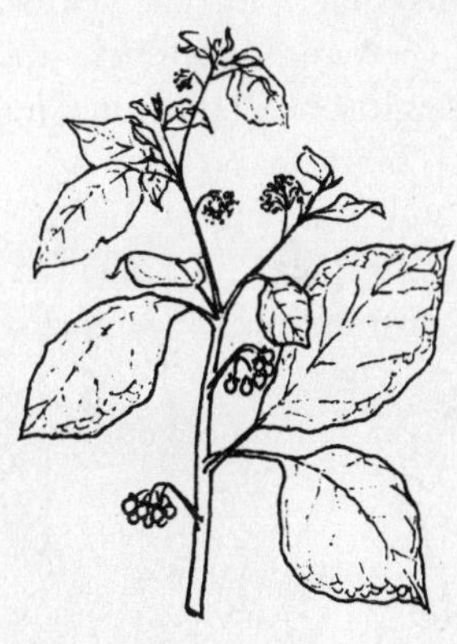

Kakamachi, the destroyer of leprosy ...
—Gunapatham

The 'Mini' Tomatoes

The fruits of the black nightshade are virtually miniature tomatoes. The dried fruits are used in the preparation of *Vattal Kuzhambu*, a hot, spicy sauce from the South, eaten with cooked rice and papad on cold nights.

The green leaves and tender shoots of the plant are also steamed and eaten like spinach.

The whole plant finds its use in native medicine, thanks to its antiseptic and anti-inflammatory properties. It is used as a mild laxative, in the preparation of rejuvenating tonics, employed in the treatment of a host of ailments: asthma, blood pressure, bronchitis, cough, dyspepsia, fevers, flatulence, general debility, haemorrhoids, heart ailments, leprosy, nausea, rheumatalgia, skin diseases, swellings, ulcer, vitiated conditions of the three *doshas*, wounds etc. It is reported that while in Rhodesia the plant is used to cure diarrhoea and cholera, it is used in the treatment of anthrax in the southern parts of Africa.

The leaves are used in poultices applied on rheumatic and gouty joints. Internal consumption of the cooked leaves is a folk remedy for dropsy. They are also found useful in the treatments of skin afflictions, particularly during the initial stages of leucoderma. Scientific experiments conducted recently confirm the antibacterial properties of the leaves: an alcoholic extract inhibits the growth of the bacteria, *E. coli* and *S. aureus*.

A decoction made of the flowers and fruits finds a place in common household remedies: in the treatment of bronchitis, cough, diarrhoea, erysipelas, fevers, hydrophobia, pulmonary tuberculosis etc.

The root bark is reported to be useful in fighting hepatitis.

The Profile

Botanical Names	:	*Solanum nigrum* Linn. *Solanum rubrum* Mill.		
English Name	:	Black nightshade		
Indian Names	:	Assamese	:	*Pichkati*
		Bengali	:	*Gurkamai, Kakmachi, Tulidan*
		Gujarati	:	*Piludi*
		Hindi	:	*Ghamai, Gurkamai, Makoi*
		Kannada	:	*Ganikesoppu, Kabigida, Kakarundi*
		Malayalam	:	*Karimtakkali, Manatakkali*
		Marathi	:	*Ghati, Kamuni, Mako*
		Punjabi	:	*Kachmach, Mako, Pilak*

	Sanskrit :	*Kakamachi*
	Tamil :	*Chukkutikirai, Manathakkali, Manithakkali. Milaguthakkali*
	Telugu :	*Kachi, Kamanchi, Kachipandu, Gojuchettu*
Family	:	Solanaceae
Appearance	:	A small and erect herb growing densely with leaves which are lobed or teethed. Flowers, 3-8 in a bunch, small, violet in colour. Fruits, pepper-sized, purplish black or red in colour, sweet when ripe. Seeds, many, disc-like, yellow.
Distribution	:	Growing wild in the drier parts of India.
Medicinal Parts	:	Whole plant, leaves, fruits.

In Tradition

Abdominal pain in children	:	Soak a handful of cleaned whole plant in 1 litre water for 2 hrs. Filter and use the infusion as an enema.
Anthrax pustules	:	Crush the whole plant into a fine paste and apply all over the affected areas.
Arthritic pain, rheumatic swelling	:	Extract 1 cup juice from fresh black nightshade leaves. Add equal amount of gingelly oil, 2 tbsp mustard oil and a crushed whole garlic. Boil the mixture thoroughly till no trace of moisture remains. Cool and bottle. Apply this oil after warming frequently on the affected parts and foment the area with a salt-bag i.e. a small piece of cloth in which 2 tbsp common salt is tied tightly.
Burns, swelling	:	Grind equal quantities of black nightshade leaves with betel leaves and turmeric into a very fine paste and apply.
Depigmentation of the skin	:	Rub the finely ground leaf paste on the affected areas frequently.
Dropsy	:	Fry the dried berries (1 tbsp) in ghee and

		take with rice or chapati or bread everyday.
❧ Fevers, dysentery and other stomach ailments	:	Soak a clean plant in 1 litre water and drink the infusion frequently.
❧ Gonorrhoea, swelling due to excessive heat in the body, urinary infection	:	Take 1 tbsp leaf juice with 1 cup warm water 2 to 3 times daily for a few days.
❧ Gum inflammation	:	Clean some leaves thoroughly in water. Chew them frequently.
❧ Gum inflammation, ulceration of the tongue	:	Cook ½ cup each of green gram (*Phaseolus radiatus*) and black nightshade leaves. Take every day with food.
❧ Halitosis, mouth ulcers	:	Soak a handful of dried berries in 1 litre water overnight. Use the infusion to gargle frequently. Chew 1 or 2 leaves of black nightshade for 10 minutes and wash the mouth with warm water. Repeat frequently.
❧ Cough, halitosis	:	Fry a handful of berries with 4 pearls of garlic, 4 cardamoms and 1 tbsp fenugreek seeds till golden brown. Now add 1 litre water and boil it till the volume is reduced to 250 ml. Gargle when bearably hot.
❧ Heart ailments	:	Boil a handful of shoots and leaves and eat in the same way as spinach.
❧ Jaundice, hepatitis	:	Soak a handful of dried berries with 1 tbsp each crushed cumin and coriander seeds in 1 litre water overnight. Dosage: 1 cup taken with 1 tbsp palm sugar two or three times a day for a few days.
❧ Indigestion, mouth ulcers	:	Fry 2 tbsp dried berries in ghee and take with meals every day for a few days.
❧ Mouth ulcers, stomatitis, ulcer on the tongue	:	Steam ½ cup leaves and add equal quantities of fresh shredded coconut. Take with meals every day for a few days. Steam ½ cup leaves with equal quantities of green gram and eat with chapati or rice for a few days.

Ringworm	:	Crush the green fruits into a paste and apply over the affected areas.
Skin eruptions	:	Extract the juice of the plant and apply over the skin.
Ulcers in the duodenum/stomach	:	Grind a mango kernel with ½ cup each of tulsi leaves and black nightshade leaves into a fine paste. Roll them into pea-sized tablets and dry in the sun. Dosage: 2 pills, twice daily with 1 cup warm water for 40 days.
Burning sensation during urination, painful and scanty urination, urinary diseases	:	Boil a handful each of the plants of black nightshade, gokhru, tal makhana, lauki and amaltas, and 1 tbsp each of amla, haritaki, vibhitaki, fennel, and cucumber seeds in 1 litre water till the volume is reduced to one-third. Dosage: 2-3 tbsp twice daily with warm water for a few days.
Whitlow	:	Apply the leaf juice.
Wounds with pus-formation	:	Grind the leaves and tie the paste on the affected parts with a cloth bandage.

Note: Individual results may vary.

A Word of Caution

In heavy doses, leaves can cause nausea, purging and nervous disturbances.

It is reported that small doses of the drug increase and large doses decrease cardiac activities. Heart patients are advised to consult a practitioner and not to indulge in any self-medication.

The plant is narcotic and sedative; its infusions and decoctions, after transient stimulation, start depressing the central nervous system and the reflexes of the spinal cord.

According to Brenen, the green and unripe berries contain a toxic substance, Solanine. The glycoalkaloids are toxic. Ripe fruits, however, contain very little alkaloids and hence in limited quantities they can be consumed without much side effect; prolonged consumption of this drug, however, is not recommended.

In Science

Afaq, S. H. et al. 1985. Predicting solasodine content in fruits of makoi (*Solanum nigrum*) by leaf nitrogen estimation. *J. Res. Indian Med.* (Jan-Jun) 13-15.

Agarwal, N. and Y. K. Bansal 1987. In vitro regeneration in *Solanum nigrum*. *Curr. Sci.* 56(17): 892-894.

Agarwal, S. S. and R. Gulati. 1996. Hepato-protective studies of *Solanum nigrum* Linn. against country-made liquor induced hepato-toxicity in albino rats fed on controversial calorie diet. *Acta Clinica Scientica*, 5&6 (I&II): 18-21.

Bezbaruah, H. P. and B. Bezbaruah. 1963. Chromosome survey of some species of *Solanum* of medicinal value. *J. Proc. Indian Acad. Sci.* 58.

Bose, B. et al. 1972. Chemical investigation of berries of *Solanum nigrum*. *J. Institn. Chem. India* 44(6): 181-182.

Brinda, P. et al. 1982. Pharmacognostic studies in *Solanum nigrum* L. an Ayurvedic drug. *J. Econ. Tax. Bot.* 3(2): 125-128.

Chakravrty, A. K. et al. 1980. Studies on Indian medicinal plants. Part 57: Constituents of some *Solanum* spp. Mass spectra of nuatigenin and isonuatigenin. *Indian J. Chem. 19B: 468.*

Chandra, V. 1967-68. Production of *Solanum* spp. for steroidal hormones. *Indian Drugs*, 5: 57-67.

Kanwar, U. et al. 1990. Glycolytic enzyme activities of human and bovine spermatozoa treated in vitro with solasodine. *J.*

Ethnopharmacol. 28(2): 249-254. (Solasodine, the steroidal alkaloid caused inhibition in motility of spermatozoa.)

Khan, F. and M. Ikram. 1983. *Solanum* species as a source of steroidal drugs. *Pakistan J. Sci. Industr. Res.* 26(3): 126-127. (Quantitative estimation of steroidal alkaloids from *Solanum* spp.; Solasodine content in leaves, fruits and seeds of black nightshade.)

Korneva, E. I. and S. P. Mikhailova, 1987. Polyploidy in the nightshade (*Solanum*) hybrid selections. *Khim. Farm. Zh.*, 21(10): 1226-1231. (Polyploid selections have far more practical value than the autoploids.)

Mahato, S. B. et al. 1975. An assay method for the estimation of solasodine from *Solanum* spp. *J. Instn. Chem. India*, 47:237.

Mital, S. P. and B. Singh. 1986. Introduction of genetic resources of some important medicinal and aromatic plants in India. *Indian J. Genet.* 46(1): 209-216.

Narkehed, M. N. et al. 1987. Cytological studies in some interspecific hybrids of *Solanum*. *J. Maharashtra Agric. Univ.* 12(3): 325-327.

Varshney, I. P. and S. C. Sharma. 1965. Saponins and Sapogenins. XXIX. Saponins of *Solanum nigrum* berries. *Phytochem.* 4(6): 967.

Varshney, I. P. and N. K. Dube. 1970. Chemical investigation of *Solanum nigrum*. *J. Indian Chem. Soc.* 47(7): 717-718.

Vishwapaul et al. 1958. Indian *Solanum* species as a possible starting material for the synthesis of cortisone and steroid sex hormones. *Indian J. Pharm* 20: 247.

Wakhloo, J. K. 1965. Evidence for indole acetic acid and tryptophan in the shoot of *Solanum nigrum* and the effect of potassium nutrition on their levels. *Planta*, 65(4): 181-182.

Yoshida, K. et al. 1987. Changes caused by the included enzymes in the constituents of *Solanum nigrum* berries. *Chem. Pharm. Bull.* 35(4): 1645-1648. (4 new steroidal alkaloids, enzymatically derived from the original constituents, were obtained.)

33

Chundakai

Solanum torvum

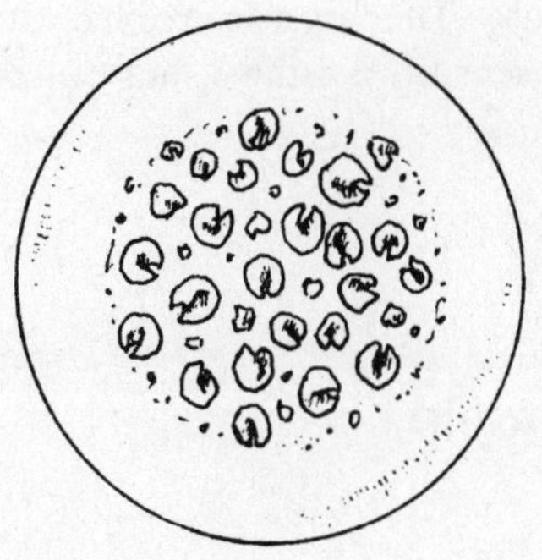

A regular intake of chundakai cures stomach ache, enlargement of stomach . . .
—From a Tamil verse

The Iron Fruit

In Cameroun, the leaves of chundakai are reported to be used as a haemostatic. The leaf juice is reported to affect the rate and amplitude of respiration and blood pressure.

In home remedies, the roots find their use for poulticing cracks in the feet.

The fresh berries of chundakai are green in colour. They are often sun-dried and preserved so that they are available throughout the year. After sun-drying, they are sprinkled with a mixture of salt and butter-milk and once again re-dried.

Chundakai is used in home remedies as a rich source of iron (22.2 mg per 100 gm) and hence forms an ideal remedy for those who suffer from anaemia. Besides iron, the berries are also rich in calcium (390 mg) and carotene (450 μgm). The berries are also prescribed for a host of ailments: asthma, chest-congestion, cold, enlargement of liver and spleen, infection of tapeworms, loss of appetite, night blindness, piles, *pitta* and *vata* aggravation, lack of taste, tuberculosis etc.

The dried berries of chundakai are the connoisseur's delight in South Indian ayurvedic cuisine for the preparation of delicacies such as *Vattal Kuzhambu* (See Recipe). They are also credited with the prevention of respiratory diseases such as asthma, lung cancer, tuberculosis etc.

The Profile

Botanical Names	:	*Solanum torvum* Swartz		
English Name	:	West Indian turkey berry		
Indian Names	:	Assamese	:	*Bhit-tita, Hathibhekuri*
		Bengali	:	*Gota Baighun, Titbaigun*
		Hindi	:	*Titbaigun, Tint*
		Manipuri	:	*Titbaigun, Tint*
		Oriya	:	*Titbaigun, Tint*
		Kannada	:	*Kadusundae, Sundaegida, Sundakayi*
		Khasi	:	*Dieng-soh-nonag*
		Malayalam	:	*Katuchunda*
		Tamil	:	*Chundaka, Sundakai*
		Telugu	:	*Chundika, Kottuvastu, Ustekaya*
Family	:	Solanaceae		
Appearance	:	A thorny shrub. Leaves oval. Flowers, white. Berries, round. Seeds, smooth.		

Distribution	:	Hot, arid and tropical zones of India. Also in the Andamans.
Medicinal Parts	:	Fruits (fresh or dried), leaves, root.

In Tradition

- Amoebiasis, fatigue, lack of taste, weight loss : Roast separately 1 tbsp each of the following, grind and bottle: ajwain, dried amla, dried chundakai, dried curry leaves, dried mango-kernel, dried rind of pomegranate, fenugreek seeds. Add ¼ tsp each asafoetida and rock salt and mix well before bottling. Dosage: ¼ tsp taken with butter milk, twice a day for 2 to 4 weeks.
- Asthma, chest congestion, diabetes, piles, tuberculosis : Fry equal quantities of the following in a little ghee till they become golden brown in colour: ajwain, amla (without seeds), curry leaves, fenugreek seeds, dried ginger, mango kernel and rind of pomegranate. Powder and bottle. Dosage: ½ tsp twice daily mixed with a little milk.
- Anaemia, chest congestion, cough : Fry 1 to 2 tsp dried berries in a little ghee and powder. Add this to every meal three times a day.
- Cough and cold : Grind a fruit into a paste with a little milk and take.
- Dog bite : Grind a handful of leaves with 1 tsp salt and apply on the bite for 3 days. (*Note*: Sour substances such as tamarind, dry mango powder etc. should be avoided in the diet.)
- Fever, malaria : Grind equal quantities of the root, sandalwood and *Achyranthes aspera* into a very fine paste. Roll into small pepper-size pills and dry in the sun. Take 2 to 4 pills with warm water, 2 to 3 times a day.
- Headache : Powder the dried berries and store. Sniff a little.

Loss of appetite, intestinal worms, tape worms, piles	:	Fry equal quantities of black pepper, cumin, curry leaves, fenugreek seeds, and dried berries in a little castor oil. Add 2 pinches of salt and powder. Dosage: 1 to 2 tsp powder with a little cooked rice preferably before a meal.
Night blindness	:	Fry 2 tsp dried berries in a little ghee and take with ragi-porridge every day for a few months regularly.
Stomach ache	:	Fry 2 tsp dried berries in a very little ghee and take. Grind a piece of root into a very fine paste. Roll it into pepper-size pills. Sun-dry and bottle. Dosage: 3 to 4 pills taken with warm water.

Note: Individual results may vary.

Vattal Kuzhambu : The Southerner's Sauce

Vattal Kuzhambu, the famous sauce in South Indian cuisine, is made of vattals (dried berries) of the Solanum species: *chundakai, manathakkali, thudhulai.* It is also made sometimes with dried cluster beans or dried bittergourd. The stepwise procedure for making this delicious ayurvedic sauce is:

Step 1: Fry 2 tsp dried chundakai in 1 tsp sesame oil and keep aside.

Step 2: Dissolve a lemon-size tamarind in hot water and keep the pulp.

Step 3: Fry in 1 tsp sesame oil, 14 fenugreek seeds, ½ tsp mustard seeds, ¼ tsp asafoetida and 2 tbsp curry leaves till the mustard seeds splutter. Now add the tamarind pulp (Step 2) and some salt, sambhar powder and sugar (to taste) and allow the concoction to boil. Add fried *chundakai* (Step 1) and remove from the fire.

Step 4: Eat with cooked rice, aappam, upma, dosai, idly, chapati, paratha or bread.

In Science

Bezbaruah, H. P. and B. Bezbaruah. 1963. Chromosome survey of some species of *Solanum* of medicinal value. *J. Proc. Indian Acad. Sci.* 58.

Bhakuni, D. S. et al. 1969. Screening of Indian plants for biological activity. Part II. *Indian J. Exptl. Biol.* 7:250. (The drug alters rate of respiration and blood pressure.)

Chakravarty, A. K. et al. 1980. Studies on Indian Medicinal Plants. Part 57: Constituents of some *Solanum* species. Mass spectra of nuatigenin and isonuatigenin. *Indian J. Chem.* 19B: 468.

Chandra, V. 1968. Production of *Solanum* spp. for steroidal hormones. *Indian Drugs Annual*, 57-67.

Dey, P. K. and B. K. Chatterjee. 1968. Neuropharmacological properties of several Indian medicinal plants. *J. Res. Indian Med.* 3(1): 9-17.

Mahato, S. B. et al. 1975. An assay method for estimation of solasodine from *Solanum* spp. *J. Instn. Chem. India*, 47:237.

Mital, S. P. and B. Singh, 1986. Introduction of genetic resources of some important medicinal and aromatic plants in India. *Indian J. Genet.* 46(1): 209-216.

Sairam, T.V. 1996. West Indian Turkey Berry. *Dignity Dialogue.* 2(8): 44-48.

Singh, S. J. et al. 1975. Studies on mosaic disease of *Solanum torvum. Indian J. Mycol. Pl. Pathol.* 5:86-90.

Vishwapaul et al. 1958. Indian *Solanum* spp. as possible starting material for the synthesis of cortisone and steroid sex hormones. *Indian J. Pharm.* 20 : 247.

34

Kantakari

Solanum xanthocarpum

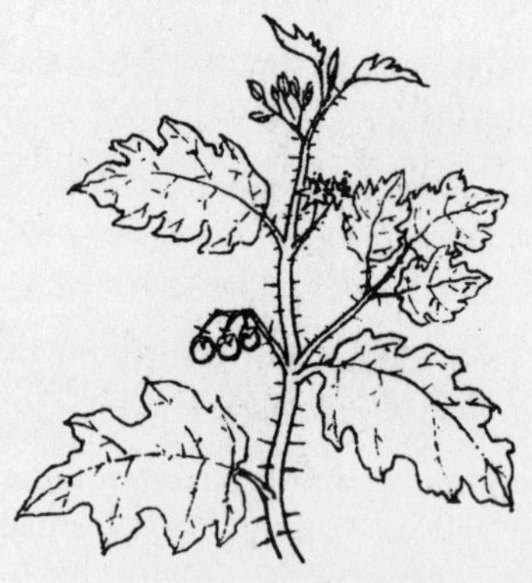

Kandankathiri is a remedy for breathing and pulmonary problems . . .
—From a Tamil verse by Agathiar

The Wealth from the Wasteland

Kantakari is a native of India. It is found throughout the subcontinent particularly on wasteland and dunghills.

The roots are largely used in ayurvedic medicines. The drug is bitter and a mild purgative. It is useful in the treatment of dropsy, a disease characterized by the accumulation of fluids in tissues and body-cavities. The drug promotes secretion and thus increases the frequency of urination.

In folk medicine, kantakari finds its use in expelling gas, phlegm and faecal accumulation and also as a diuretic. Common diseases such as asthma, bronchitis, cough, fevers, indigestion, intestinal worms, lung afflictions, rheumatism, and tuberculosis, etc. are challenged by this humble plant, which is a very common weed in hot and humid climates.

The fruits and seeds possess laxative properties.

The fruits are used to combat several ailments: bronchitis, cough, difficulties in breathing, fevers, gum diseases, exhaustion, itching, muscular pain, phlegm-accumulation, sore throat, swellings, wheezing etc. They strengthen the weak and induce appetite by improving the process of digestion.

The seeds find their application in the treatment of asthma, breathing difficulties, feverishness, indigestion, loss of appetite, lung disease and rheumatism.

The whole plant has its application in asthma, breathing difficulties, catarrh, dropsical swellings and phlegm-accumulatioin

Experiments have endorsed the antibacterial capabilities of the drug.

In several tribal pockets, the roots find their application in the treatment of scorpion and snake bites. However, pharmacological investigations conducted in this regard are yet to prove the drug's efficacy. The plant's anti-fertility activity—a traditionally glorified phenomenon—has been rated as 'mild' by laboratory experimenters.

The Profile

Botanical Names	:	*Solanum xanthocarpum* Schrad and Wendl. *Solanum surattense* Sch. and Wendl.		
English Name	:	Yellow-berried nightshade		
Indian Names	:	Assamese	:	*Katsareya*
		Bengali	:	*Kentakari*
		Kannada	:	*Kentakari*
		Sanskrit	:	*Kentakari*

		Gujarati : *Bhoyaringani*
		Hindi : *Kateli, Kateri, Ringni*
		Oriya : *Brihatibengani*
		Punjabi : *Kandiyari, Mokryan*
		Tamil : *Kandankathiri*
		Telugu : *Challanmulaga, Nelamulaka*
Family	:	Solanaceae
Appearance	:	A prickly, spreading herb with young branches covered with minute star-shaped hairs. Leaves with their midribs and veins with sharp yellow prickles. Flowers purple, a few forming a bunch opposite the leaves. Fruits yellow, round with green veins. Seeds, smooth.
Distribution	:	Throughout India in wastelands and on roadsides.
Medicinal Parts	:	The root of the plant is the chief drug. Flower-buds, flowers, fruits, leaves, seeds and the whole plant also find their use in several folk medicines.
Ayurvedic Preparations	:	*Amritrarishta, Chyavanaprasha, Dasamula-rishta, Kantakari avaleha.*

In Tradition

Boils	:	Boil a flower in a little almond oil. Cool and apply over the affected parts.
Headache, joint swelling, bad odour in armpits	:	Boil a handful of leaves in 2 tbsp gingelly oil. When luke warm apply over the affected parts.
Cold, cough, phlegm-accumulation		Boil 1-2 pinches of powdered root in water. Add 1 tsp honey and a pinch of powdered cubebs. Drink when bearably hot.
Cracks in heels	:	Extract the leaf juice from a handful of leaves. Add 1 tbsp ghee and 2 tbsp crushed inseeds and boil the mixture thoroughly. Cool and apply over the affected parts.

❧ Dysuria (difficulty in passing urine)	:	Mix ¼ tsp fruit juice with 1 tsp honey and take.
❧ Ear ache	:	Crush the fruits and expel the juice. Use as ear drops. (*Note*: This is a common practice among the tribals of Bastar.)
❧ Ear ache, white leprosy	:	Steam 1 cup fruit pulp with ¼ cup gingelly oil. Cool and filter. Apply the oil every day. (*Note*: The same oil can be used as ear drops to cure ear ache.)
❧ Gum infection, tooth ache	:	Burn the seeds and inhale the smoke. Boil a handful of leaves with ½ tsp crushed mustard seeds in 1 litre of water. Cool and when lukewarm gargle frequently.
❧ Scorpion sting, snake bite	:	Grind the roots into a fine paste. Mix in some lime juice and apply. (*Note*: Rush the patient to medical help.)
❧ Throat problems	:	Boil a handful of leaves in 1 litre of water till the volume is reduced to half. Cool and when lukewarm, use the decoction for gargling frequently.

Note: Individual results may vary.

In Science

Ansari, M. S. et al. 1971. Pharmacognostical studies on *Solanum surattense* Burm. (Kantakari) *J. Res. Indian Med.* 6(2): 143-158.

Basu, A. and S. C. Lahiri. 1977. Some pharmacological actions of Solanine. *Indian J. Exptl. Biol.* 15(4): 285-289. (Hypotensive, vasoconstrictor activity of solanine, isolated from kantakari.)

Bector, N. P. et al. 1971. New approach to the treatment of some chronic respiratory diseases, *Indian J. Med. Res.* 59(5): 739-742. (Whole plant in dose of 1gm 2 to 3 times a day for one month on 305 patients suffering from chronic bronchial asthma cured 50% of patients completely without showing any side-effects.)

Central Council for Research in Ayurveda and Siddha. 1996. *Pharmacological Investigations of Certain Medicinal Plants and Compound Formulations Used in Ayurveda and Siddha.* New Delhi, 165-169. (The drug, a muscle relaxant, lowers blood pressure.)

Deshmukh, P. B. et al. 1982. Study of insecticidal activity of twenty indigenous plants. *Pesticides.* 16(12): 7-10. (Kantakari, an effective insecticide.)

Dharmadhikari, S.V. 1976. Antiseptic action of *Solanum xanthocarpum. Nagarjun.* 20(3): 4-5.(Protective action of the plant with experimental rats.)

Gujaral, M. L. et al. 1960. Oral contraceptives, Part I. Preliminary observations on the anti-fertility effect of some indigenous drugs. *Indian J. Med. Res.* 48(1): 46-57. (Stems and leaves exhibit a very mild i.e. 10% anti-fertility activity in female albino rats.)

Gupta, S. S. 1966. Cardiac stimulating effects of kantakari (*Solanum xanthocarpum) Indian J. Med. Sci.* 20(8): 554-559. (Saponin obtained from the leaf and stem extract increased the force of contraction of hypodynamic heart significantly.)

Handa, S. S. et al. 1986. Natural products and plants as liver-protecting drugs, *Filoterapia.* 57(5): 307-351. (Hepato-protective role of the drug observed.)

Jaggi, R. K, et al. 1987. Static callus cultures of fruit of *Solanum xanthocarpum. Indian J. Pharm. Sci.* 49(6): 210-212.

Jaggi, R. K. et al. 1987. Static callus cultures of fruit of *Solanum platanifolium. Indian Drugs.* 25(3): 98-101.

Jain, S. P. 1980. A clinical trial of kantakari (*Solanum xanthocarpum*) in cases of *Tamak Swasa* (some respiratory diseases) *J. Res. Ayur. Siddha.* 1(3): 447-460.

Joshi, C. G and N. G. Nagar. 1952. Antibiotic activity of some Indian medicinal plants. *J. Sci. Industr. Res.* 11B(6):261. (Kantakari as an antibiotic.)

Pal, M. N. et al. 1983. Ayurvedic way to get a son or daughter at will. *Ancient Sci. Life.* 3(2): 98- 100. (Fruitful effect on parents.)

Setty, B. S. et al. 1977. Screening of Indian medicinal plants for biological activity (Pt.VII) (Spermicidal activity of Indian plants.) *Indian J. Exptl. Biol.* 15(3):231-232.(The plant exhibited spermicidal effect on rats.)

Sharma, K. et al. 1971. Role of kantakari (*Solanum xanthocarpum*) in *shwas* and *kas* – bronchial asthma and non-specific cough. *J. Res. Indian Med.* 6(2): 200-201.

Shukla, S. P. 1986. Indigenous drugs and their utilization by human beings. *Nagarjun* 29(5): 10-11. (Efficacy of leaf juice against rheumatism; roots against cough and anthelmintic property of a mixture of powdered roots of kantakari and calamus.)

Swarnkar, P. L. et al. 1987 Alpha-amylase acitivity and morphogenetic potential in callus cultures of *Solanum surattense. Curr. Sci.* 56(17): 905-906.

Vohora, S. P. and M. S. Y. Khan. 1981. Diuretic studies on plant principles. *Indian Drugs Pharm. Ind.* 16(1): 39. (Plant as a diuretic.)

35

Chirata

Swertia chirata

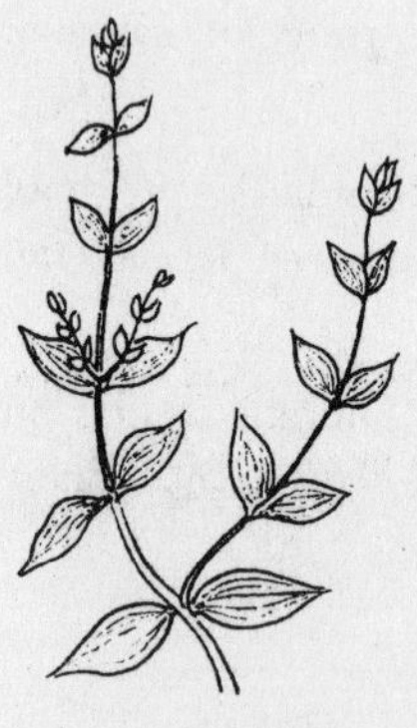

Nepalanimba cures all fevers...
—Raja Nighantu

The Neem of Nepal

Chirata is an ancient Ayurvedic drug, more commonly known as 'Nepali Neem' as it is mostly obtained from the forests of Nepal.

It was only in the year 1839 that English medical practitioners started prescribing chirata to their patients.

Unlike the neem tree, which spreads its branches towards the sky, the neem of Nepal is quite humble: it sticks firmly to the ground. Several varieties of the plant are found in Himalayan forests. The plant is collected at the flowering stage and dried and preserved for medicinal use.

The drug is found useful in overcoming fatigue, in improving appetite, removing acidity, and eliminating biliousness and nausea. Its blood-purifying quality has been exploited while treating acne, pimples and other skin rashes which are often caused by the presence of impurities and toxic substances in the blood.

The drug which is devoid of any aroma or astringency, is a specific remedy for intermittent fevers.

The bulk of the drug consists of the stem and a small portion, the root, which is actually its most potent part. Medicinally, it is akin to the Western herb, gentian.

Some botanists identify *Andrographis paniculata* (Nees.) with the drug chirata, as this plant exhibits properties identical with that of *Swertia chirata.*

The Indian vaids often prescribe it in combination with *neem* or *guduchi* or both.

The Profile

Botanical Names	:	*Swertia chirata* (Wall) C.B. Clarke *Swertia chirayita* (Roxb. ex Flem.) Karst.		
English Names	:	Chirata, Chirayta, Brown chiretta, White chiretta		
Indian Names	:	Bengali	:	*Chirata, Chirayata, Chirayita*
		Gujarati	:	*Chirata, Chirayata, Chirayita*
		Marathi	:	*Chirata, Chirayata, Chirayita*
		Hindi	:	*Nepalineem, Chirata, Chirayita*
		Kannada	:	*Nilabevu*
		Malayalam	:	*Nilaaveppa, Uttarakiriyattu*
		Marathi	:	*Chiragita*
		Sanskrit	:	*Bhunimba, Kiratatikta*
		Tamil	:	*Nilavembu, Chirathakutchi*
		Telugu	:	*Neelavemu, Neelaveru*
Ayurvedic Name	:	*Chirayta*		

Unani Name	:	*Chirayatah*
Family	:	Gentianaceae
Appearance	:	A branched robust annual. Stems cylindrical at the base and quadrangular towards the top. Leaves, lance-like and 4-nerved. Flowers, greenish yellow with a tinge of purple, in bunches. Fruits, egg-shaped capsules. Seeds, smooth, many-angled.
Distribution	:	Found in the Himalayas in temperate zones (1200 to 3000 m height) from Kashmir to Bhutan; also found in Meghalaya (Khasi hills).
Medicinal parts	:	The whole plant collected at the flowering stage and dried.
Medicinal Preparations	:	Fluid-extract, infusion (usually prepared in hot water in combination with cinnamon, cloves etc.), powder, tincture.
Dosage	:	¼ to ½ tsp, preferably with honey.
Ayurvedic Preparations	:	*Chandanasava, Chandraprabhavati, Chaturbhadrakvata, Gorochanadi-gulika, Lodhrasava, Mahasudarshan powder, Panchatikta kashaya, Sarvajvaraharalauha, Sudarshana churna, Tiktaghrita* etc.
Unani Preparations	:	*Arq chirata, Jawarish-jalinoos, Ma'jun juzam, Roghan kallan.*

In Tradition

Fatigue, weakness	:	Soak 1 clove, ½ inch cinnamon and ¼ tsp chirata in 1 cup hot water for 15 minutes. Drink the filtrate with 1 tsp honey.
Fever, indigestion, skin diseases		Fresh juice of the plant or an infusion of the dried parts (¼ tsp).
Hiccups, nausea	:	Take a pinch of root powder with 1 tsp honey.
High fever	:	Mix 1 cup decoction in 1 litre cold water and wipe the body or use the solution as a

		cold compress to bring down the temperature.
		Boil ¼ tsp dried chirata in 2 cups water till the volume is reduced to ½ cup. Filter. Add 1 tsp honey and 1 tsp dried ginger powder. Drink when bearably hot.
❧ Intestinal worms	:	Take ¼ tsp chirata powder in 1 cup hot water at bed time. Repeat if necessary.

Note: Individual results may vary.

A Word of Caution

Certain clinical experiments conducted recently have not confirmed the plant's febrifuge role. (Jain, 1968.)

Chirata may cause nausea and vomiting in excess.

It is reported that the commercially available chirata is heavily adulterated. The commonly used adulterants are: *Enicostema litorale, Exacum bicolor, Exacum tetragonum, Swertia angustifolia* etc. These adulterants are characterised by their inferior, bitter tonic properties.

In Science

Ainapura, S. S. et al. 1985. Hypoglycaemic activity of an indigenous preparation. *Indian J. Pharmacol.* 17(4): 238-239. (Caused reduction in blood sugar of alloxanised rats.)

Aiyer, K. N. and M. Kolammal. 1962. *Pharmacognosy of Ayurvedic Drugs.* Trivandrum, 5:64.

Biswas, K. 1956. *Common Medicinal Plants of Darjeeling and Sikkim Himalayas.* Calcutta, 70. (Chirata in Sikkim Himalayas.)

Chaturvedi, G. N. et al. 1983. Clinical studies on kalmegh (*Andrographis paniculata* Nees.) in infective hepatitis. *Anc. Sci.*

Life, 2(4): 208-215. (*Andrographis paniculata* is found medicinally useful.)

Chopra, R. N. et al. 1956. *Glossary of Indian Medicinal Plants.* CSIR. New Delhi, 237. (Bitter, febrifuge, laxative, stomachic and tonic properties of the drug.)

Chopra, R. N. et al. 1958. *Indigenous drugs of India.* Calcutta: U. N. Dhur & Sons. 2nd edn. 250.

Council of Scientific and Industrial Research. *The Wealth of India.* Raw Materials. New Delhi, X, 78.

Dalal, S. R. et al. 1953. Chemical examination of Indian medicinal plants I. Investigation of *Swertia decussata.* Isolation of decussation and swertinin. *J. Indian Chem. Soc.* 30:457.

George, M. et al. 1947. Investigation of plant antibiotics (Part II). A search for antibiotic substances in some Indian medicinal plants. *J. Sci. Industr. Res.* 6B(3): 42-46. (Antibiotic activity of the drug.)

Ghosal, S. et al. 1973. Chemical constituents of *Gentianaceae. V.* Tetraoxygenated xanthones of *Swertia chirata* Buch.—Ham. *J. Pharm. Sci.* 62:926. (Chemistry of the aerial parts and the roots of chirata.)

Gopal, H. et al. 1981. Anti-malarials from Indian medicinal plants. *J. Res. Ayur. Siddha.* 2(3): 286-295. (Absence of anti-malarial properties.)

Gopal, H. et al 1981. Activity of mangiferin on malarial parasite, bacteria and fungi. *J. Nat. Integ. Med. Ass.* 23(4): 109-112. (No antibacterial, antifungal and anti-malarial properties of mangiferin, extracted from *Swertia chirata.*)

Handa, S. S. et al. 1986. Natural products and plants as liver protecting drugs. *Filoterapia*, 57(5): 307-351. (Hepatoprotective activity of the drug.)

Harwell, J. L. 1969. Plants used against cancer—A survey. *Lloydia.*

32 (2): 153-205. (Anti-cancer activity of the drug.)

Inouye, H. and Y. Nakamura. 1971. Monoterpene glucosides and related natural products. XIV. Structure of two strongly bitter glucosides—amarogentin and amaroswerin from *Swertia japonica. Tetrahedron*, 27: 1967.

Jain, S. K. 1968. *Medicinal Plants.* New Delhi: National Book Trust, 164.

Kirtikar, K. R. and B. D. Basu, 1935. *Indian Medicinal Plants.* Allahabad: Lalit Mohan Basu, 2nd edn. III:1666.

Komatsu, M. et al. 1971. Xanthones from *Swertia.* Japan 7127, 558 (Patent); *Chem. Abstr.* 1971,75:P 143990. (Xanthones in chirata are found to possess anti-tuberculous properties.)

Prakash, A. et al. 1982. Chemical constituents of *Swertia paniculata*, Part 29 of Series Chem. Const. of Gentianaceae. *Planta Med.* 45: 61.

Purohit, V. P. et al. 1985. Ethnobotanical studies of some medicinal plants used in skin diseases from Rath Garhwal Himalaya, *J. Sci. Res. Pl. Med.* 61(1-4): 39-47. (Decoction of chirata roots along with camphor and shilajit was found effective in various skin ailments: leprosy, leucoderma, scabies etc.)

Purushothaman, K. K. et al. 1983. *Leather Sci. Madras*, 20:132. (Study of pigments isolated from chirata.)

Tajuddin, S. A. and M. Tariq. 1983. Anti-inflammatory activity of *Andrographis paniculata* Nees. (Chirayata), *Nagarjun*, 27(1): 13-14.

Takino, Y. et al. 1980. Quantitative determination of bitter principles in *Swertia* herb: Studies on evaluation of crude drugs. (IX). *Planta Med.* 38:351.

Thakur, R. S. *Major Medicinal Plants of India.* Lucknow: CIMAP, 475-478.

Vohora, S. B. et al. 1979. Gastro-enterological, diuretic and anti-microbial studies on *Jawarish Jalinoos*, *J. Res. Indian Med. Yoga and Homoeo.* 14(3-4): 34-43. (Jawarish Jalinoos, a compound preparation of 20 herbs, increased appetite and raised body weight.)

36

Arjuna

Terminalia arjuna

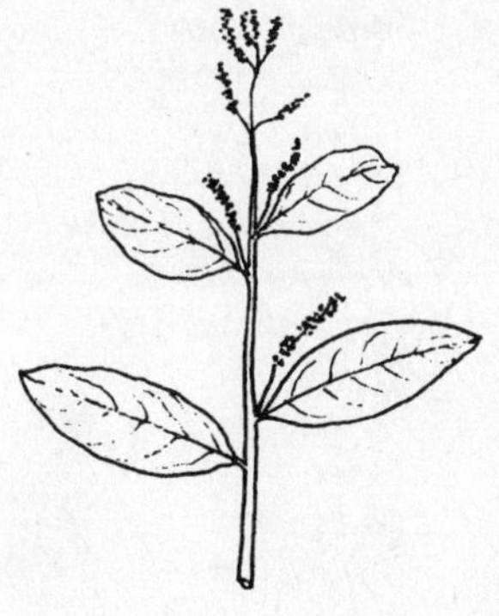

Arjunah . . . for all vitiated conditions of pitta
—Madanadi Nighantu

Medicine for the Heart

The discovery of arjuna as a medicine dates back to ancient tribal folk-lore. However, both Charaka and Sushruta, in their samhitas have referred to the medicinal use of the plant. The plant's use in the treatment of heart ailments has particularly been dealt with by Vagabhatta and re-confirmed by Bhavamishra and Chakradutta.

The bark of arjuna, known as a cardiac stimulant, is often prescribed in the form of powder together with milk and sugar. The mechanism of the cardio-tonic effect of the bark was scientifically investigated and it was found that there was a dose-dependent decrease in blood pressure and heart rate.

The plant is also prescribed in the treatment of asthma, bronchitis, cardiopathy, cirrhosis of the liver, diabetes, dysentery, fatigue, fracture, inflammation, haemorrhage, hypertension, leucorrhoea, ulcer, vitiated conditions of *pitta* etc.

The Profile

Botanical Name	:	*Terminalia arjuna* (Roxb.) Wight & Arn.		
English Name	:	Arjuna		
Indian Names	:	Assamese	:	*Orjun*
		Bengali	:	*Arjhan*
		Gujarati	:	*Sadado*
		Hindi	:	*Arjun*
		Kannada	:	*Maddi, Vaidairya*
		Malayalam	:	*Neermaruthu, Maruthu, Vennmaruthu*
		Marathi	:	*Sanmadat, Sadura, Vellamatta*
		Oriya	:	*Arjuno, Sahajo*
		Punjabi	:	*Arjan*
		Tamil	:	*Kulamaruthu, Vellaimaruthu*
		Telugu	:	*Erumaddi, Erramaddi, Tellamuddi, Yermaddi*
Ayurvedic and Unani	:	Arjun		
Family	:	Combretaceae		
Appearance	:	A large evergreen tree with buttressed trunk and smooth bark, greyish outside and flesh-coloured inside, flaking off in large flat pieces. Leaves, opposite, usually carrying a pair of oil glands on their lower surface, close to the top of the leaf-stalk. Flowers, cup-shaped, cream-coloured in bunches, attracting bees with their honey. Fruits ovoid, with leathery wings, tan-coloured when dry.		

Distribution	:	Throughout India. In central parts of the country, the tree grows near streams. Cultivated generally on road sides, as it gives excellent shade.
Medicinal Parts	:	Bark, leaves, fruits, gum.
Ayurvedic Preparations	:	*Arjunarishtam, Arjunaghritam.*

In Tradition

Cirrhosis of liver, high blood pressure	:	Take 1 to 2 pinches of bark powder with 1 cup warm water for a few days continuously.
Diarrhoea	:	Mix 1 to 2 pinches of bark powder in 1 cup warm water and drink two or three times.
Diarrhoea, menorrhagia, weakness of the heart	:	Boil ¼ tsp bark powder in 2 cups water till the volume is reduced to ¼ cup. Dosage: 2 to 3 tbsp taken with 1 tsp honey, twice daily for a few days.
Ear ache	:	Extract fresh leaf juice. Put 1 or 2 drops into the ears.
Mouth ulcers	:	Chew a twig of arjun for 10 minutes and wash the mouth with warm water. Do this three times a day. Dry the twigs of arjun, powder and bottle. Apply a little on the affected portion. Allow it to remain for 10 minutes. Wash the mouth with warm water three times a day.
Heart problems	:	Mix 1 to 2 pinches of bark powder and 1 tsp honey in 1 cup milk and drink for a few days continuously.
Menorrhagia	:	Grind ½ tsp bark into a very fine powder and mix with 1 litre of drinking water. Use this water for drinking purposes.
Pimples, skin eruptions	:	Dust the fine powder of the bark frequently on the affected areas.
Spermatorrhoea	:	Mix 1 to 2 pinches of bark powder with a little sandal paste in 1 cup warm water and drink for a few days continuously.

- Wounds : Boil 1 tsp bark powder in ½ cup water. Allow it to cool. Use this decoction for washing wounds.

Note: Individual results may vary.

A Word of Caution

The bark is often found adulterated with that of other species of Terminalia; the bark of *Lagerstroemia flos-reginae, and Sterculia urens* etc., are also at times used as adulterants.

In Science

Ali, M. E. et al. 1979. Chemical investigation on *Terminalia arjuna* Bedd. Part II. Examination of Bark. *Bangladesh Sci. Industr. Res.* 14: 237.

Anjaneyulu, A. S. R. and A.V. K. Prasad. 1982. Chemical examination of roots of *Terminalia arjuna* (Roxb.) Wight & Arn. Part I. Characterization of two new triterpenoid glycosides. *Indian J. Chem.* 21B:530.

Bardham, P. et al. 1985. In vitro effects of an ayurvedic liver remedy on hepatic enzymes in carbon tetrachloride treated rats. *Indian J. Med. Res.* 82: 359-364. (Livol and Liv-52 are found to show significant effects in liver disorders.)

Bhatia, K. and K. S. Ayyar. 1980. Barks of *Terminalia* species—A new source of oxalic acid. *Indian Forester,* 106:363. (Oxalic acid, tannins and complex glycosides are the constituents of the bark.)

Burkill, I. H. 1935. *A Dictionary of the Economic Products of the Malay Peninsula.* London: The Crown Agents for the Colonies, Vol II. 2136.

Chopra, R. N. et al. 1956. *Glossary of Indian Medicinal Plants*, New Delhi: CSIR, 241. (Arjun, a tonic, is useful in the disorders of heart and liver.)

Colabawalla, H. M. 1951. An evaluation of cardiotonic and other properties of *Terminalia arjuna*. *Indian Heart J.* 3: 205-230.

Gaind, P. P. et al. 1985. Effects of Livol(R) on some biochemical parameters in relation to improvement of liver functions. *Indian Vet. J.* 62(1): 870-874.

Kamboj, V. P. and B. N. Dhawan. 1982. Research on plants for fertility regulation in India. *J. Ethno-Pharmacol.* 6(2): 102-104.

Kirtikar, K. R. and B. D. Basu. 1935. *Indian Medicinal Plants.* Allahabad: Lalit Mohan Das, Vol II, 1024.

Mahli, B. S. and V. P. Trivedi. 1972. Vegetable anti-fertility drug of India. *Quart. J. Crude Drug Res.* 12(3): 1922-1928.

Pandey, G. P. et al. 1983. Studies on histo-pathological changes in carbon tetrachloride induced hepatotoxicity and protective effect of Livol in dogs. *Indian Vet. J.* 60(12): 978-980.

Patney, N. L. et al. 1973. New therapeutic agents in the management of steatorrhoea of cirrhosis of liver. *J. Res. Indian Med.* 8(3): 28-34.

Prakash, A. O. and R. Mathur. 1976. Screening of Indian plants for anti-fertility activity. *Indian J. Exptl. Biol.* 14(5): 623-626.

Satyavati, G. V. 1984. Indian plants and plant-products with anti-fertility effect. *Ancient Sci. Life*, 3($): 193-202.

Seshadri, I. C. et al. 1981. Anti-fertility activity of a compound ayurvedic preparation. *J. Sci. Res. Pl. Med.* 2(1&2): 1-3.

Sharma, P. N. et al. 1982. Arjunolone—a new flavone from stem-bark of *Terminalia arjuna*. *Indian J. Chem.* 21B: 263 (Anti-fertility and oxytocic effects of the flavone.)

Singh, N. et al. 1982. Mechanism of cardio-vascular action of

Terminalia. Planta Med. 45:102. (Hypotensive and bradycardiac effects of arjuna.)

Soma, S. K. et al. 1976. Efficacy of an indigenous compound preparation (Liv-52) in acute viral hepatitis. A double blind study. *Indian J. Med. Res.* 64(5): 738-742.

37

Guduchi

Tinospora cordifolia

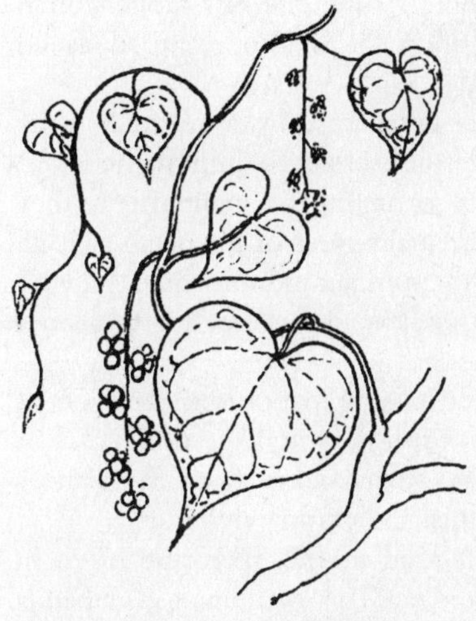

Guduchi, an aphrodisiac . . .
—Raja Vallabham

Everything in a Name!

In the Sanskrit language, a plant is known by various names, almost all of them lauding its unique features and the characteristics that distinguish it from others—a phenomenon akin to the way a Hindu devotee would worship his god by using a thousand names (*sahasranama*) with awe and admiration.

One such name for this plant is '*Amrita*', the heavenly elixir. The name seems to have been derived from the plant's quality of imparting longevity, vitality and youthfulness, besides improving the intellect. Other names, for example, '*Madhuparni*' refers to it as 'sweet leaves'; '*Kundali*' refers to it being a creeper; '*Vishalya*' refers to its smoothness of surface, it is without thorns, spines or other damaging outgrowths and so on.

The drug has been in use in native medicine from time immemorial. In folk medicine, it is used often to cure anaemia, bleeding piles, consumption, diabetes, chronic dysentery, diarrhoea, enteric fevers, erysipelas, gonorrhoea, heart diseases, helminthiasis, hypertension, itching, jaundice, leprosy, rheumatoid arthritis, skin infections, thirst, syphilis, vomiting and worm-infection. It is also considered useful in promoting longevity and is used as a tonic. Being a bitter tonic, it often finds its application in the preparation of blood purifiers. It is also regarded as an aphrodisiac.

Although the fresh stems are considered by some vaids to be more potent than the dried ones, it is easier to employ the latter. The plants that grow on neem trees are much sought after as they are said to incorporate the medicinal virtues of the neem as well. The stems are collected during the summer months and dried with the bark intact. The dried stems are popular as the drug tinospora or gilo.

The drug is often administered in combination with the roots of ginger and pippali (*Piper longum*) for improving digestion.

The starch obtained from the stems and roots of the plant is used in the treatment of diarrhoea and chronic dysentery.

A decoction of the drug is used in folk medicine often in combination with other ingredients. This combination depends on the type of treatment involved. Thus, the drug finds its partner in castor oil when it is aimed at the treatment of arthritic conditions, ghee for neurological problems, ginger for rheumatism, honey for respiratory diseases, jaggery for constipation and candy-sugar for *pitta*-aggravation.

The bitter principle of the plant has produced hypoglycaemic effects in rats and increased the glucose uptake of the tissues. It was also found effective in the dissolution of urinary calculi. A chemical analysis of the drug has indicated that giloinin, a non-glycoside bitter, gilosterol and tinosporine are the active constituents. There are conflicting views about the presence of berberine in certain fractions of the drug.

The Profile

Botanical Names	:	*Tinospora cordifolia* (Willd.) Miers. Ex Hook. & Thoms. *Menispermum cordifolium* Willd. *Tinospora glabra (*N.Burm.) Merr.
English Name	:	Glauncha Tinospor
Indian Names	:	Bengali : *Gadancha, Giloe, Gulancha, Guluncho, Nimgilo*
		Gujarati : *Gado, Galo, Gulo, Gulwel*
		Hindi : *Ambarvel, Gilo, Giloya, Gulancha, Gulbel, Gulve, Gurach, Gurcha*
		Kannada : *Anebule*
		Kashmiri : *Bark Bekhgilo*
		Malayalam : *Amrytu, Peyamrtam, Sittamrytu*
		Marathi : *Ambervel, Gharol, Giroli, Gulwel, Wulavel gulo*
		Oriya : *Gulochi*
		Punjabi : *Batino, Gilo, Zakhmihayat*
		Sanskrit : *Amrita, Amritalata, Amritavalli, Amritavallari, Bhishakapriya, Chakrala-kshana, Chakrangi, Chandrahasa, Dhira, Guduchi, Kandaruha, Madhuparni, Pittaghni, Sivanthika, Somavalli*
		Sindhi : *Satgilo*
		Tamil : *Amirdavalli, Kaipruchindil, Sindal*
		Telugu : *Guduchi, Somida*
		Arabic : *Gilo*
		Burmese : *Singomone*
		Persian : *Gulbel*
Ayurvedic Name	:	*Guduchi*
Unani Name	:	*Gilo*
Family	:	Menispermaceae

Appearance	:	A climbing shrub with rough corky bark, reaching great heights and sending down long thread-like aerial roots, green when young and greyish when mature. Leaves, shiny and round with 7-9 nerves and long stalk. Flowers, minute and yellow, male and female separate. Fruits, pea-sized, red, when ripe.
Distribution	:	Throughout the warmer parts of the country, particularly in Andhra Pradesh, Assam, Kerala, Tamil Nadu and Uttar Pradesh upto an altitude of 1500 m. Also in Bangladesh and Sri Lanka.
Medicinal Parts	:	Stem, root, leaves.
Preparations	:	Powder, decoctions (often in combination with one of the following: castor oil, ghee, ginger, honey, jaggery or mishri.)
Dosage	:	10-15 gm powder (or 15-20 ml decoction) with 15 ml honey twice daily.
Ayurvedic Preparations	:	*Amrtarishtam, Dhanavantaram tailam, Cheriya Rasanadi Kasshayam, Valiya marmagulika.*

In Tradition

Dyspepsia, joint pain, oedema	:	Boil 1-2 pinches of powdered stem with ¼ tsp ginger in 1 cup water and drink.
Excessive urination	:	Mix a few drops of the plant extract in 1 tsp cow's ghee and take twice daily.
Gonorrhoea, pus in urine	:	Mix 1-2 pinches of the drug extract in 1 glass milk and 1 tsp sugar. Take 3 times a day.
Fever, indigestion	:	Mix a pinch each of ginger, pippali and guduchi in 1 cup water and boil. Add 1 tsp honey and take.

- Excessive thirst due to diabetes; fever caused by *pitta*-aggravation : Mix 1-2 pinches of crushed citronella grass, dried ginger, guduchi, hribera, nut grass, sandalwood powder and vetiver in 3 cups water and boil thoroughly till the volume is reduced to 1 cup. Take ½ cup in the morning and the remaining half in the evening.
- Jaundice : Boil 1-2 pinches of powdered stem with 1 tbsp raisins and 1 tsp sugar in 1 cup water. Drink.
- Migraine : Extract a few drops of fresh juice from the plant. Add 1 tsp honey and take.
- Vaginal inflammation : Boil 1 tsp each of guduchi, triphala and Danti seeds in 1 litre water. Filter and cool. Use it as a vaginal douche.
- Wounds : Warm the leaves over a flame and apply on the wound.

Note: Individual results may vary.

In Science

Ainapure, S. S. et al. 1985. Hypoglycaemic activity of an indigenous preparation (1) *Picrorhiza kurroa* (2) *Caesalpinia bonducella* (3) *Mallotus philippensis* (4) *Tinospora cordifolia. Indian J. Pharmacol.* 17(4): 238-239. (The compound preparation exhibited significant hypoglycaemic property on clinical trials.)

Atta-ur-Rahman. 1986. Isolation, structural and synthetic studies on the chemical constituents of medicinal plants of Pakistan. *Pure Appl. Chem.* 38:663.

Bhupinder Singh, et al. 1981. Anti-hepatotoxic activity of *Tinospora cordifolia* Miers. *Indian J. Pharmacol.* 13(1): 96. (The protector of the liver.)

Bisset, N. G. and J. Nwaiwa. 1983. Quaternary alkaloids of *Tinospora* species. *Planta Med.* 48:225.

Central Council for Research in Ayurveda and Siddha. 1996. *Pharmacological Investigations of Certain Medicinal Plants and Compound Formulations used in Ayurveda and Siddha*. New Delhi. 119-122. (Hypoglycaemic effects of the bitter principle contained in the drug; efficacy in dissolution of urinary calculi; antipyretic, anti-arthritic and anti-inflammatory activities.)

Chopra, R. N. et al. 1956. *Glossary of Indian Medicinal Plants*. New Delhi: CSIR, 244. (Traditional use as an anti-periodic, aphrodisiac, bitter, nutrient, stomachic and in the treatment of diarrhoea, dysentery and gonorrhoea.)

Deshmukh, R. R. 1980. Clinical trial of Gasex in the post-operative gastro-intestinal symptoms. *Probe* 19(4): 277-279. (Usefulness of a preparation containing guduchi in the treatment of dysentery.)

Dixit, S. N. and R. L. Khosla. 1971. Chemical investigation on *Tinospora cordifolia*. *Indian J. Appl. Chem.* 34:46. (Steroids in the leaves.)

Dhar, M. L. et al. 1968. Screening of Indian plants for biological activity. Part I. *Indian J. Exptl. Biol.* 6(4):232-247. (Antibacterial activity.)

Gulati, O. D. et al. 1980. Clinical trial of *Tinospora cordifolia* in rheumatoid arthritis. *Rheumatism.* 15(4): 143-148. (Anti-rheumatic activity.)

Gulati, O. D. and D. C. Pandey. 1982. Anti-inflammatory activity of *Tinosporia cordifolia* in rheumatoid arthritis. *Rheumatism*. 15(4): 143-148. (Anti-inflammatory activity.)

Gupta, S. S. et al. 1967. Anti-diabetic effect of *Tinospora cordifolia*, Part I. Effect on fasting blood sugar level, glucose tolerance and adrenalin-induced hyperglycaemia. *Indian J. Med. Res.* 55(7): 733-745. (Hypoglycaemic activity.)

Handa, S. S. et al. 1986. Natural products and plants as liver-protecting drugs. *Filoterapia,* 57(5): 307-351. (The liver-protector.)

Khosla, R. L. and S. Prasad. 1971. Pharmacognostical studies on guduchi (*Tinospora cordifolia* Miers.) *J. Res. Indian Med.* 6(3): 261-269.

Mhaisker, V. B. et al. 1980. Clinical evaluation of *Tinospora cordifolia* in *Amvata* and *Sandhigat vata. Rheumatism.* 16(1): 35-39. (Stems an effective remedy for the two types of *vata: Amavata* and *Sandhigatvata*; anti-allergic and anti-rheumatic activities are also reported.)

Nayampalli, S. S. et al. 1982. Study on anti-allergic and bronchodilator effects of *Tinospora cordifolia. Indian J.Pharmacol.* 14:64. (Increase of glucose tolerance by administering water extract.)

Patel, S. R. et al. 1978. Studies on pharmacological effects of *Tinospora cordifolia, J. Res. Indian Med. Yoga and Homoeo.* 13(2): 46-47. (Clinical trial showed marked decrease in blood urea in experimental animals.)

Pendse, V. K. et al. 1981. An experimental study of water extract of *Tinospora cordifolia* in acute and chronic inflammation. *Indian J. Pharmacol.* 13(1): 73. (Significant analgesic and anti-inflammatory activity reported.)

Pillai, N. R. et al. 1980. On *Amritarishtam* and *Tinospora cordifolia* in albino rats. *Nagarjun*, 23(12): 262-263 (Antipyretic activity.)

Prem Kishore et al. 1980. Role of Suntlu-Guduchi in the treatment of *Amavata* (Rheumatoid arthritis). *J. Res. Ayur. Siddha* 1(3): 417-428. (Anti-allergic and anti-rheumatic activity.)

Raghunathan, K. and P. V. Sharma. 1969. Effect of *Tinospora cordifolia* Miers (guduchi) on alloxan-induced hyperglycaemia. *J. Res. Indian Med.* 3(2): 203-209. (Water extract helped in reducing the blood sugar.)

Quadrat-I-Khuda, M. et al. 1964. *Tinospora cordifolia* I. Constituents of the plant fresh from the field. *Sci. Res.* (Dacca) 1:177; *Chem. Abstr.* 1964, 61: 12331.

Quadrat-I-Khuda, M. et al. 1966. Studies on *Tinospora cordifolia* II. Isolation of tinosporin, tinosporic acid and tinosporol from the fresh creeper. *Sci. Res.* (Dacca) 3:9. *Chem. Abstr.* 1966, 65: 10549a.

Rege, N. et al. 1984. Hepato-protective effects against carbon tetrachloride-induced liver damage, *Indian Drugs.* 21(12): 544-546. (Repairing the damaged liver.)

Sastry, M. M. 1977. Clinical trial of Guduchi and Suntee in *Amavata. Rheumatism.* 12(2): 29-31. (Anti-allergic and anti-rheumatic activity)

Shal, D. S. and D. C. Pandeya, 1976. Preliminary study about the anti-inflammatory activity of *Tinospora cordifolia. J. Res. Indian Med. Yoga and Homoeo.* 11(4): 77-83. (Anti-inflammatory activity.)

Sharma, A. K. and R. H. Singh. 1980. Screening of anti-inflammatory activity of certain indigenous drugs on Carragenin-induced hind paw oedema in rats. *Bull. Medico-ethno-bot. Res.* 1(2): 262-271. (Confirmation of the anti-inflammatory role.)

Singh, K. P. et al. 1975. Experimental and clinical studies on *Tinospora cordifolia. J. Res. Indian Med.* 10(1): 9-14. (Water extract increased the urine output and ventricular contractions; reduced blood urea.)

Singh, R. H. 1978. Critical analysis of the studies done on indigenous anti-inflammatory and anti-arthritic drugs during the post-Independent era. *Rheumatism.* 13(3): 99-108. (Anti-rheumatic activity.)

Singh, R. H. et al. 1979. Comparative biochemical studies on the effect of four medhya rasayana drugs described by Charaka on some central neuro-transmitters in normal and stressed rats. *J. Res. Indian Med. Yoga. and Homoeo.* 14(3&4): 7-13. (Drug as CNS depressant.)

Singh, R. H. and G. N. Chaturvedi. 1974. On the antibacterial activity of some ayurvedic drugs. *J. Res. Indian Med.* 9(2):65-66. (Antibacterial activity.)

Thakur, R. S. et al. 1989. *Major Medicinal Plants of India.* Lucknow: CIMAP. 499-502. (Chemistry and pharmacology of guduchi.)

38

Vetiver

Vetivera zizanioides

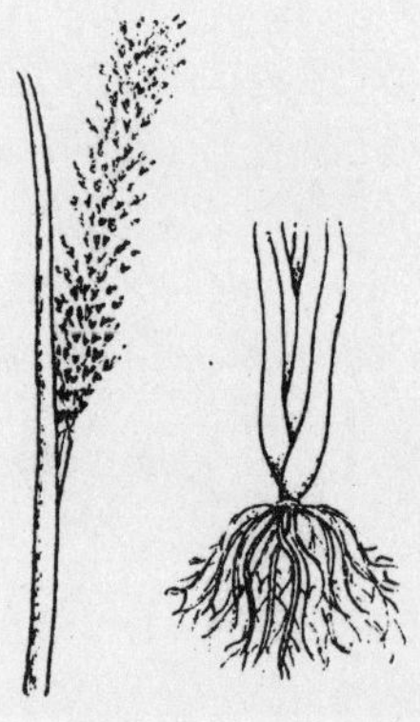

Vetiver, one of the ten great aids in improving the complexion . . .
—Charaka Samhita

Tall and Fragrant

Vetiver is a tall, fragrant grass that grows naturally in India and Sri Lanka. It is also cultivated in other parts of the world for commercial use.

Vetiver is a popular medicine in rural Tamil Nadu. It gains in importance during the summer months when the sun is at its unkindest in the tropics. Rural folk medicines use its roots in the preparation of hair oil, powder (Churanam), jam (Lehyam) and sherbet, which are prescribed as a 'cooling medicine' in 'burning' fevers, inflammation, venereal diseases etc.

The hand fans made of vetiver were quite popular before the arrival of electricity. These fans not only brought in breeze, but also a whiff of fragrance, which had a soothing impact on people, especially those suffering from depression and behavioural problems.

There are two varieties of vetiver: one with cream-coloured roots and the other, black-coloured.

In folk remedies vetiver finds its use as a circulation stimulant. Its rubefacient role makes it an ideal pain-reliever in the case of rheumatic arthritis and muscular aches. It is also useful in skincare treatments, thanks to its antiseptic and de-toxifying properties. It is useful in clearing acne and as it promotes skin regeneration, it assists in wound healing and rejuvenates ageing skin.

The sedative effect of vetiver makes it a welcome ingredient in bath oils and massage oils. In aroma therapy, it is known for its anti-stress and anti-anxiety usage. It is also reported to be a cure for insomnia, nervous tension etc.

Vetiver is much sought after by the great perfumers of the world, as it conjugates admirably with cedarwood, clarysage, lavender, jasmine, mandarin, petitgrain, rose, sandalwood, ylang ylang and a host of other perfumes to produce new magic in aroma-blending.

Oil of Vetiver

Oil of vetiver, an essential which is distilled from the dried roots, is known for its smoky, intense, earthy aroma – a fragrance which is ideal for those who indulge in meditation, thanks to its relaxing effect. It is this quality that has rendered its popular name 'oil of tranquility'. The aroma is believed to help people in getting back to normality after having suffered shocks, disappointments and frustrations in life. Negative emotions such as anger, jealousy, greed etc. are easily conquered with a few drops of vetiver oil!

A Word of Caution

Vetiver oil may damage the eyes on direct contact. Its internal use is not recommended.

The Bath Oil: A Recipe for Relaxation

Whenever you are tense and emotionally upset, try this recipe:

Add to your bath water, 2 drops each of lavender, rose and vetiver oils with 2 tsp sweet almond oil. Then bathe, concentrating on the aroma that surrounds you for 10 minutes.

Feel the difference yourself! If you are convinced, let others know about it so that people around you start behaving in a positive way.

The Profile

Botanical Names	:	*Vetiveria zizanoides* (L.) Nash *Phalaris zizanodies* L. *Andropogon muricatus* Retz.		
English Name	:	Vetiver		
Indian Names	:	Hindi	:	*Gandar, Khas, Khuskhus*
		Kannada	:	*Vettiveru, Lamanchi,*
			:	*Karidappa sajjehallu*
		Malayalam	:	*Ramacham*
		Sanskrit	:	*Sugandhimula, Sevyah, Ushara*
		Tamil	:	*Vetiver*
		Telugu	:	*Kuruveru, Vetiveru.*
Ayurvedic Name	:	Ushira		
Unani Name	:	Khas		

Family	:	Poaceae
Appearance	:	A perennial grass with thick fibrous aromatic roots, light or dark brown in colour.
Distribution	:	Grows wild in the plains, particularly in sandy soils and in river-beds; cultivated chiefly in Punjab, Rajasthan and Uttar Pradesh and the West Coast.
Medicinal Part	:	Root.
Ayurvedic Preparations	:	*Brihatkasturibhairava rasa, Ushira asana, Ushiradi kvatha.*

In Tradition

Excessive thirst, jaundice, *pitta*-aggravation, semen-loss, Rakthapittam	:	Soak ½ cup cleaned and crushed vetiver roots for 24 hours in an earthenware pot containing drinking water and drink it frequently.
Boils and burning sensation caused by excessive heat, burning sensation during urination, excessive thirst, pain in the neck, semen loss	:	In an eartherware pot, soak ½ cup cleaned and crushed vetiver roots and ¼ cup Thiruneetrupachai (*Ocimum basilicum*) in 2 litres boiled water for 24 hours. Drink the water frequently.
Boils caused by summer heat	:	Powder 1 cup vetiver and 1 cup sandalwood scraps and bottle. Mix 1 tbsp of this powder-mixture in water or rose-water and apply on the affected areas. Allow it to remain for at least 1 hour before washing it away.
	:	Soak some crushed sandalwood scraps and vetiver in a mud pot containing drinking water. Drink this water frequently.
	:	Boil 1 tsp vetiver powder in 1 cup water. Drink along with 1 cup buttermilk or milk every day for a month.

Burning sensation due to excessive heat and also during urination, stomach upset	:	Clean, dry, powder and bottle the roots. Take 2 pinches with 2 pinches of powdered saunf with 1 cup hot water.
Headache, high fevers	:	Soak a handful of roots in a jug of water and apply the infusion over the forehead.
Prickly heat	:	Grind equal quantities of the following into a very fine paste: vetiver, sandalwood and coriander seeds. Dry the paste and bottle. Mix rose-water and apply all over the affected parts frequently.
Swelling	:	Appy a paste of the root.
Boils and swellings	:	Grind equal quantities of sandal wood, vetiver and turmeric and apply on the affected areas.

Note: Individual results may vary.

In Science

Anderson, N. H. et al. 1970. Structure of vetiverones and vetispirenes. *Tetrahedron Lett.* 1755.

Dikshit, A. and A. Hussain. 1984. Antifungal action of some essential oils against animal pathogens. *Filoterapia.* 55: 171-176.

Anderson, N. H. and M. S. Falcone. 1971. Vetiver oil constituents. IV. Prezizaenes and the biogenesis of zizaene. *Chem. Ind.* 74: 7654b.

Ganguly, R. N. et al. 1978. Khusinol: A biogenetically significant component of vetiver oil. *Indian J. Chem.* 16 B: 23.

Hanayama, N. et al. 1968. Minor acidic constituents of vetiver oil. *Tetrahedron Lett.* 6099.

Jain, S. C. et al. 1972. Insect repellants from vetiver oil. I. Zizanal and epizizanal. *Tetrahedron Lett.* 23: 4639. (Vetiver oil possesses potent topical activity on cockroaches and flies, thanks to its constituents: zizanal and epizizanal.)

Kaiser, R. and P. Naegali. 1972. Biogenetically significant compound in vetiver oil. *Tetrahedron Lett.* 2009.

Kalsi, P. S. et al. 1962. Structure of isobisabolene, new sesquiterpenoid hydrocarbon from vetiver oil. *Tetrahedron*, 18: 1165.

Kalsi, P. S. et al. 1972. Terpenoids. LIII. Structure of Khusilal: a novel aldehyde from vetiver oil. *Tetrahedron* 20: 2617.

Kalsi, P. S. et al. 1972. Structure and absolute configuration of epikhusinol—a new sesquiterpene alcohol from vetiver oil. *Indian J. Chem.* 10: 1127.

Karkhanis, D. W. et al. 1978. Minor sesquiterpene alcohols of North Indian vetiver oil. *Indian J. Chem* 16B: 260.

Kido, F. et al. 1967. Structure of zizanoic acid—a novel sesquiterpene in vetiver oil. *Tetrahedron Lett.* 2817.

Kido, F. et al. 1969. Minor acidic constituents of vetiver oil. II. Cyclocopacamphenic acid and 'epicyclocopacamphenic acid. *Tetrahedron Lett.* 3169.

Komae, H. and I. C. Nigam, 1968. Essential oils and their constituents: Structure of khusenic acid and isokhusenic acid, two sesquiterpenic constituents of oil of vetiver. *J. Org. Chem.* 33: 1771.

Lemberg, S. and R. B. Hale, 1978. Vetiver oil *v.* oils of different geographical origins. Int. Congr. Essent. Oil. 1978. *Perfumer flavorist*, 3: 23.

Manchanda, S. K. et al. 1969. Complete elimination of khusinol from vetiver oil. *Perfum. Essent. Oil Res.* 59: 363.

Nigam, I. C. et al. 1968. Essential oils and their constituents. Isolation and structure of khusinol, a new sesquiterpenic primary alcohol from vetiver oil. *J. Pharm. Sci.* 57: 1029.

Rao, A. A. et al. 1963. Structure of khusinol, a new sesquiterpene from vetiver oil (Vetiveria zizanoides). *Tetrahedron.* 19: 233.

Shaligram, A. M. et al. 1961. Abstracts of papers presented at the Symposium on Production and Utilization of Medicinal and Aromatic Plants in India, held at RRL, Jammu on November 27-29, p 25.

Singh, G. et al. 1978. Anti-microbial activity of essential oils against keratinophilic fungi. *Indian Drugs*, 16 (2): 43-45.

Thakur, R. S. et al. 1989. Major Medicinal Plants of India. Lucknow: CIMAP. pp. 521-527.

Tirodkar, S. V. et al. 1969. Khusinol: Location of hydroxyl group. *Sci. Cult.* 35: 27.

Uma Rani, D. C. et al. 1969. Terpenoids. LXVII. Isokhusinol—a sesquiterpene primary alcohol from vetiver oil. *Perfum. Essent. Oil Res.* 69: 314.

39

Grape

Vitis vinifera

Draksha, one of the ten drugs most useful for the throat . . .
—Charaka Samhita

The Good Old Grape

Grapes come to us from the dark abysm of time. Archaeologists have dug out several specimens of fossilized grape plants from the wombs of the earth. They are also found entombed with the mummies in Egypt. Egyptian hieroglyphics record details of grape cultivation and wine-making. Wine-making was an art in Greece during the time of Homer (700 BC). The Bible has a reference to the vineyard tended by Noah. Back in India, Charaka and Sushruta have extensively referred to grapes in their early medical treatises (1st Century AD).

Out of the total world output of grapes, 80% is consumed by the wine industry and 7% goes in the making of raisins. The remaining produce is consumed as fresh fruits or as processed juice.

For table wines, grapes with high acidity and a moderate sugar content are preferred. Dessert (sweet) wines are made out of those which have a high sugar content and low acidity. Depending on the sugar content, the alcoholic content in wine ranges between 8 to 24%.

Raisins are preferred when soft in texture, with little tendency to stickiness, of uniform colour and distinctive flavour. They contain 73% reducing sugars and minerals such as calcium, phosphorous and iron.

Not long ago, two Canadian researchers conducted an experiment to learn how viruses react to a medium of grapes: grapes, raisins (dried grapes) and wine (red, white and rosé) were used. When they added viruses to the grape extract made from pulp and skins, to the infusion of raisins, and to the wines, they noted that all of them inactivated the viruses. Interestingly, grapes were found to be deadly against those virsuses which cause herpes infection and polio. In 1928, Ms. Johanna Brandt from South Africa wrote a popular book *The Grape Cure* in which she eulogised grapes for curing her abdominal ulcer. The 'grape cure' is still popular in Europe.

Grape juice is also known to battle bacteria and studies made on animals confirm that the tooth decay process could be successfully thwarted by chewing grapes regularly.

The fruits possess a very high concentration of caffeic acid, a polyphenol compound known to prevent cancer in animals. An American study confirms that raisin intake could be linked to a low rate of cancer deaths.

Grapes, either fresh or dried, are considered to be blood-purifiers. Fresh grapes are cooling, demulcent, diuretic, laxative and stomachic.

The leaves are astringent, sometimes used in diarrhoea. The juice of the unripe fruits is used as an astringent in throat affections.

Attempts to grow grapes in India have been quite successful thanks to the application of modern technology in horticulture: in peninsular India, two crops mature in a year. Thompson Seedless is popular due to the absence of seeds and for its pleasing flavour. Anab-e-Shahi enjoys a formidable reputation as a choice table variety.

The Profile

Botanical Name	:	*Vitis vinifera* Linn.
English Name	:	Grape
Indian Names	:	Hindi : *Angoor*
		Sanskrit : *Draksha*
		Tamil : *Drakshai*
Family	:	Vitaceae
Appearance	:	A large climber with tendrils. Leaves, palm-like, 3 or 5 or 7-lobed, irregularly toothed with fine hairs beneath. Flowers, green in dense clusters. Fruits vary in size, shape and colour. Globose or ovoid. Greenish, purplish or bluish black. Edible and sweet when ripe.
Distribution	:	Cultivated in several parts of India.
Medicinal Part	:	Fruits.
Ayurvedic Preparations	:	*Chyavanaprasha, Drakshasava.*

In Tradition

- Acidity, anaemia, asthma, constipation, heartburn, gastritis, jaundice, loss of appetite, *pitta*-aggravation, stomach ache, loss of taste : SEE 'Drakshai Churanam'. (Page 237)

Blood pressure, rheumatism, ulcers	:	Drink 1 cup fresh grape juice.
Burning sensation in body and limbs and dizziness due to aggravation of *pitta*	:	Take 1 cup of fresh grape juice every day.
Cold and fever in children at the time of teething	:	Expel the fresh juice and give 1 tsp twice daily.
Constipation	:	Soak 2 tbsp raisins in ½ cup water for 1 hour and take with the water 2 or 3 times a day.
Diarrhoea at the time of teething in infants	:	Express the juice from fresh fruits and administer 1 tsp 2 or 3 times daily.
Diarrhorea caused by indigestion	:	Grind 1 tsp leaf juice with 2 pinches each of black pepper and cumin and boil the mixture in 1 glass water. Filter and drink.
Eye ailments	:	Boil 1 tbsp raisins and 2 pieces of fruit in 1 cup milk and drink every day.
Dry cough	:	Fry 3 tbsp raisins in 1 tsp ghee and take.
For improvement in eye sight and brain functions	:	Boil 2 tbsp raisins and 1 fig in a glass of milk and drink every day.
Fevers, general debility, spermatorrhoea, sexual debility, to improve the complexion	:	Extract ½ cup juice from ripe, yellow-coloured neem fruits. Add 1 tbsp each of the following after thoroughly crushing or powdering: cucumber-seeds, almonds, cashew nuts, pista, coriander seeds, tarbooz seeds, saunf, liquorice; mix with ¼ cup raisins, 1 cup mishri and 1 cup ghee. Now, boil the mixture thoroughly till all traces of moisture go and the mixture reaches a jam-like consistency. Cool and bottle. Dose: 1 to 1½ tsp twice daily. (*Note*: This jam cannot be preserved for long due to the possibility of fungal attack.)
Hypertension, joint pain, liver problems	:	Take 1 cup juice of fresh grapes once a day.
Impure blood	:	Take grapes or raisins every day.

Jaundice, liver disorders	:	Take 1 cup fresh grape juice every day.
Jaundice, liver disorders, *pitta*-aggravation	:	Eat a portion (1 cup) fresh grapes every day.
Loss of appetite or taste after recovery from fever and illness	:	Boil 1 crushed seed of amla with 1 tsp each crushed raisins and sugar. Filter. Use the decoction as a mouth wash or a gargle.
Menopause, problems due to	:	Daily intake of 1 cup fresh grape juice.
Palpitation, weak heart		Soak a few grapes (about 10 in number) in 2 tbsp rose water for 10 minutes and take.
Pre-menstrual syndrome	:	In the days just before or during the menstrual cycle, chew well before dinner 1 tbsp each of roasted sesame seeds with raisins. (*Note*: Frequent intake of fresh ginger tea recommended; salt, sugar and fermented foods to be avoided.)
Prickly heat	:	Take grapes or raisins frequently.
Skin diseases	:	Apply the sap extracted from the young branches.
Spermatorrhoea	:	Soak a few grapes in ½ cup water for an hour. Take the water with some milk at bed time.
Stomach ulcers	:	Take 1 glass of fresh grape juice twice daily.
To improve memory	:	Boil 2 figs and 1 tsp raisins in 1 cup milk and drink.
Ulcers in stomach/ duodenum	:	Take 1 cup fresh grape juice twice daily.
Venereal diseases	:	Eat fresh grapes daily.

Note: Individual results may vary.

Note: Some nutritionists recommend that grape juice should not be drunk at one go. One should sip a small quantity of the juice and 'chew' it thoroughly so that enough saliva gets mixed to enable the beneficial reaction of salivary enzymes.

Drakshai Churanam: A Home Remedy for Keeping the Stomach Fit and Functional

Churanam (or churan) is constituted of a mixture of various herbs, brought together to maintain health or to fight diseases. Household churanams are part of the kitchen in many traditional communities throughout the length and breadth of the subcontinent. Here is a South Indian version for enabling the stomach to achieve its peak performance!

Step I: Roast slightly (each item separately) 4 tsp dried ginger and 2 tsp each of the following and keep aside after grinding them into a very fine powder: ajwain, black pepper, cinnamon, cloves, jatamanshi, koshtam (Kushta; *Saussurea lappa*), liquorice and manjishta.

Step II: Roast slightly (again separately) 1 tsp each of the following and keep aside after grinding the mixture into a very fine powder: amla, coriander seeds, cubebs, haritaki, karungaalipattai, jaadipatri, kodivelipattai, lavangapathiri, moongiluppu, nutmeg, sandalwood flakes, vibhitaki, vetiver.

Step III: Grind together 2 tsp each dates and raisins into a fine paste. Add 2 tsp karkandu, 2 cups sugar, 1 cup ghee, ½ cup honey and mix thoroughly.

Step IV: Mix thoroughly all the ingredients from Steps I to III and bottle when cool.

Dosage: 1 to 2 tsp, twice daily for 1 or 2 months continuously.

In Science

Allen, 1948. *Commercial Organic Analysis.* Philadelphia: The Blakistan Co. 5th edn. 238. (Chemistry of grapes.)

Cormier, F. and C. Ambid, 1987. Extractive bioconversion of geraniol by a *Vitis vinifera* cell suspension employing a two phase system. *Plant Cell Rep.* 6(6): 427-430.

Chopra, R. N. et al. 1958. *Indigenous Drugs of India.* Calcutta: U. N.

Dhur & Sons. 2nd edn. 530.

Cruess, W.V. 1958. *Commercial Fruits and Vegetable Products.* New York: McGraw Hill. 4th edn. 592.

Girdhari Lal et al. 1960. *Preservation of Fruits and Vegetables.* New Delhi: ICAR. 130.

Hilditch, T. P. and P. N. Williams. 1964. *The Chemical Constitution of Natural Fats.* London: Chapman & Hall. 4th edn.

Hulme, A. C. (ed.) 1971. *The Biochemistry of Fruits and their Products.* London: Academic Press. II: 202.

Joshi, S.V. 1998. *Ayurveda and Panchakarma: The Science of Healing and Rejuvenation.* Delhi: Motilal Banarsidas. 277.

Kertesz, Z. I. 1951. *The Pectic Substances.* New York: Interscience Publishers Inc. 306.

Uphof, J. C. Th. 1968. *Dictionary of Economic Plants.* 2nd edn.

Williams, K. A. 1966. *Oils, Fats and Fatty Foods.* London: J. & A. Churchill. 4th edn. 353.

Winkler, A. J. 1962. *General Viticulture.* Berkeley: Univ. of California Press. 133. (Grape cultivation.)

Glossary of English Medical Terms

Abortifacient: Causing abortion.

Abcess: Local inflammation.

Acne: Infection of glands of skin, characterized by blackheads and found usually in adolescents.

Amenorrhoea: Delayed menstruation.

Amylases: Enzymes capable of hydrolysing starch and carbohydrates.

Anaemia: A deficiency of red-cells or their haemoglobin in blood, resulting in pallor.

Analgesic: Relieving pain.

Anaesthesia: Loss of sensation.

Anaesthetics: Agent producing complete or partial lack of sensation.

Anthelmintic: Destroying intestinal worms.

Anticarcinogenic: Reducing and preventing cancer.

Antidote: A substance that counteracts poison.

Antiemetic: Preventing vomiting.

Antiepileptic: Preventing epilepsy.

Antifungal: Reducing and preventing fungal growth.

Anti-microbial (also, *antiseptic*): Reducing and preventing microbial growth.

Anti-oxidant: An agent that inhibits oxidation.

Antiprotozoal: Reducing and preventing the growth of protozoans e.g., amoeba.

Antipyretic: Reducing fever.

Anti-tumour: Reducing and preventing the growth of tumours.

Aphrodisiac: Enhancing sexual activity.

Artery: One of the vessels that convey blood from the heart to the body.

Arthritis: Inflammation in the joints.

Asthma: An allergic respiratory disease.

Astringent: Causing contraction of body tissues.

Bactericidal: Destroying bacteria.

Bile: Thick, oily fluid excreted by the liver, helpful in digestion of fats.

Biliousness: Disorder of bile production (to excess).

Blood pressure, High: See Hypertension.

Blood pressure, Low: See Hypotension.

Bronchitis: An inflammation of the mucous lining of the bronchial tubes.

Carbuncle: Large boil.

Carcinoma: Cancer, especially of epithelial origin.

Cardiac: Of the heart.

Cardio-vascular: Pertaining to the heart and the blood vessels.

Carminative: Expelling gas from the stomach and the intestines.

Cataract: Clouding of the lens, preventing clarity of vision.

Catarrh: Inflammation of the nasal membranes with mucus discharge.

Chancre: Venereal sores.

Cholesterol: Steroid alcohol present in cells and body fluids. Excess can lead to gallstones.

Cirrhosis: Hardening of the tissues, particularly in the liver.

CNS: Central Nervous System.

Compress: A pad that is soaked in hot or cold substances and applied to the body for relief of swelling and pain.

Constipation: Condition of bowels in which defecation is irregular and difficult.

Convulsion: Generalized involuntary spasm of the voluntary muscles.

Cramp: Painful, spasmodic contraction.

Cystitis: Inflammation of the urinary bladder, accompanied by painful urination.

Decoction: A herbal preparation, where the plant material (usually bark, roots etc.) is boiled in water and reduced to make a concentrated extract.

Diabetes: Disease characterized by excessive discharge of glucose-containing urine, with thirst and emaciation, caused by the failure of the pancreas to secrete an adequate amount of insulin and the resultant accumulation of glucose in the blood.

Diarrhoea: Excessive looseness of the bowels.

Diuretic: Increasing the formation of urine.

Dropsy: Generalized accumulation of fluid in body; oedema.

Dysentery: Disease with inflammation of mucous membrane and glands of large intestine with mucous and bloody evacuations.

Dysmenorrhoea: Painful and difficult menstruation.

Dyspepsia: Indigestion or impaired digestion.

Dyspnoea: Laboured breathing.

Eczema: An itching disease of the skin.

Elephantiasis: Tropical disease leading to massive swelling of the tissues especially in the lower limbs.

Embrocation: Medicated oils to relieve muscular pain.

Emetic: Producing vomiting.

Emmenagogue: An agent that stimulates the menstrual flow in women.

Enzymes: Catalysts produced by living cells.

Epilepsy: A nervous disorder, usually chronic, with characteristic convulsions of sudden onset, a tonic spasm often with crying and arrest of breathing followed by twitching, biting of tongue, frothing at the mouth, relaxation of the sphincter.

Expectorant: Causing or stimulating expectoration to cough up and spit.

Fatigue: Exhaustion.

Febrifuge: Eliminating fever.

Fever: Elevation of body temperature.

Fistula: Unusual passage leading from body surface to its interior.

Flatulence: Wind or gas in the stomach or intestine.

Fungus: Mould.

Galactagogue: Increasing milk secretion.

Gastritis: Inflammation of the stomach.

Gastro-enteritis: Inflammation of the mucous membrane of the stomach and the intestine.

Goitre: An enlargement of the thyroid, usually caused by a lack of iodine in the diet.

Gram-positive: Said of bacteria which stain when treated with methyl violet, followed by iodine and then by acetone or ethanol. Bacteria which do not stain are 'Gram-negative'.

Haemorrhage: Severe loss of blood from a blood vessel.

Haemorrhoids: Varicose dilation of veins at the lower end of the rectum and the anus; piles.

Haematuria: The passing of blood in urine.

Halitosis: Bad breath.

Heartburn: Burning sensation especially on the left side of the chest, usually after a meal.

Hepatitis: Inflammation of liver.

Hydrocele: Accumulation of serous fluid in a body sac.

Hypertension: High arterial pressure.

Hypoglycaemia: A below normal concentration of sugar in the blood.

Hypotension: A fall in the blood pressure below the normal range.

Impotency: Inability to copulate; sterility.

Inflammation: The reaction of living tissue to injury or infection; swelling.

Insomnia: Inability to sleep.

Itch (also, *Itching*): An irritating cutaneous disorder involving a persistent impulse to scratch.

Jaundice: Increase in bile pigments in blood.

Laxative: Promoting bowel movements.

Leprosy: Chronic, endemic bacterial disease caused by *Mycobacterium lepriae*, characterized by ulceration and thickening of the skin with loss of sensation and in severe cases, deformity and blindness.

Leucorrhoea: An abnormal mucous discharge from the vagina.

Liniment: An embrocation, made with oil.

Lipid: Fat.

Liver: An organ secreting bile which plays a key role in digestion.

Mastitis: Inflammation of mammary glands or breasts.

Menorrhagia: Irregular profuse bleeding irrespective of menstrual cycle in women.

Menoschesis: Suppression of menstruation in women.

Menstruation: Periodic shedding of the lining of uterus.

Migraine: A pathological headache, often on only one side, characterized by nausea and sensory disturbances.

Mucus: A thick, white liquid secreted by mucous glands.

Neuralgia: Pain along the course of a nerve, especially in the head or face; intense, intermittent pain.

Obesity: A bodily condition in which there is an excess of fat in relation to other bodily components; presumed to exist when an individual is 20% or more over the normal weight.

Oedema: Accumulation of tissue fluid in excess.

Oxytocic: Stimulating contraction of the uterine muscle, accelerating childbirth.

Oxytocin: Hormone produced by the pituitary glands, stimulating muscles of uterus.

Pathogen: Anything capable of producing disease.

Pharmacognosy: Science relating to medicinal products in their raw or unprepared forms.

Pharmacology: The study of drugs.

Pharmacopoeia: Containing a list of drugs with directions for their use.

Phlegm: Thick mucus from the respiratory tract.

Piles: Enlarged painful veins in the rectum or around the anus.

Pleurisy: Inflammation of the membrane covering the lungs.

Pneumonia: Infection of the lungs.

Poliomyelitis: Infantile paralysis.

Polyp: Outgrowths usually in bladder, nose or intestines.

Poultice: A soft mush prepared from various substances with oily or watery fluids.

Psoriasis: Chronic skin disease in which red, scaly patches develop.

Purgative: Relieving constipation.

Pus: A resultant of infection containing dead cells.

Pyoderma: A skin inflammation producing pus.

Pyorrhoea: A gum infection.

Rectum: Lowest six-inch portion of the intestinal tract adjoining the anus.

Rejuvenation: The process of restoring vitality, especially the renewal of youthful physiological vigour in the aged and the senescent.

Rheumatism: Pain, swelling and deformity of joints of unknown cause.

Ringworm: A fungal infection.

Salve: A healing ointment.

Saponins: A group of glycosides, useful as detergents.

Scabies: A skin disease caused by mites.

Sciatica: Inflammation of the sciatic nerve in the back of the thigh.

Sciatic nerve: The largest nerve in the body located in the back of the thigh.

Sedative: Tending to soothe.

Sore: An ulcer or wound.

Spermatorrhoea: Frequent, involuntary discharge of semen, in the absence of sexual excitement or intercourse.

Spleen: A ductless gland situated at the left side of the cardiac end of the stomach.

Sprain: An injury caused by over-stretching of ligaments in joints.

Suppository: Solid medication inserted in cavities other than mouth.

Steroids: Fat soluble organic compounds that occur naturally in flora and fauna and play many important functional roles.

Strangury: Painful urination.

Sty (also, *stye*): Inflammation on the edge of an eye lid.

Styptic: Checking bleeding.

Syphilis: A contagious venereal disease, spreading from genitals to skin and mucous membranes and eventually to the muscles, bones and brain.

Tannin: Widespread in plants, particularly in bark, leaves etc. it prevents bacterial growth and thus helps in healing.

Tonsilitis: Inflammation of tissues at the root of the tongue.

Toxin: Poison.

Ulcer: A slow healing wound with superficial loss of tissues.

Urethra: A tube that eliminates urine from the bladder.

Urine: Excretion of kidneys, stored in the bladder and eliminated through urethra.

Uroschesis: Urine-retention.

Venereal sores: Diseases transmitted through coitus.

Vermifuge: Expelling worms from the intestine.

Veterinary: Of or for ailments related to animals and their treatments.

Virus: Minute organism that causes diseases such as common cold, chicken pox, measles, mumps, poliomyelitis etc.

Vitamin: Any of the numerous substances, essential for nutrition, occurring naturally in food; also synthesized.

Wart: Skin growth usually caused by a virus.

Wheeze: Sound in chest due to lung problems.

Wound: An injury or break in the skin.

Glossary of Non-English Terms

Ama: toxin; undigested food or uneliminated waste materials.

Ayurveda: 'The Veda of Life', the Indian system of medicine, as dealt with in the Atharva Veda.

Bhavaprakasa: a 16th century text on Indian medicines.

Charaka Samhita: a medical compilation by Charaka.

Churan (also, *Churna, Churnam*): powder.

Dhatu: the basic tissue-elements of the body.

Dosha: the essential factor or humour.

Gulkand: a confection made of petals, usually of rose petals.

Kapha (also, *Sleshma*): water-humour.

Katha: catechu.

Kayakalpa: a treatment that arrests or retards the ageing process.

Leha (also, *Leham*): a medicinal jam.

Panchakarma: five types of detoxification.

Pitta: fire-humour.

Purana: the ancient treatises of India.

Rasayana: a rejuvenative drug or therapy.

Siddha (also *Chittar, Siddhar, Sitthar*): a Tamil yogi or sadhu; the Tamil system of medicine, somewhat akin to Ayurveda.

Sloka: a distich verse.

Sushruta Samhita: a compilation by Sushruta.

Tailam (also, *Taila*): medicated oil.

Triphala: a mixture of three myrobalans: emblic (amlaki), chebulic (haritaki) and beleric (vibhitaki).

Unani: conventional Arabian system of medicine.

Vagabhatta: the author of the treatise *Ashtanga Hridaya.*

Vaid (also, *Vaidya, Vaidyar, Baid):* one who is trained in medical science.

Vata: air-humour.

Vattal kuzhambu: a South Indian soup made of tamarind and dried fruits, somewhat bitter in taste, having medicinal value.

Yoga: a methodology of the practical and coordinated application of knowledge; science of self-realization.

Glossary of Plants and Other Ingredients

This glossary covers only those plants which are not discussed in a separate chapter in this book. Abbreviations used: (E)=English; (H)=Hindi; (Mal)=Malayalam; (S)=Sanskrit; and (T)=Tamil.

Adhatodai (T): *Adhatoda vasica.* Malabar nut (E). Vasaka (H). Leaves are used as an expectrant and relieve cough. (T).

Ajwain (H): *Trachyspermum ammi.* Omum (T). Fruits are used as carminative stimulant, tonic and in indigestion.

Almond (E): *Prunus amygdalus.* Badam (H & T). The seed oil is used in perfumery.

Amaltas (H): *Cassia fistula.* Indian Laburnum (E). Aavaram (T). The fruit-pulp is used as a purgative.

Amla (H): *Emblica officinalis.* Emblic myrobalan (E). Nellikai (T). One of the Three Great Myrobalans used in *triphala.*

Anar: SEE Pomegranate.

Aniseed (E): *Pimpinella anisum.* Saunf, Saurif (H). Fruits are used as carminative and to prevent flatulance.

Asafoetida (E): *Ferula asafoetida.* Hing (H). Perungayam (T). The gum-resin is used in the treatment of asthma, cough and indigestion.

Babchi (H): *Psoralea corylifolia*. Karbogam (T). Seeds used in the treatment of leprosy, leucoderma and other skin diseases.

Banana (E): *Musa paradisiaca*. Kela (H). Vaazhai (T). The banana stem is a good source of starch.

Banyan (E): *Ficus benghalensis*. Bargad (H). Aal (T). A large tree cultivated as a hedge plant.

Betel leaf (E): *Piper betel*. Paan (H). Vettilai (T). Leaves are used as a masticatory.

Bottle gourd (E): *Lagenaria siceraria*. Lauki (H). Surai (T). Fruits are used as a vegetable.

Black cumin (E): *Nigella sativa*. Kalonji, Kalajira (H).

Black pepper (also, Pepper) (E): *Piper nigrum*. Kali mirch (H). Milagu (T). Fruits are used as spice and condiment.

Broccoli (E): *Brassica oleracea var. Botrytis*. The inflorescence is edible.

Brussels sprout (E): *Brassica oleracea var. gemmifera*. The young shoots, buds and leaves are edible.

Caraway (E): *Carum carvi*. Shiajira (H). A native of Europe newly cultivated in India, the fruits of this plant are used medicinally as stomachic and carminative.

Cardamom (E): *Elettaria cardamomum*. Elaichi (H). Elam (T). Stimulates spleen and heart.

Carrot (E & T): *Daucus carota*. var. *sativa*. Gaajar (H). The roots are edible.

Castor (E): *Ricinus communis.* Arandi (H). Aamanakku (T). The seed oil is used as a purgative.

Chamomille (also spelled, camomille) (E): Recent studies show that chamomille has a healing effect when applied to skin wounds, abrasions and infections.

Chana (H): *Cicer arietinum.* Gram (E). Kadalai (T). The seeds are edible and the vegetative parts are used as salad and fodder.

Chapati (H): Unleavened bread.

Chilli (also Red chilli, Green chilli) (E): *Capsicum frutescens.* Mirch (H). Milagai (T). Known for its pungent fruits.

Chinese hibiscus (E): *Hibiscus rosa-sinensis.* Jaba (H). Chemparuthy (T). Its definitive action in the treatment of arterial hypertension stands confirmed by clinical trials.

Chirchita (H): *Achyranthes aspera.* Prickly chaff-flower (E). Naayuruvi (T). Achyranthine, an alkaloid extracted from this plant is reported to lower blood pressure and heart-rate by dilating the blood vessels and increasing the rate of respiration.

Cinnamon (E): *Cinnamomum zeylanicum.* Dalchini (H). Lavangapattai (T). Fights toxins.

Citronella (E): *Cymbopogon winterianus.* The scented grass.

Climbing brinjal (E): *Solanum trilobatum.* Popular drug in Sidda.

Cloves (E): *Syzygium aromaticum.* Laung (H). Kraambu (T). The dried flower buds are used medicinally as stimulant, carminative and in flatulance.

Coconut (E): *Cocos nucifera.* Nariel (H). Thengai (T). Coconut oil tends to promote hair growth.

Coriander (E): *Coriandrum sativum.* Dhania (H). Kothmalli (T). 'A cure for all diseases' —Prophet Muhammad (s.a.w.s.)

Cubebs (E): *Piper cubeba.* Kabab-chini (H). The fruits are used in perfumory and also as a spice and condiment.

Cucumber (E): *Cucumis sativus.* Khira (H). Vellari (T). The fruits are useful in vitiated conditions of *pitta.*

Cumin (E): *Cuminum cyminum.* Zeera (H). Seeragam (T). Used to season certain cheese varieties.

Curry leaf (E): *Murraya koenigii.* Kadi patta (H). Karuveppilai (T). 'The germ killer', Guna Paadham.

Danti (S): *Baliospermum montanum.* Nagadanti (Mal). Niradimuttu (T). Seeds used externally as stimulant.

Dhatura (H): *Datura stramonium.* Umathai (T). Dhatura is a highly poisonous plant.

Dhoop (H): *Jurinea macrocephala.* An extract from the roots of this plant is used as an incense.

Dronapushpi (S): *Leucas aspera.* Thumbai (T). The plant juice induces vomiting.

Durva: *Cynodon dactylon.* Doob (H). Arugampul (T). 'A complexion promoter'. Charaka.

Fennel (E): *Foeniculum vulgare.* Saunf (H). Sombu (T). An excellent stomach and intestinal remedy.

Fenugreek (E): *Trigonella foenum-graecum.* Methi (H). Vendhayam,

Mendhayam (T). The seeds are loaded with iron.

Fig (E): *Ficus carica.* Anjir (H). Athi (T). 'The ideal food for those who are brought low by long sickness…' Pliny, the Roman naturalist.

Galangal: *Alpinia galanga.* Kulinjan (H). Arathai (T). Charaka includes this drug in the category of ingredients which impart youthful vigour.

Garlic (E): *Allium sativum.* Lasan (H). Poondu (T). The bactericidal effect of garlic oil was found 24 times greater than that of carbolic acid.

Ghee (H): Clarified butter, preferably made of cow's milk. Old ghee finds its application as an ideal vehicle for many a herbal medicine.

Gingelly oil (also Sesame oil) (E): obtained from the seeds of *Sesamum indicum.* Til-ka-tel (H). Nallennai (T).

Ginger (E): *Zingiber officinale.* Adrak, Sonth (H). Inji, Chukku (T). The outer rind of both fresh as well as dried ginger needs to be discarded before consumption.

Gokhru (H): *Tribulus terrestris.* Nerunji (T). The fruit possesses antibacterial properties.

Green gram (E): *Phaseolus aureus.* Mung (H). Pacha payaru (T). The grains are eaten as 'dal'.

Gulkand (H): A confection made of rose petals.

Haritaki (H & S): *Terminalia chebula.* Chebulic myrobalan (E). Kadukkai (T). One of the three ingredients in *triphala.*

Henna (E): *Lawsonia inermis.* Mehndi (H). Marudhani (T). Its use in leprosy finds mention in ancient Indian texts.

Horse purslane (E): *Trianthema portulacastrum*. Santhi (H). Pushkaramul (S). A common succulant herb used as a vegetable.

Hribera (Also, Bala) (S): *Pavonia odorata*. Iruveli (M). Peramutiver (T). Preparation of the root with 'bel' fruit (*Aegle marmelos*) is used in dysentery.

Indian frankincense (E): *Boswellia serrata*. Luban (H). Saambiraani (T). An oleo-gum-resin obtained from the bark is used in rheumatism.

Indian sarsaparilla (E): *Hemidesmus indicus*. Magrabu (H). The roots are used as substitute for sarsaparilla—as tonic, diaphoretic, diuretic and demulcant.

Indian senna (E): *Cassia senna*. Sonamukhi (H). Nila aavaarai (T). Leaves and fruits are used as laxative and purgative.

Jaggery (E): Unrefined cane sugar. Often used in folk medicine as a cheap substitute for honey.

Java Plum (E): *Eugenia jambolana*. Jamun, Jambu (H) Naaval (T). Leaves, fruits, seeds and barks have medicinal application.

Kala chana: SEE Chana.

Karanda: *Carissa caranda*. Karaunda (H).

Katha: (H) Catechu. Black cutch (E). The cutch obtained from the heart-wood is used as a masticatory.

Katurohini (also, Katki) (H): *Picrorhiza kurroa*. Yellow gentian (E). Kadugu rogini (T). 'Katurohini drives away fevers . . .' Bhavaprakasa Nighantu.

Keezhanelli (T): *Phyllanthus niruri*. Wild emblic (E). Jungli amli (H). Bhumyamlaki (S). A single drug remedy for jaundice.

Lauki (H): *Lagenaria vulgaris*. Calabash cucumber. Bottle gourd. (E). The fruit of this climber is used as a vegetable.

Lime (E): *Citrus aurantifolium*. Nimbu (H). Elumichai (T). 'Lime adds beauty and properity to a house.' Matsya Purana.

Linseed (also, flax seed) (E): *Linum usita tissimum*. Alsi (H). Aali (T). The green pods are edible.

Liquorice (also, Licorice) (E): *Glycyrrhiza glabra*. Mulethi (H). Yashtimadhu (S). Adhimadhuram (T). The Chinese consider it an aphrodisiac.

Long pepper (E): *Piper longum*. Pippali (H). Tippali (T). The fruits are used as a spice and condiment.

Mango (E): *Mangifera indica*. Aam (H). Maa (T). 'The year in which I didn't eat enough mangoes should be deleted from my life-span'. Tagore.

Mishri (H): Candy.

Moringa (also, Drumstick) (E): *Moringa pterygosperma*. Sahijan (H). Murungai (T). The leaves are loaded with Beta-carotene.

Neem (H): *Azadirachta indica*. Margosa (E). Vembu (T). Regular massaging of body with neem oil is advised for rheumatic patients.

Nut grass (E): *Cyperus rotundus*. Motha (H). The dried tuberous roots are used in perfumery.

Nutmeg (E): *Myristica fragrans*. Jaiphal (H). Jaadhikka (T). Beware of nutmeg poisoning!

Palash (also, Palas) (H): *Butea monosperma.* Flame of the Forest (E). Palaasu (T). The ripe fruits are edible.

Palm sugar (also, Palm candy, Palmyrah sugar) (E): Sugar obtained from the palm, *Borassus flabellifer.*

Pippali: SEE Long pepper.

Pista (H & T): *Pistacia vera.* Native of W. Asia, cultivated in N. India for its edible seeds.

Pomegranate (E): *Punica granatum.* Anar (H). Maadulai (T). The peel from the edible fruit is used to control diarrhoea and dysentery.

Pudina (H & T): *Mentha arvensis.* Fieldmint (E). One of the three Great mints.

Purslane (E): *Portulaca oleracea.* Kulfa (H). A common herb used as a vegetable.

Ragi (T): *Elensine coracana.* Finger millet (E). Mandal, Mandua (H). It is the staple food of the agricultural class in south India. The hill tribes brew a beer.

Rock salt (E): Common salt as a solid mineral.

Rose (E): *Rosa* spp. Gulan (H). Roja (T). There are many varieties of roses in India.

Saffron (E): *Crocus sativus.* Kesar (H). Kungumapoo (T). The dried stigmas and tops of the styles are used as spice and medicine.

Sandal (E): *Santalum album.* Chandan (H). Chandanam (T). The powdered heartwood and the essential oil extracted from it are used as cosmetics and medicine.

Saunf (H): SEE Fennel.

Senna (E): SEE Indian senna.

Sesame (E): *Sesamum indicum.* Til (H). The edible seed oil is also used in the manufacture of soaps and cosmetics.

Sickle senna (E): *Cassia tora.* Chakramardah (S). Takara (Mal). Chakunda (H). The young tender leaves are used as a vegetable.

Slaked lime (E): Calcium hydroxide produced when caustic lime is mixed in water. Chuna (H). Chunnambu (T).

Soap nut (E): *Sapindus emarginatus.* Ritha (H). Cultivated in North India. The fruits are used for washing woollen clothes.

Spinach (E): *Spinacia oleracea.* Paalak (H). Keerai (T). The leaves are eaten as a vegetable.

Sweet basil (E): *Ocimum basilicum.* Barbari (H). Vibhuthi pachai (T). The extracts of the seeds show antibacterial properties.

Sweet marjoram (E): *Origanum majorana.* Marua (H). Dried leaves and flowering tops are used medicinally as carminative and stimulant.

Tal-makhana (H): *Asteracantha longifolia.* Neermulli (T). The leaves, roots and seeds are used for dropsy, jaundice and rheumatism.

Tamarind (E): *Tamarindus indica.* Imli (H). Puli (T). The seeds are used medicinally as carminative and laxative. The unripe fruits are a rich source of tartaric acid.

Tobacco (E): *Nicotiana tabacum.* Tambaku (H) Pugayilai (T). The leaves contain alkaloids and are used as insecticides.

Tree cotton (E): *Gossypium arboreum.* Kapas (H). The fibre obtained from the surface of the seeds is used by the textile industries.

Triphala: A mixture of three myrobalans: amla, haritaki and vibhitaki.

Tulsi (H): *Ocimum sanctum*. Holy basil (E). Tulasi (T). 'To be sought after and cherished.' Puranas.

Turmeric (E): *Curcuma longa*. Haldi (H). Manjal (T). 'The turmeric paste can drive away all poisons from the body'. Matsya Purana.

Urad (H): *Phaseolus mungo*. Ulundu (T). Cultivated as a pulse crop in Punjab, Madhya Pradesh, Uttar Pradesh and West Bengal.

Vibhitaki (also Bibhitaki): *Terminalia bellirica*. Bahera (H). Taanikkai (T). Belleric Myrobalan, Bastard Myrobalan (E). A constituent of triphala, myrobalan pulp is also used as an adhesive.

Water melon (E): *Citrullus vulgaris*. Tarbooz (H). Tarpooshni (T). Native of tropical Africa but cultivated throughout India for the edible fruits.

Index